Copyright © 2021 by J&J Test Prep, LLC

All rights reserved. No part of this book may be reproduced, distributed, published, or licensed in any manner without written permission of the copyright owner.

Cover design by Jacqueline Pollina

ISBN 979-8773406167

SAT® is a registered trademark of the College Board, which does not endorse this publication.

The graphs featured in this publication were produced with Desmos.

The content provided within this book is to be used solely for educational purposes. No liability is assumed for damages or losses due to any of the material provided.

This book is dedicated to all our amazing tutoring colleagues who have been there for us from inception to present. None of this would be possible without your endless support.

Understanding this Book

No B.S. SAT Math is exactly as it sounds – all the math you need to ace your SAT without any of the B.S.

Concepts are explained clearly with our unique methodology – the same one we utilize with our private tutoring clients.

This workbook is suited for all levels: concepts are explained thoroughly with no prior knowledge of a topic assumed. For students aiming for a 700+ math score, specific concepts and problems are labeled as "700+" either due to their difficulty or due to them being lower-yield topics.

Answers to problems are provided at the end of each chapter. To access **detailed** solutions, scan the QR code at the beginning of each answer page using your phone's camera.

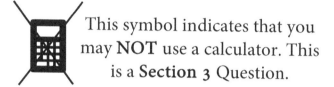 This symbol indicates that you may **NOT** use a calculator. This is a **Section 3** Question.

 This symbol indicates that you may use a calculator. This is a **Section 4** Question.

About the Authors

Josh and Jackie are the founders of J&J Test Prep, a company that offers test preparation, subject tutoring, and essay services. As full-time test prep professionals, Josh and Jackie have helped thousands of students achieve success on the SAT. They also run a successful test prep TikTok account: @testpreptips.

Errors

What makes us human is that none of us are perfect! Spot an error? Please let us know by submitting a form, and we will fix it:

testpreptips.org/bookerrors

Thank you!

Table of Contents

Topic 1: Expressions
- Expressions vs. Equations
- Combining Like Terms
- Distributing a Term
- "FOIL"
- Picking Numbers

Page 1

Topic 2: Solving Equations & Isolating Variables
- Isolating a Single Variable: The Basics
- Variables in Terms of Other Variables
  - Using Factoring to Get a Variable in Terms of Other Variables
- Square Roots
  - Expressions vs. Equations
  - Square Roots vs. Squaring
  - Squaring to Get Rid of a Square Root
  - Extraneous Solutions
  - Using a Square Root to Get Rid of a Square

Page 10

Topic 3: Exponents
- Exponent Rule Table
- Making the Bases Identical
- Radicals ↔ Exponents
- Operations with Radicals
- Radical Reduction for Square Roots
- Radical Reduction for Higher Roots
- Applying the "Heart Method" to Exponents

Page 25

Topic 4: Lines
- Slope-Intercept Form
- Calculating the Slope
- The y-intercept
- The x-intercept
- What Does the Slope Mean?
- Interpreting slope, y-intercept, and x-intercept
- Finding the Equation of a Line
- Parallel and Perpendicular
- Standard Form

Page 45

Topic 5: Functions
- Function Notation
- Table Functions
- Graphical Functions
- Characteristics of Functions
- Equations with Functions
- Undefined Functions
- Composition of Functions
- Functions in Terms of Another Function
- Translation of Functions
- Interpreting Functions in a Linear Context
- Interpreting Functions in Real-World Scenarios
- Changing the Input

Page 67

Topic 6: Polynomials
- Definitions
- Degree
- Factoring Polynomials
  - The Relationship Between Roots and Factors
- Questions Involving Polynomials
- Factoring Polynomials of a Degree Greater Than 2
- Graphing Polynomials

Page 87

Topic 7: Quadratics

- Standard Form
- Solving Quadratics in Standard Form
- The Quadratic Formula
- Factored Form
- Vertex Form
- Converting Between the Forms
  - Standard → Factored; Standard → Vertex; Factored → Vertex
  - Summary of the Three Forms
- Sum and Product of Roots
- The Discriminant
- Real-Life Applications

Page 98

Topic 8: Factoring

- Finding the Greatest Common Factor (GCF)
- The Three Must-Know Factored Forms
  - Recognizing Direct Versions of the Three Factored Forms
  - Recognizing Less-Direct Versions of the Three Factored Forms
- Solving for Entire Expressions

Page 131

Topic 9: Fractions

- Fractions without Variables
  - Addition and Subtraction
  - Finding the Least Common Denominator (LCD)
  - Reducing (Simplifying) Fractions
  - Multiplication and Division
- Fractions with Variables
  - Addition and Subtraction
  - Multiplication and Division
- Splitting Fractions
- Solving Equations with Fractions
  - Cross-Multiplication
  - Clearing Denominators

Page 144

Topic 10: Systems of Equations
- Methods of Solving Systems
  - Elimination
  - Substitution
  - Clever Combination
- Word Problems
- Meaning of the Solutions

Page 161

Topic 11: Types of Solutions – Two Lines
- No Solutions
- Infinitely Many Solutions
- One Solution
- Solving More Advanced Examples

Page 174

Topic 12: Inequalities
- Symbols
- Solving Inequalities
  - Compound Inequalities
- Inequalities on a Number Line
- Graphing Inequalities
- Graphing Constants
- Decoding Word Problems

Page 186

Topic 13: Ratios
- "Recipe" Ratios – A Simple Explanation
- Explicit Ratios
- Order is Important
- 3+ Ratios
- Standard vs. Total Ratios
- Unit Conversions
- Rates
- Degrees ↔ Radians
- Map Unit Conversions

Page 202

ASA
AAS
SSS
SAS

Topic 14: Percentages
- Taking a Percent
- Word Problems
- Fractions as Percentages
- Percentages from Tables and Graphs
- Percent Increase / Decrease
- Consecutive Percentages
- What is the Percent Increase / Decrease?

Page 222

Topic 15: Exponentials
- Linear vs. Exponential Functions
- Linear vs. Exponential Situations
- Exponential Functions
- Accounting for Time
- Exponential Graphs
- Exponential Tables

Page 240

Topic 16: Statistics
- Measures of Central Tendency
  - Mean, Median, and Mode
- Measures of Spread
  - Range and Standard Deviation
- Modifying Statistics
  - Least and Greatest Values Changing
  - Inserting an Equal Number of Values Above and Below the Median
- Frequency Charts (Histograms)
- The Median Position Formula
- Box Plots
- Table Probability
- Surveys
  - Accurate Surveys
  - Survey Response Generalization
- Margin of Error

Page 257

Topic 17: Geometry

Part I: Definitions, Area, and Perimeter
- Terms and Symbols
  - Symbols on Shapes
- Area and Perimeter of Shapes
  - Triangles, Squares, Rectangles, Parallelograms, and Trapezoids

Page 287

Part II: Lines and Angles
- Rules Regarding Angles
  - Line Split
  - Right Angles
  - Triangles
  - Opposite Angles
  - Parallel Lines
  - General Shapes

Page 294

Part III: Triangles
- Angles and Sides
- Types of Triangles
- The Pythagorean Theorem
- Special Right Triangles
- Similar Triangles
- The Triangle Inequality

Page 306

Part IV: Circles
- Area and Circumference
- Equation of a Circle
- Endpoints and Midpoints
- Completing the Square
- Tangent Lines
- Circle Ratios (arc length and sector area)

Page 322

Topic 18: Right Triangle Trigonometry
- SOHCAHTOA
- The Unit Circle
- Sine and Cosine Properties

Page 340

Topic 19: Imaginary and Complex Numbers
- Imaginary Numbers
  - Powers of Imaginary Numbers
  - Operations with Imaginary Numbers
- Complex Numbers
  - Addition & Subtraction, Multiplication, and Division
  - The Conjugate

Page 352

Topic 20: Absolute Value
- Solving Absolute Value Equations

Page 360

Topic 1: Expressions

An <u>expression</u> is a combination of numbers and variables linked by a mathematical operation (addition, subtraction, division, or multiplication).

$3x + 5$, xy, and $2a - b$ are all examples of expressions.

Expressions vs. Equations

Equations have an equal sign; **expressions** do **NOT**.

Unlike equations, expressions **CANNOT** be solved. We can, however, manipulate expressions (combine like terms, distribute a term, etc.).

Expression (unsolvable)	Equation (solvable)
$3x + 5$	$3x + 5 = 10$
xy	$xy = 5$
$2a - b$	$2a - b = c$

Combining Like Terms

We can only **add** or **subtract** terms with the **exact** same variable.

This means that the terms must be…

1. Of the same variable (x, y, a, b)
2. Raised to the same power ($x^5 \neq x^2$)

Expression	Common Variable	Simplified Form
$2x + 4x$	x	$6x$
$7y - 0.5y$	y	$6.5y$
$143x^3 - 18x^3$	x^3	$125x^3$
$17y + 20x$	**NONE** y and x are <u>NOT</u> the same variable, so we cannot simplify the expression	$17y + 20x$
$30x^3 + 12x^2$	**NONE** x^3 and x^2 are NOT raised to the same power, so we cannot simplify the expression	$30x^3 + 12x^2$
$6x^2y^2z + 6x^2y^2z^2$	**NONE** x^2y^2z and $x^2y^2z^2$ are NOT the same (the power attached to "z" is inconsistent), so we cannot simplify the expression	$6x^2y^2z + 6x^2y^2z^2$

> Simplify the following expression:
> $24x^2z - 8xz + 16y^3 + 14y^3 + 2x^2z$

All x^2z terms: $24x^2z + 2x^2z = 26x^2z$
All xz terms: $-8xz$
All y^3 terms: $16y^3 + 14y^3 = 30y^3$

Final Simplification: $26x^2z - 8xz + 30y^3$

Drill

1

Instructions: Combine like terms. If the terms cannot be combined, leave them as is.

A. $5x - 7x$ _____

B. $3x^5 + 4x^5$ _____

C. $5a^2b - 2ab^2 + 8a^2b + 10ab^2$ _____

D. $7x^5y - 13xy^5$ _____

Distributing a Term

A term sitting **outside** a set of parentheses should be distributed to **ALL** terms inside of the parentheses.

<u>RULE</u>: Distribute first. Add and subtract later.

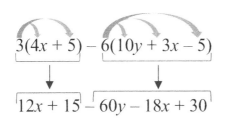

$3(4x + 5) - 6(10y + 3x - 5)$

$12x + 15 - 60y - 18x + 30$

*<u>NOTE</u>: We must distribute not only the term but also the **SIGN** (+ / -) attached to the term. For the second distribution, we distribute "-6" and not just "6"

Now that we've distributed, we can further simplify by combining like terms:

$12x + 15 - 60y - 18x + 30 = -6x - 60y + 45$

> Simplify the following expression:
>
> $y(2x - 7) - 8(y + 15x)$

<u>Step 1</u>: Distribute

$2xy - 7y - 8y - 120x$

<u>Step 2</u>: Combine Like Terms

$2xy - 15y - 120x$

 Drill

1

Instructions: Perform all necessary distributions. Combine all like terms after distributing.

A. $3(x^2 - 7)$ _____

B. $5x + 4 - 2(x + 3)$ _____

C. $4(3x - 1) - (2x - 5)$ _____

D. $2y(5 - x) + 7(x + 3y)$ _____

"FOIL"

A <u>binomial</u> is an expression with **two** terms that are added or subtracted.

$2x + 5$, $b - 3c$, and $x^2 - 6$ are all examples of binomials.

To multiply two binomials, we use a method called **"FOIL,"** which involves four different multiplications.

$(2x + 6)(4x - 5)$

- <u>F</u>IRST (terms)
- <u>O</u>UTER (terms)
- <u>I</u>NNER (terms)
- <u>L</u>AST (terms)

We will address exponent rules later (in Topic 3). All that you need to know now is that $(x)(x) = x^2$.

<u>First</u>: $(2x)(4x) = 8x^2$
<u>Outer</u>: $(2x)(-5) = -10x$
<u>Inner</u>: $(6)(4x) = 24x$
<u>Last</u>: $(6)(-5) = -30$

We get $8x^2 - 10x + 24x - 30$

Now we can combine like terms: $8x^2 + 14x - 30$

Simplify the following expression:

$-2(x + 4)(3x - 8)$

<u>Step 1</u>: FOIL Terms Inside Parentheses

$-2(3x^2 - 8x + 12x - 32)$

<u>Step 2</u>: Combine Like Terms

$-2(3x^2 + 4x - 32)$

<u>Step 3</u>: Distribute Term Outside Parentheses

$-6x^2 - 8x + 64$

Drill

1

<u>Instructions</u>: Use the "FOIL" method on each of the following examples. Perform all necessary distributions and combine all like terms.

A. $(x - 3)(2x + 5)$ _____

B. $(x - 4)^2$ _____

C. $3(4x - 2)(x + 1)$ _____

D. $2(x - 3)^2$ _____

Picking Numbers

When we are asked for an equivalent expression, we can, of course, try to simplify or expand the expression as needed to find an equivalent version.

Sometimes, however, it's easiest to try plugging in numbers.

> Which of the following expressions is equivalent to $(3x - 4)^2 - (3x - 4)$?
> A) $9x^2 - 24x + 20$
> B) $3x^2 - 27x + 12$
> C) $(3x - 4)(3x - 4)$
> D) $(3x - 4)(3x - 5)$

Step 1: Plug in $x = 0$

<u>Original</u>: $(3[0] - 4)^2 - (3[0] - 4) = (-4)^2 - (-4) = 16 + 4 = 20$

A) $9(0)^2 - 24(0) + 20 = 20$ ✓
B) $3(0)^2 - 27(0) + 12 = 12$
C) $(3[0] - 4)(3[0] - 4) = (-4)(-4) = 16$
D) $(3[0] - 4)(3[0] - 5) = (-4)(-5) = 20$ ✓

*<u>NOTE</u>: You cannot stop and select an answer just because one of your choices matched with the original expression. You must test **ALL** choices.

As we can see, both Choices A and D, like the original expression, equal 20 when we plug in $x = 0$.

To decide between Choices A and D, we will now plug in $x = 1$.

Step 2: Plug in $x = 1$

<u>Original</u>: $(3[1] - 4)^2 - (3[1] - 4) = (-1)^2 - (-1) = 1 + 1 = 2$

A) $9(1)^2 - 24(1) + 20 = 9 - 24 + 20 = 5$
D) $(3[1] - 4)(3[1] - 5) = (-1)(-2) = 2$ ✓

Choice D is correct.

 Drill

1

What is $\dfrac{5}{x-4} - \dfrac{2}{4-x}$?

A) $\dfrac{-28}{(x-4)^2}$

B) $\dfrac{3}{4-x}$

C) $\dfrac{7}{x-4}$

D) $\dfrac{7}{4-x}$

 Drill

2

Which of the following is equivalent to $\dfrac{x^2-5}{x+\sqrt{5}}$?

A) $x-5$
B) $x+5$
C) $x-\sqrt{5}$
D) $x+\sqrt{5}$

Answers

For **detailed solutions**, scan the QR code with your phone's camera

or

visit testpreptips.org/expressions

Drill (Page 2)

A. $-2x$
B. $7x^5$
C. $13a^2b + 8ab^2$
D. $7x^5y - 13xy^5$ (no like terms)

Drill (Page 4)

A. $3x^2 - 21$
B. $3x - 2$
C. $10x + 1$
D. $31y - 2xy + 7x$

Drill (Page 6)

A. $2x^2 - x - 15$
B. $x^2 - 8x + 16$
C. $12x^2 + 6x - 6$
D. $2x^2 - 12x + 18$

Drills (Page 8)

1. C [No Calculator]
2. C [Calculator]

Topic 2: Solving Equations & Isolating Variables

Isolating a Single Variable: The Basics

Rule 1: If a variable is linked to another term by addition or subtraction, perform the opposite operation on the term to "move" it to the other side of the equation.

term added → subtract it
term subtracted → add it

Term Added → Subtract Term
$$x + 5 = 3$$
$$ -5 -5$$
$$x = -2$$

Term Subtracted → Add Term
$$x - 5 = 3$$
$$ +5 +5$$
$$x = 8$$

Rule 2: If a variable is linked to another term by multiplication or division, perform the opposite operation on the term.

term multiplied → divide it
term divided → multiply it

Term Multiplied → Divide Term
$$\frac{5x}{5} = \frac{10}{5}$$
$$x = 2$$

Term Divided → Multiply Term
$$2\left(\frac{x}{2}\right) = 10(2)$$
$$x = 20$$

Rule 3: Add or subtract before multiplying or dividing.

We want to first isolate 4x by subtracting 7 from both sides. Once 4x is isolated, we can isolate x by dividing both sides by 4.

$$4x + 7 = 23$$
$$ -7 -7$$
$$\frac{4x}{4} = \frac{16}{4} \longrightarrow x = 4$$

Rule 4: First, combine like terms. Then solve.

We want to get the variables on one side of the equation and the numbers on the other side of the equation. Then, we can solve the equation.

$$5x - 15 = 2x + 4$$
$$-2x -2x$$
$$3x - 15 = 4$$
$$ +15 +15$$
$$\frac{3x}{3} = \frac{19}{3}$$
$$x = \frac{19}{3}$$

Drill

1

A. Solve for x:

$x - 9 = 4$

D. Solve for y:

$3y = 21$

B. Solve for x:

$\dfrac{x}{4} = 5$

E. Solve for y:

$5y - 11 = 29$

C. Solve for x:

$3 - \dfrac{x}{6} = 2$

F. Solve for x:

$7x + 11 = 3x - 13$

Variables in Terms of Other Variables

We can use the rules we learned to write one variable in terms of other variables.

> Solve for a in terms of b and c:
> $5a + 3b = c$

Use **Rule 3**: Add or subtract before multiplying or dividing.

$$5a = -3b + c$$

$$a = \frac{-3b + c}{5}$$

> Solve for v in terms of d and m:
> $d = \dfrac{m}{v}$

Use **Rule 2**: If a variable is linked to another term by multiplication or division, perform the opposite operation on the term.

term divided → multiply it

$$v(d) = \left(\frac{m}{\cancel{v}}\right)\cancel{v}$$

$$dv = m$$

term multiplied → divide it

$$v = \frac{m}{d}$$

> Solve for C in terms of F and A:
> $$F = \frac{A}{1-C}$$

Use **Rule 2**: If a variable is linked to another term by multiplication or division, perform the opposite operation on the term.

term divided → multiply it

$$(1-C)F = \frac{A}{\cancel{1-C}}\cancel{(1-C)}$$

$$F(1-C) = A$$

term multiplied → divide it

$$\frac{\cancel{F}(1-C)}{\cancel{F}} = \frac{A}{F}$$

$$1 - C = \frac{A}{F}$$

Use **Rule 1**: If a variable is linked to another term by addition or subtraction, perform the opposite operation on the term to "move" it to the other side of the equation.

term added → subtract it

$$-C = \frac{A}{F} - 1$$

We can multiply both sides by -1 to make C positive

$$-1(-C) = \left(\frac{A}{F} - 1\right) \cdot -1$$

$$C = -\frac{A}{F} + 1$$

13

Questions

1
Solve for a in terms of b and c.
$$6a - 3b = 5c$$

2
Solve for F in terms of B and H.
$$H(F - 5) = B$$

3
Solve for c in terms of b and a.
$$3a = \frac{b}{c}$$

4
Solve for B in terms of A and C.
$$3C = \frac{A}{B - 1}$$

5
Solve for h in terms of v and r.
$$v = \pi r^2 + 2\pi r h$$

Using Factoring to Get a Variable in Terms of Other Variables

***NOTE**: Sometimes, we will need to **factor out** a term to isolate a variable.

$$\boxed{\begin{array}{c}\text{Solve for } x \text{ in terms } k: \\ kx + x = 5\end{array}}$$

We can do this by factoring x out of both kx and x. Because x perfectly factors into x, it will become 1:

$$kx + x = 5 \longrightarrow x(k+1) = 5$$

Then we can divide both sides by $k + 1$ to isolate x entirely: $x = \dfrac{5}{k+1}$

 Drill

1

Solve for x in terms of a and c.

$$cx - 10x = 4a$$

Square Roots

Expressions vs. Equations

	Expression	Equation
Example	$\sqrt{49}$	$x^2 = 49$ $\sqrt{x^2} = \sqrt{49}$
Solution	7	$x = \pm 7$
Meaning	Taking the square root of an **expression** gives **only a positive** solution.	When we use a square root as a **way to solve** an equation, we must account for the **positive AND negative** solutions of a square root.

Drill

1

A. What is $\sqrt{25}$?

B. Solve for x:

$x^2 = 25$

Square Roots vs. Squaring

Square Root ←――― opposite ―――→ Squaring

When we square a square root, the operations (which are opposite) cancel each other out:

$$\sqrt{4} \longrightarrow (\sqrt{4})^2 \longrightarrow 4$$

When a **square root is squared**, we will always just be left with the number, variable, or expression that is inside the square root:

$$(\sqrt{x+2})^2 \longrightarrow x+2 \quad\quad (\sqrt{7a})^2 \longrightarrow 7a$$

We can use this property to solve equations involving square roots

Squaring to Get Rid of a Square Root

What is the value of x if $\sqrt{2x} = 6$?

$$(\sqrt{2x})^2 = 6^2$$
$$2x = 36$$
$$x = 18$$

*RULE: The square root term must be isolated before we can square both sides of the equation.

What is the value of x if $\sqrt{4x-7} + 6 = 9$?

First isolate the square root term by subtracting 6 from both sides:

$$\sqrt{4x-7} = 3$$

Now we can square both sides:

$$(\sqrt{4x-7})^2 = 3^2$$
$$4x - 7 = 9$$
$$4x = 16$$
$$x = 4$$

What is the value of x if $3\sqrt{5x-1} - 4 = 2$?

First isolate the square root term by adding 4 to both sides. Then divide both sides by 3:

$$3\sqrt{5x-1} = 6$$
$$\sqrt{5x-1} = 2$$

Now we can square both sides:

$$(\sqrt{5x-1})^2 = 2^2$$
$$5x - 1 = 4$$
$$5x = 5$$
$$x = 1$$

 **Drills**

1

Instructions: Solve for x in each of the following examples.

A. $\sqrt{x} = 3$

C. $(\sqrt{x-2})^2 = (10)^2$

$x - 2 = 100$

$x = 98$

B. $\sqrt{4x + 1} - 5 = 2$

D. $6\sqrt{x - 3} - 4 = 44$

2

Solve for B in terms of A and C.

$$A = \sqrt{\frac{B-1}{C}}$$

3

Solve for D in terms of H, F, and K.

$$H = F\sqrt{\frac{K}{D}}$$

Extraneous Solutions

Square root equations can have extraneous (false) solutions.

For this reason, we must plug our answer choices back into the original equation to ensure that each one is a valid solution.

> What value(s) of x satisfy the following equation: $\sqrt{2x} = x - 4$?

$$\left(\sqrt{2x}\right)^2 = (x-4)^2$$
$$2x = x^2 - 8x + 16$$
$$x^2 - 10x + 16 = 0$$
$$(x-8)(x-2) = 0$$
$$x = 8, x = 2$$

It appears this equation has two solutions: 2 and 8.

However, we must plug them both back in to ensure they are valid:

$\underline{x = 2}$:

$$\sqrt{2(2)} = 2 - 4$$
$$\sqrt{4} = -2$$
$$2 \neq -2$$

$x = 2$ is **extraneous**

$\underline{x = 8}$:

$$\sqrt{2(8)} = 8 - 4$$
$$\sqrt{16} = 4$$
$$4 = 4$$

Therefore, only $x = 8$ is a valid solution to this equation.

Factoring Quadratics is discussed in extensive detail on pages 100-109 in Topic 7: Quadratics

> Which of the following is a solution to the equation $\sqrt{x+12} = -x$?
>
> I. -3
> II. 4
>
> A) I
> B) II
> C) I and II
> D) Neither I nor II

***NOTE**: When we are provided with potential solutions in a multiple choice question like the one above, there is no need to actually square both sides and solve the equation. Instead, simply plug in the two options.

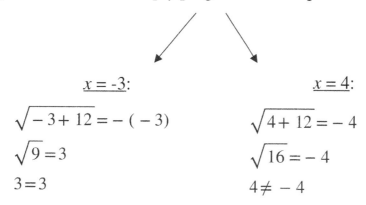

Therefore, only $x = -3$ is a solution to this equation, making **Choice A** correct.

1

Which of the following is a solution to the equation $\sqrt{10-3x} = -x$?

I. -5
II. 2

A) I only
B) II only
C) I and II
D) Neither I nor II

2

What value(s) of x satisfy the following equation: $\sqrt{6-2x} = x-3$?

21

Using a Square Root to Get Rid of a Square

What value(s) of x satisfy the following equation: $36 = (x + 4)^2$?

Recall that when we use a square root as a **way to solve** an equation, we must take both the **positive** and **negative** solutions of the square root, giving us two equations to solve.

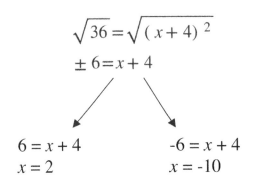

 Drills

1
What value(s) of x solve(s) the equation shown below?

$$(x - 1)^2 = 25$$

2
What value(s) of x solve(s) the equation shown below?

$$5(x + 3)^2 = 20$$

Answers

For **detailed solutions**, scan the QR code with your phone's camera

or

visit testpreptips.org/equations

Drills (Page 11)

A. $x = 13$
B. $x = 20$
C. $x = 6$
D. $y = 7$
E. $y = 8$
F. $x = -6$

Questions (Page 14)

1. $a = \dfrac{3b + 5c}{6}$

2. $F = \dfrac{B}{H} + 5$

3. $c = \dfrac{b}{3a}$

4. $B = \dfrac{A}{3C} + 1$

5. $h = \dfrac{v - \pi r^2}{2\pi r}$

Drill (Page 15)

1. $x = \dfrac{4a}{c - 10}$

Drill (Page 16)

A. 5
B. $x = \pm 5$

Drills (Page 19)

1.

A. $x = 9$
B. $x = 12$
C. $x = 102$
D. $x = 67$

2. $B = A^2C + 1$

3. $D = \dfrac{KF^2}{H^2}$

Drills (Page 21)

1. A
2. $x = 3$

Drills (Page 22)

1. $x = 6$ and $x = -4$
2. $x = -1$ and $x = -5$

Topic 3: Exponents

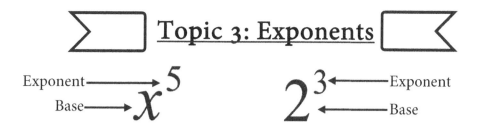

Exponent Rule Table

Rule	Demonstration
Zero Rule Any number or variable raised to the power of zero will be 1 (excluding the number zero itself)	A. $x^0 = \boxed{1}$ B. $15^0 = 1$ C. $6256.5^0 = 1$
Negative Exponents To make a negative exponent positive, **flip** it over the fraction bar. *<u>CAUTION</u>: Make sure you are only moving the number or variable **with** the negative exponent attached to it (shown in Demonstrations E and F).	A. $x^{-2} = \dfrac{1}{x^2}$ B. $5^{-1} = \dfrac{1}{5}$ C. $\dfrac{1}{\boxed{y^{-5}}} = y^5$ D. $5^{-a}x^{-b} = \dfrac{1}{5^a x^b}$ E. $4x^{-6} = \dfrac{4}{x^6}$ F. $\dfrac{6}{7^{-2}x} = \dfrac{6(7)^2}{x}$
Product Rule When multiplying exponential terms of the <u>same base</u>, **add** the exponents.	A. $(x^a)(x^b) = x^{a+b}$ B. $(2^3)(2^5) = 2^8$ C. $(a^{-4})(a^{-3}) = a^{-7} = \dfrac{1}{a^7}$ D. $(108^2)(108^{-1}) = 108$

25

Quotient Rule When dividing exponential terms of the <u>same base</u>, **subtract** the exponents.	A. $\dfrac{x^a}{x^b} = x^{a-b}$ B. $\dfrac{3^8}{3^3} = 3^5$ C. $\dfrac{s^{-9}}{s^{-2}} = s^{-7} = \dfrac{1}{s^7}$ D. $\dfrac{4k^3}{k^{-4}} = 4k^7$ E. $\dfrac{x^3}{x^9} = x^{-6} = \dfrac{1}{x^6}$
Power Rule When raising an exponential term to a power, **multiply** the exponents.	A. $(x^a)^b = x^{ab}$ B. $(2^5)^3 = 2^{15}$ C. $(s^5)^2 = s^{10}$
Distribution Rule When raising a product to an exponent, **distribute** the exponent to all the terms being multiplied / divided. *__CAUTION__: We can only distribute a power when the terms inside the parentheses are **multiplied** or **divided**. We CANNOT distribute the power to terms that are **added** or **subtracted**. $\left(\dfrac{x^5 y^2}{z^{-1}}\right)^3$ ✓ 3 **can** be distributed to each of the terms $(x - 100)^3$ ✗ 3 **CANNOT** be distributed to each of the terms	A. $(xy)^a = x^a y^a$ B. $(sr)^5 = s^5 r^5$ C. $(5x)^6 = 5^6 x^6 = 15{,}625 x^6$ D. $\left(4x^2 y\right)^3 = 4^3 x^6 y^3 = 64 x^6 y^3$ E. $\left(\dfrac{5x^8}{6y^2}\right)^3 = \dfrac{5^3 x^{24}}{6^3 y^6} = \dfrac{125 x^{24}}{216 y^6}$ F. $\left(\dfrac{2a^2 b^{-4}}{c^{-3}}\right)^{-3} = \dfrac{2^{-3} a^{-6} b^{12}}{c^9} = \dfrac{b^{12}}{2^3 a^6 c^9} = \dfrac{b^{12}}{8 a^6 c^9}$

Drills

Instructions: For all drills below, express your final answer in terms of **positive exponents**. For example, if your answer is $\frac{1}{x^{-3}}$, express it as x^3.

Zero Rule

1. 5^0

1

2. $a^0 b^5$

b^5

3. $(425^0)(32)$

32

Negative Exponents

1. $\frac{1}{x^{-7}}$

x^7

2. $\frac{4}{a^{-3}}$

$4a^3$

3. $\frac{5x^{-1}}{y^{-2}}$

$\frac{y^2}{5x^1}$

4. $7a^{-1}$

$\frac{7}{a^1}$

5. If $c > 0$, which of the following expressions is equivalent to c^{-3}?

(A.) $\frac{1}{c^3}$
B. $\frac{1}{\sqrt[3]{c}}$
C. $\sqrt[3]{c}$
D. $-3c$

Product Rule

1. $(z^5)(z^2)$
z^7

2. $(x)(x^4)$
x^5

3. $(a^9)(a^{-2})$
a^7

4. $(d^4)(d^{-7})$
$\dfrac{1}{d^3}$

5. $6(y^{-9})(y^{-5})$
$\dfrac{6}{y^{14}}$

Quotient Rule

1. $\dfrac{8x^4}{2x^3}$
$4x^1$

2. $\dfrac{x^7}{x^3}$
x^4

3. $\dfrac{b^5}{b^9}$
$\dfrac{1}{b^{-4}}$

4. $\dfrac{2a^6}{4a^7}$
$\dfrac{1}{2a^{-1}}$

5. $\dfrac{c^{-11}}{c^{-3}}$
$\dfrac{1}{c^8}$

6. $\dfrac{8a^{11}}{4a^{13}}$
$2a^{-7}$

7. $\dfrac{a^1}{a^{15}}$
$\dfrac{1}{a^{14}}$

$\begin{array}{r} {}^0\!\!/\!\!/^{10} \\ -13 \\ \hline 7 \end{array}$

Power Rule

1. $(x^3)^2$

x^6

2. $(5^3)^4$

5^{12}

3. $(y^3)^a$

y^{3a}

Distribution Rule

Instructions: For the following drills, circle YES or NO to indicate if the power can be distributed.

1. $(xy)^3$ — **YES** / NO

2. $(x+y)^3$ — YES / **NO**

3. $(x-7)^2$ — YES / **NO**

4. $(7x)^{-2}$ — **YES** / NO

5. $(10+x)^{-8}$ — YES / **NO**

6. $\left(\dfrac{3x}{y^2}\right)^5$ — **YES** / NO

Instructions: For the following drills, use the Distribution Rule.

1. $(ab)^2$

$a^2 b^2$

2. $(2a^3 b^5)^4$

$2^4 a^{12} b^{20}$

3. $(x^{-2} y^7)^{-3}$

$x^6 y^{-21}$

4. $\left(\dfrac{5x^5}{y^2 z}\right)^2$

$\dfrac{25 x^{10}}{y^4 z^2}$

5. $\left(\dfrac{2xy^5}{4z^3}\right)^{-3}$

$\dfrac{2^{-3} x^{-3} y^{-15}}{4^{-3} z^{-9}}$

6. $\left(\dfrac{6a^{-1} c^3}{4b^{-5}}\right)^{-2}$

$\dfrac{6^{-2} a^2 c^{-6}}{4^{-2} b^{10}}$

7. $\left(\dfrac{2}{3}\right)^2$

$\dfrac{4}{9}$

Combined Exponent Rules

1

$$\frac{a^3 b^9 c^{-2}}{a^{-4} b^5 c^3}$$

2

$$\left(\frac{6a^8 c^{-2}}{4ac^5}\right)^{-2}$$

Making the Bases Identical

Product Rule: $(x^a)(x^b) = x^{a+b}$

Quotient Rule: $\dfrac{y^a}{y^b} = y^{a-b}$

As discussed, to use either the Product Rule or the Quotient Rule, the **bases** of each term must be **identical**.

To make our bases identical, we may have to rewrite them:

$$(8^5)(2^2) = ?$$

We can make the bases identical by realizing that both bases are perfect powers of the same number.

If both bases are powers of the same number, we can reduce each base to that number.

Because $8 = 2^3$....

$$(8)^5 (2)^2$$
$$= (2^3)^5 (2)^2$$
$$= (2^{15})(2^2)$$
$$= 2^{17}$$

Which expression is equivalent to $\dfrac{4^{2c}}{8^{d}}$?

A) 4^{2c-2d}
B) 2^{4c-3d}
C) 2^{2c-d}
D) $\dfrac{1}{2^{2c-d}}$

Step 1: Make the bases identical

$$\dfrac{\left(2^{2}\right)^{2c}}{\left(2^{3}\right)^{d}} \rightarrow \dfrac{2^{4c}}{2^{3d}}$$

Step 2: Subtract the exponents

Choice B: 2^{4c-3d}

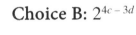

1
Express $(16^{4})(2^{6})$ as a single exponent.

32

2
Express $(4^{x-2})(8^{5x})$ as a single exponent.

3
If $2x - y = 5$, what is the value of $\dfrac{4^{x}}{2^{y}}$?

A) 4
B) 8
C) 16
D) 32

Radicals ⟷ Exponents

Radicals to Exponents

When going from a radical to an exponent, the number inside the radical (here, 2) becomes the top of the fraction. The number outside the radical (here, 3) becomes the bottom of the fraction.

"Inner, Upper"/ "Outer, Under"

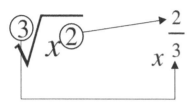

Exponents to Radicals

When going from an exponent to a radical, execute the process in reverse: move the number on the top of the fraction to the inner part of the radical and the number on the bottom of the fraction to the outer part of the radical.

"Upper, Inner"/ "Under, Outer"

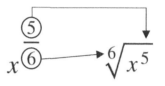

*__NOTE__: If we see a radical without a number written on the outside, such as $\sqrt{x}$, we assume there is a 2:

$$\sqrt{x} = \sqrt[2]{x} = x^{\frac{1}{2}}$$

Operations with Radicals

For performing operations on radicals, you can refer to the table listed below:

Radical Rule Table

Rule	Demonstration
N/A	N/A
N/A	N/A
N/A	N/A

There's **no such thing** as a radical rule table, simply because it's so much easier to manipulate exponents. If we're presented with terms in a radical form, we want to convert them to exponents before we attempt to manipulate them:

$$(\sqrt[4]{x^2})(\sqrt[8]{x^7}) \rightarrow x^{\frac{2}{4}} x^{\frac{7}{8}}$$

$$x^{\frac{2}{4}+\frac{7}{8}} \rightarrow x^{\frac{4}{8}} + x^{\frac{7}{8}}$$

$$x^{\frac{11}{8}}$$

Radicals → Exponents [Part I]

$\dfrac{Power}{root}$

Instructions: Convert each of the following radicals to exponents.

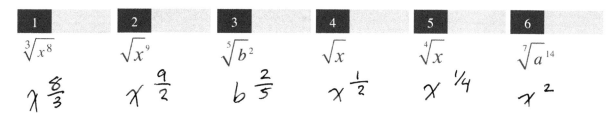

1. $\sqrt[3]{x^8}$ → $x^{\frac{8}{3}}$
2. $\sqrt{x^9}$ → $x^{\frac{9}{2}}$
3. $\sqrt[5]{b^2}$ → $b^{\frac{2}{5}}$
4. $\sqrt{x}$ → $x^{\frac{1}{2}}$
5. $\sqrt[4]{x}$ → $x^{1/4}$
6. $\sqrt[7]{a^{14}}$ → x^2

Exponents → Radicals [Part II]

Instructions: Convert each of the following exponents to radicals.

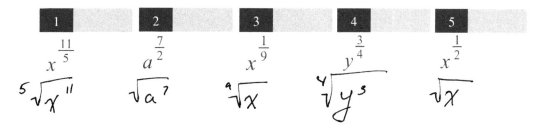

1. $x^{\frac{11}{5}}$ → $\sqrt[5]{x^{11}}$
2. $a^{\frac{7}{2}}$ → $\sqrt{a^7}$
3. $x^{\frac{1}{9}}$ → $\sqrt[9]{x}$
4. $y^{\frac{3}{4}}$ → $\sqrt[4]{y^3}$
5. $x^{\frac{1}{2}}$ → $\sqrt{x}$

Desired Operation [Part III]

Instructions: Perform the desired operation.

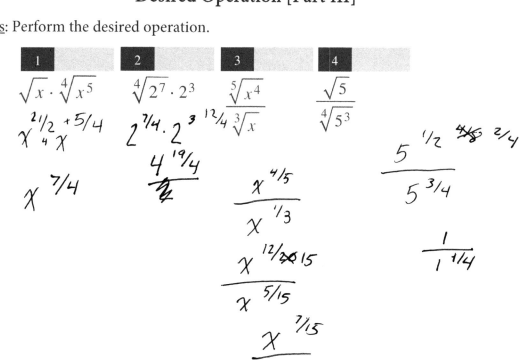

1. $\sqrt{x} \cdot \sqrt[4]{x^5}$

$x^{2/4} \cdot x^{5/4}$ ← $x^{1/2 + 5/4}$

$x^{7/4}$

2. $\sqrt[4]{2^7} \cdot 2^3$

$2^{7/4} \cdot 2^3$

$4^{19/4}$

3. $\dfrac{\sqrt[5]{x^4}}{\sqrt[3]{x}}$

$\dfrac{x^{4/5}}{x^{1/3}}$

$\dfrac{x^{12/15}}{x^{5/15}}$

$x^{7/15}$

4. $\dfrac{\sqrt{5}}{\sqrt[4]{5^3}}$

$\dfrac{5^{1/2}}{5^{3/4}}$ $\dfrac{2/4}{}$

$\dfrac{1}{1^{1/4}}$

Radical Reduction for Square Roots

When we are presented with the expression $\sqrt{50}$, our aim is to pull out the perfect square and leave the rest under the square root sign, as there's nothing more we can simplify:

$$\sqrt{50} \to \sqrt{25}\sqrt{2} \to 5\sqrt{2}$$

When we are presented with an expression with variables, there are two ways that we may be asked to express an answer:

Type 1: Radical Remaining Method

We will pull out all perfect squares, combine the rest, and leave those combined terms under the radical sign.

$$\sqrt{x^7 y^5} \to \sqrt{x^6}\sqrt{x}\sqrt{y^4}\sqrt{y} \to x^3 y^2 \sqrt{xy}$$

Type 2: Fractional Exponents Method

We will convert the radical to an exponent.

$$\sqrt{x^7 y^5} \to x^{\frac{7}{2}} y^{\frac{5}{2}}$$

*<u>NOTE</u>: $x^3 y^2 \sqrt{xy} = x^{\frac{7}{2}} y^{\frac{5}{2}}$. These are two ways of expressing the **same** answer.

*<u>CAUTION</u>: Just as we could only distribute a power when the terms inside of the parentheses were **multiplied** or **divided** (NOT added or subtracted), we can only distribute a radical to terms that are **multiplied or divided** (NOT **added** or **subtracted**).

$\sqrt{\dfrac{9x^2}{4y^2}} \to \dfrac{\sqrt{9x^2}}{\sqrt{4y^2}} \to \dfrac{3x}{2y}$ ✓ The radical **can** be distributed to each of the terms

$\sqrt{9x^2 + 4y^2}$ ✗ The radical **CANNOT** be distributed to each of the terms

Drills

Instructions: For the following drills, circle YES or NO to indicate if the radical can be distributed.

1. $\sqrt{4x^2}$ — (YES) / NO

2. $\sqrt{x^2+4}$ — YES / (NO)

3. $\sqrt[7]{8x^3-27}$ — YES / (NO)

4. $\sqrt[7]{8x^3 y^6}$ — (YES) / NO

5. $\sqrt[3]{\dfrac{8a^{12}}{b^3}}$ — (YES) / NO

Instructions: For the following drills, simplify by the **Radical Remaining Method**.

Example: $\sqrt{18x^3y^4} \to \sqrt{9}\sqrt{2}\sqrt{x^2}\sqrt{x}\sqrt{y^4} \to 3xy^2\sqrt{2x}$

1. $\sqrt{32}$

$\sqrt{\cancel{9}}\sqrt{4}$
$\sqrt{8}\sqrt{4}$
$2\sqrt{8}$

2. $\sqrt{\dfrac{4}{9}}$

$\dfrac{2}{3}$

3. $\sqrt{x^8 y^{20}}$

$x^4 y^{10}$

4. $\sqrt{25a^{12}b^2}$

$5a^6 b$

5. $\sqrt{\dfrac{36x^2}{25y^6}}$

$\dfrac{6}{25y^3}$

6. $\sqrt{a^{13}}$

$a^{\frac{13}{2}}$

7. $\sqrt{15x^{11}y^{19}}$

$\sqrt{15}\, x^{11/2} y^{19/2}$

8. $\sqrt{50x^9 y^6}$

$\sqrt{50}\, x^{9/2} y^3$

Instructions: For the following drills, simplify by the **Fractional Exponent Method**.

Example: $\sqrt{9x^6 y^{11}} \to 3x^{\frac{6}{2}} y^{\frac{11}{2}} \to 3x^3 y^{\frac{11}{2}}$

1. $\sqrt{a^{13}}$

$a^{13/2}$

2. $\sqrt{49x^{11}y^{19}}$

$7x^{11/2} y^{19/2}$

3. $\sqrt{25x^9 y^6}$

$5x^{9/2} y^3$

Radical Reduction for Higher Roots

The same process applies when we change a square root to a cube root and beyond.

Here, we can also express an answer in two ways:

Type 1: Radical Remaining Method

We will pull out all perfect powers, combine the rest, and leave those combined terms under the radical sign.

$$\sqrt[3]{x^7 y^5} \rightarrow \sqrt[3]{x^6}\left(\sqrt[3]{x}\right)\sqrt[3]{y^3}\left(\sqrt[3]{y^2}\right) \rightarrow x^2 y \left(\sqrt[3]{xy^2}\right)$$

Type 2: Fractional Exponent Method

We will convert the radical to an exponent.

$$\sqrt[3]{x^7 y^5} \rightarrow x^{\frac{7}{3}} y^{\frac{5}{3}}$$

*__NOTE__: $x^2 y \left(\sqrt[3]{xy^2}\right) = x^{\frac{7}{3}} y^{\frac{5}{3}}$. These are two ways of expressing the **same** answer.

Instructions: For the following drills, simplify by the **Radical Remaining Method**.

Example: $\sqrt[3]{27x^3y^5} \rightarrow \sqrt[3]{27}\left(\sqrt[3]{x^3}\right)\left(\sqrt[3]{y^3}\right)\left(\sqrt[3]{y^2}\right) \rightarrow 3xy\left(\sqrt[3]{y^2}\right)$

1. $\sqrt[3]{8}$

2. $\sqrt[3]{27x^3}$

3. $\sqrt[3]{\dfrac{x^6}{y^9}}$

4. $\sqrt[3]{\dfrac{27x^{12}}{64y^9}}$

5. $\sqrt[4]{a^6b^7c^8}$

6. $\sqrt[3]{16x^{10}y^{21}}$

7. $\sqrt[5]{64x^{12}y^{19}z^{10}}$

Instructions: For the following drills, simplify by the **Fractional Exponents Method**.

Example: $\sqrt[3]{8x^9y^{14}} \rightarrow 2x^{\frac{9}{3}}y^{\frac{14}{3}} \rightarrow 2x^3y^{\frac{14}{3}}$

1. $\sqrt[4]{a^6b^7c^8}$

2. $\sqrt[3]{27x^{10}y^{21}}$

3. $\sqrt[5]{32x^{12}y^{19}z^{10}}$

Applying the "Heart Method" to Exponents

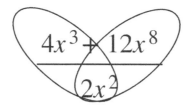

We need to evaluate each term individually, dividing each term in the top of the fraction by the single term in the bottom of the fraction:

$$\frac{4x^3}{2x^2} + \frac{12x^8}{2x^2}$$

$$= 2x + 6x^6$$

Drills

<u>Instructions</u>: Simplify each of the following expressions.

1

$$\frac{12x^5 - 8x^7}{x^2}$$

$$\frac{12x^5}{x^2} - \frac{8x^7}{x^2}$$

$$\frac{4x^{-2}}{x^2}$$

$$\boxed{4}$$

2

$$\frac{15a^4 + 5a^9}{5a^4}$$

$$\frac{15a^4}{5a^4} + \frac{5a^9}{5a^4}$$

$$3a + a$$

$$3 + a^5$$

Questions

1

Which of the following is equivalent to $2^{\frac{3}{2}}$?

A) 3
B) 4
C) $2\sqrt{2}$
D) 8

2

Which of the following is equivalent to $\dfrac{(3a^{-3}\sqrt{b})^2}{a^2 b^{-2}}$ if a and b are both positive real numbers?

A) $\dfrac{9b^3}{a^8}$
B) $\dfrac{9b^3}{a^{10}}$
C) $9a^8 b^3$
D) $9a^4 b^3$

3

If $a > 0$ and $b > 0$, $(a^2 b^3)^{\frac{1}{2}}(a^4 b^6)^{\frac{1}{2}} = a^c b^d$. What is the value of $|c - d|$?

A) $\dfrac{27}{2}$
B) $\dfrac{3}{2}$
C) $\dfrac{15}{2}$
D) 3

4

$x(x^2)^3 = x^a$. What is the value of a?

A) 5
B) 6
C) 7
D) 9

5

If $s > 0$, then which of the following is equivalent to $\sqrt{s}(s^{\frac{1}{3}})$?

A) $s^{\frac{1}{5}}$
B) $s^{\frac{1}{6}}$
C) $s^{\frac{5}{6}}$
D) $s^{\frac{2}{3}}$

6

What is the value of $\dfrac{2^b}{16^a}$ if $b = 4a + 4$?

A) 4
B) 8
C) 16
D) 32

7

If $x > 0$, $\dfrac{5x(3x)^2}{(2x)^3}$ is equal to what value?

$$5x(9x^2)$$

$$\dfrac{45x^3}{8x^3}$$

8

What is the value of $\left(\dfrac{\sqrt{3}}{2}\right)^2$?

$$\left(\dfrac{3^{1/2}}{2}\right)^2 \qquad \begin{array}{c} 1/2 \cdot 1/2 \\ \uparrow \\ 1/4 \end{array}$$

$$\dfrac{3^{1/4}}{2^4}$$

$$\dfrac{3}{2^{3\,3/4}}$$

Answers

For **detailed solutions**, scan the QR code with your phone's camera

or

visit **testpreptips.org/exponents**

Drills (Page 27)

Zero Rule
1. 1
2. b^5
3. 32

Negative Exponents
1. x^7
2. $4a^3$
3. $\dfrac{5y^2}{x}$
4. $\dfrac{7}{a}$
5. A

Drills (Page 28)

Product Rule
1. z^7
2. x^5
3. a^7
4. $\dfrac{1}{d^3}$
5. $\dfrac{6}{y^{14}}$

Quotient Rule
1. $4x$
2. x^4
3. $\dfrac{1}{b^4}$
4. $\dfrac{1}{2a}$
5. $\dfrac{1}{c^8}$
6. $\dfrac{2}{a^2}$
7. $\dfrac{1}{a^{14}}$

Drills (Page 29)

Power Rule
1. x^6
2. 5^{12}
3. y^{3a}

Distribution Rule [Part I]
1. YES
2. NO
3. NO
4. YES
5. NO
6. YES

Distribution Rule [Part II]
1. a^2b^2
2. $16a^{12}b^{20}$
3. $\dfrac{x^6}{y^{21}}$
4. $\dfrac{25x^{10}}{y^4z^2}$
5. $\dfrac{8z^9}{x^3y^{15}}$
6. $\dfrac{4a^2}{9b^{10}c^6}$
7. $\dfrac{4}{9}$

Drills (Page 30)

Combined Exponent Rules
1. $\dfrac{a^7b^4}{c^5}$
2. $\dfrac{4c^{14}}{9a^{14}}$

Drills (Page 31)

1. 2^{22}
2. 2^{17x-4}
3. D

Drills (Page 33)

Radicals → Exponents [Part I]	Exponents → Radicals [Part II]	Desired Operation [Part III]
1. $x^{\frac{8}{3}}$	1. $\sqrt[5]{x^{11}}$	1. $x^{\frac{7}{4}}$
2. $x^{\frac{9}{2}}$	2. $\sqrt{a^7}$	2. $2^{\frac{19}{4}}$
3. $b^{\frac{2}{5}}$	3. $\sqrt[9]{x}$	3. $x^{\frac{7}{15}}$
4. $x^{\frac{1}{2}}$	4. $\sqrt[4]{y^3}$	4. $\dfrac{1}{5^{\frac{1}{4}}}$
5. $x^{\frac{1}{4}}$	5. $\sqrt{x}$	
6. a^2		

Drills (Page 35)

Part I	Radical Remaining [Part II]	Fractional Exponent [Part III]
1. YES	1. $4\sqrt{2}$	1. $a^{\frac{13}{2}}$
2. NO	2. $\dfrac{2}{3}$	2. $7x^{\frac{11}{2}} y^{\frac{19}{2}}$
3. NO	3. $x^4 y^{10}$	3. $5x^{\frac{9}{2}} y^3$
4. YES	4. $5a^6 b$	
5. YES	5. $\dfrac{6x}{5y^3}$	
	6. $a^6 \sqrt{a}$	
	7. $x^5 y^9 \sqrt{15xy}$	
	8. $5x^4 y^3 \sqrt{2x}$	

Drills (Page 37)

Radical Remaining [Part I]

1. 2
2. $3x$
3. $\dfrac{x^2}{y^3}$
4. $\dfrac{3x^4}{4y^3}$
5. $abc^2\left(\sqrt[4]{a^2b^3}\right)$
6. $2x^3y^7\left(\sqrt[3]{2x}\right)$
7. $2x^2y^3z^2\left(\sqrt[5]{2x^2y^4}\right)$

Fractional Exponent [Part II]

1. $a^{\frac{3}{2}}b^{\frac{7}{4}}c^2$
2. $3x^{\frac{10}{3}}y^7$
3. $2x^{\frac{12}{5}}y^{\frac{19}{5}}z^2$

Drills (Page 38)

1. $12x^3 - 8x^5$
2. $3 + a^5$

Questions (Pages 39-40)

1. C
2. A
3. B
4. C
5. C
6. C
7. $\dfrac{45}{8}$
8. $\dfrac{3}{4}$

Topic 4: Lines

Slope-Intercept Form

$$y = mx + b$$

m = slope b = y-intercept

The <u>slope</u> of a line tells us how **steep** the line is and in what **direction** it is going

Steepness

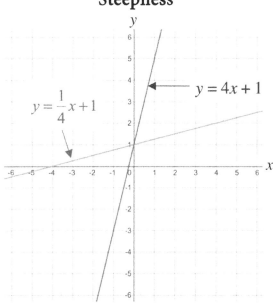

Direction

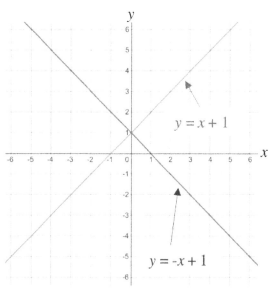

Lines with **larger slopes** (like 4) rise at a **faster** rate (are **steeper**).

Lines with **smaller slopes** (like $\frac{1}{4}$) rise more **gradually** (are **less steep**).

Lines with **positive slopes** (like 1) **increase** from **left-to-right**.

Lines with **negative slopes** (like -1) **decrease** from **left-to-right**.

Calculating the Slope

The slope can be calculated from any two points with the **Slope Formula**:

$$m = \frac{y_2 - y_1}{x_2 - x_1}$$

(0, 5) and (2, 15) are points on Line *L*. What is the slope of Line *L*?

(0, 5)   (2, 15) $m = \frac{15-5}{2-0} = \frac{10}{2} = 5$
$x_1\ y_1$ $x_2\ y_2$

Drills

1

Find the slope of a line with the following points:

A. (2, 7) and (6, 15)

B. (5, -3) and (-1, 21)

C. (-5, 8) and (19, 8)

2

Find the slope of the line shown below <u>using the Slope Formula</u> by picking 2 points on the line.

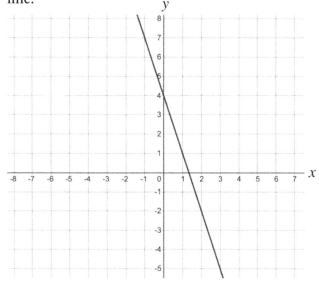

The y-intercept

The y-intercept is where a line crosses the y-axis

The y-intercept occurs when x = 0

Therefore, the y-intercept can always be written as (0, y-intercept)

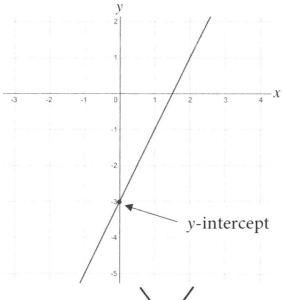

The y-intercept of this line is -3.

The y-intercept of this line occurs at the point (0, -3).

Drill

1

Write the equation of the line shown to the right in $y = mx + b$ form.

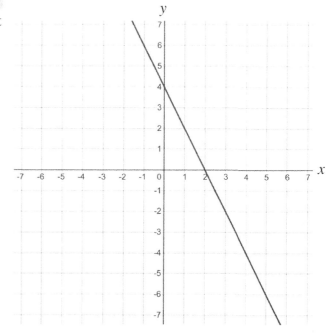

A. First, find the slope:

$m = $ _____

B. Second, identify the y-intercept:

$b = $ _____

C. Third, write the line's equation in $y = mx + b$ form:

_____

D. Write the y-intercept as a coordinate point:

(____ , ____)

The *x*-intercept

The *x*-intercept does not appear in slope-intercept form ($y = mx + b$), but it still is significant

The *x*-intercept is where a line crosses the *x*-axis

The *x*-intercept occurs when $y = 0$

↓

Therefore, the *x*-intercept can always be written as (*x*-intercept, 0)

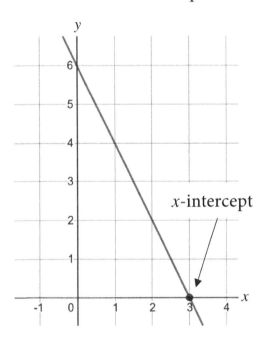

The *x*-intercept of this line is 3.

The *x*-intercept of this line occurs at the point $(3, 0)$

What Does the Slope Mean?

The slope tells us how much y increases (or decreases) each time x increases by 1

Equation	When x increases by 1, y...
$y = 2x$	Increases by 2
$y = -3x + 8$	Decreases by 3
$y = \frac{1}{3}x$	Increases by $\frac{1}{3}$

Graphs

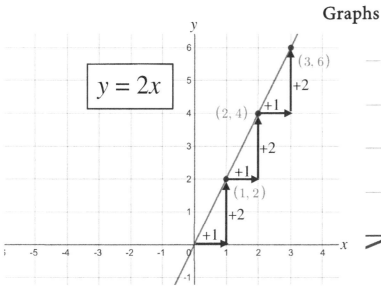

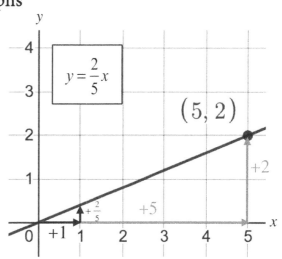

Interpretation

When x increases by 1, y increases by 2

Interpretation

A. When x increases by 1, y increases by $\frac{2}{5}$

B. When x increases by 5, y increases by 2

Drills

1

Interpret the slope of the following line:

$$y = 5x - 1$$

As *x* increases by 1, *y* …

   INCREASES / DECREASES **(circle one)**

   by _____ **(specify amount)**

2

Interpret the slope of the following line:

$$y = \frac{2}{7}x$$

A. As *x* increases by 1, *y* …

   INCREASES / DECREASES **(circle one)**

   by _____ **(specify amount)**

B. As *x* increases by 7, *y* …

   INCREASES / DECREASES **(circle one)**

   by _____ **(specify amount)**

3

Interpret the slope of the following line:

$$y = -4x$$

As *x* increases by 1, *y* …

   INCREASES / DECREASES **(circle one)**

   by _____ **(specify amount)**

4

Interpret the slope of the following line:

$$y = \frac{3}{5}x + 6$$

A. As *x* increases by 1, *y* …

   INCREASES / DECREASES **(circle one)**

   by _____ **(specify amount)**

B. As *x* increases by 5, *y* …

   INCREASES / DECREASES **(circle one)**

   by _____ **(specify amount)**

Interpreting slope, y-intercept, and x-intercept
Real-Life Scenarios

> Roger is saving up money for a vacation. The total amount of money M, in dollars, Roger has in his vacation fund account can be modeled by $M = 100w + 550$, where w represents the number of weeks Roger has been saving.

A. What does 100 represent in this context?

100 represents the slope

Step-by-Step Procedure for Interpreting the Slope:

Step 1: Replace variables in the equation with x and y

$$M = 100w + 550 \longrightarrow y = 100x + 550$$

Step 2: Interpret slope as usual

Each time x increases by 1, y **increases** by 100

Step 3: Swap slope interpretation into real-life scenario

After each week, the total amount of money in Roger's vacation fund, M, increases by $100

B. What does 550 represent in this context?

550 represents the y-intercept

> ***NOTE:** In a physical scenario, the y-intercept represents the starting point

That means Roger started off with $550 in his vacation fund **before** adding any additional money each week.

> A bird sitting on a perch begins descending to the ground. The bird's height h, in meters, can be modeled by the equation $h = -2m + 50$, where m represents the time in minutes.

What is the significance of the m-intercept?

$$h = -2m + 50 \longrightarrow y = -2x + 50$$

In the above equation, m is the x-variable, so the m-intercept is the x-intercept.

As discussed, the x-intercept is the x-value when $y = 0$.

Based on this scenario, the m-intercept is the m-value when $h = 0$. Therefore, it is the number of minutes it takes for the bird's height to be 0 meters (when the bird hits the ground).

Drill

1

Walter, who is standing on top of a building, throws a football to his friend on ground-level. The height of the football, h, relative to the ground, in feet, can be modeled by the following equation: $h = -0.5t + 20$, where t represents the time in seconds for the interval $0 \leq t \leq 40$.

A. What does -0.5 represent in this context?

-0.5 represents the *y*-intercept / *x*-intercept / slope **(circle one)**

Step 1: Replace variables in the equation with x and y

$$h = -0.5t + 20 \longrightarrow \underline{\hspace{3cm}}$$

Step 2: Interpret slope as usual

Each time x increases by 1, y increases / decreases **(circle one)** by _____ **(specify quantity)**

Step 3: Swap slope interpretation into real-life scenario

Each second, the height, h, increases / decreases **(circle one)** by _____ feet **(specify quantity)**

B. What does 20 represent in this context?

20 represents the *y*-intercept / *x*-intercept / slope **(circle one)**

This means that before the football is thrown, its height is _____ feet **(specify quantity)**

C. What is the significance of the *t*-intercept?

The *t*-intercept occurs when t / h **(circle one)** equals 0

The *t*-intercept is the number of seconds it takes for the height of the football to become _____ feet **(specify quantity)**

Finding the Equation of a Line

As discussed, the equation of a line can be easily found if the slope **and** *y*-intercept are provided.

However, we will need to use <u>Point-Slope Form</u> to determine the equation of the line if we are only provided with either…

A. the slope and one point

or

B. two points

Point-Slope Form

$$y - y_1 = m(x - x_1)$$

where y_1 is the *y*-coordinate of point, m is the slope, and x_1 is the *x*-coordinate of point.

A. Slope and One Point

> The slope of Line *J* is -3. The point (3, 5) falls on Line *J*. What is the equation of Line *J*?

$m = -3$
$x_1 = 3$
$y_1 = 5$

$\longrightarrow$

$y - y_1 = m(x - x_1)$
$y - 5 = -3(x - 3)$
$y - 5 = -3x + 9$
$y = -3x + 14$

B. Two Points

The points (-3, 5) and (6, 0) fall on a given line. What is the equation of this line?

Step 1: Use the two points provided to find the slope with the Slope Formula

$$m = \frac{y_2 - y_1}{x_2 - x_1} = \frac{0 - 5}{6 - (-3)} = -\frac{5}{9}$$

Step 2: Take the slope and either one of the two points provided and plug them into Point-Slope Form

$$y - y_1 = m(x - x_1)$$

$$y - 0 = -\frac{5}{9}(x - 6)$$

$$y = -\frac{5}{9}x + \frac{10}{3}$$

***NOTE**: If one of the points has a 0 as either x or y, use that point for Point-Slope Form – it'll make plugging in easier.

Drills

1

What is the equation of the line that has a slope of 5 and passes through the point (1, 4)?

2

What is the equation of the line that passes through the points (-2, -3) and (7, 15)?

55

Parallel and Perpendicular
Parallel Lines

Parallel Lines run side-by-side.

Parallel Lines have the **identical slopes**.

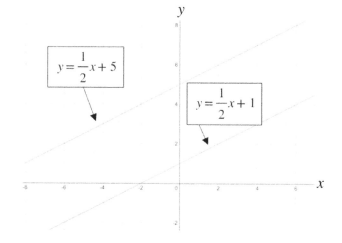

Perpendicular Lines

Perpendicular Lines form right angles with one another.

Perpendicular lines have slopes that are **negative reciprocals**.

$$\frac{1}{3} \longrightarrow \frac{3}{1} \longrightarrow -\frac{3}{1} \longrightarrow -3$$

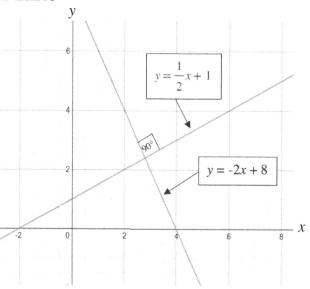

56

Line R has the equation $y = 3x - 4$. If Line S is **parallel** to Line R and passes through the point $(1, 3)$ when graphed in the xy-plane, what is the equation of Line S?

1. Slope of Line S = same slope as Line R = 3
2. Use Point-Slope form to find the equation of Line S

$$y - y_1 = m(x - x_1)$$
$$y - 3 = 3(x - 1)$$
$$y - 3 = 3x - 3$$
$$y = 3x$$

Line R has the equation $y = 3x - 4$. If Line S is **perpendicular** to Line R and passes through the point $(1, 3)$ when graphed in the xy-plane, what is the equation of Line S?

1. Slope of Line S = negative reciprocal of Line R's slope = $-\dfrac{1}{3}$
2. Use Point-Slope form to find the equation of Line S

$$y - y_1 = m(x - x_1)$$
$$y - 3 = -\frac{1}{3}(x - 1)$$
$$y - 3 = -\frac{1}{3}x + \frac{1}{3}$$
$$y = -\frac{1}{3}x + \frac{10}{3}$$

Drills

1

Line M has equation $y = 2x + 5$. If line N is <u>parallel</u> to line M and the graph of line N in the xy-plane passes through the point $(3, 8)$, what is the y-intercept of line N?

2

Line M has equation $y = 2x + 5$. If line N is <u>perpendicular</u> to line M and the graph of line N in the xy-plane passes through the point $(3, 8)$, what is the y-intercept of line N?

Standard Form

When a line is in the following form, it is said to be in Standard Form:

$$ax + by = c$$

Example: $3x + 4y = 7$

If provided with a line in Standard Form, rearrange it into $y = mx + b$ form:

$$3x + 4y = 7 \longrightarrow y = -\frac{3}{4}x + \frac{7}{4}$$

> Lines p and n are parallel in the xy-plane. The equation of line p is $6x + 2y = 20$. Line n passes through the point $(4, 7)$. What is the value of the y-intercept of line n?

Step 1: Rearrange equation into $y = mx + b$ form

$$6x + 2y = 20 \longrightarrow y = -3x + 10$$

***NOTE**: Once rearranged, the slope of the line becomes **visible**

Step 2: Consider what it means for lines to be parallel

Parallel lines have the same slope, so the slope of Line n will also be -3

Step 3: Use Point-Slope Form

$$y - 7 = -3(x - 4)$$
$$y - 7 = -3x + 12$$
$$y = -3x + 19$$

y-intercept = 19

Drills

1

Lines g and h are perpendicular in the xy-plane. The equation of Line g is $10x + 5y = 12$. Line h passes through the point $(6, 3)$. What is the value of the y-intercept of Line h?

2

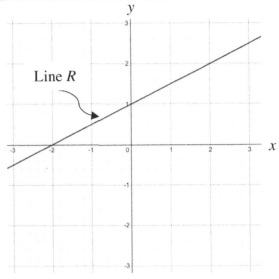

Line R is displayed in the xy-plane above. Which of the following is the equation of Line R?

A) $-x + 2y = 2$
B) $-x - 2y = 2$
C) $x + 2y = 2$
D) $x - 2y = 2$

Questions

1

x	y
5	8
6	11
7	14
8	17

The table above shows some pairs of corresponding x and y values. Which of the following accurately represents the relationship between the 2 variables?

A) $y = 7x - 3$
B) $y = 3x - 7$
C) $y = 2x + 1$
D) $y = \dfrac{x}{5} + 3$

2

The height y, in inches, of a certain species of animal can be modeled by $y = 24x + 19$, where x is the number of years that have passed since the animal was 3. What is the meaning of the y-intercept?

A) The animal's height at birth
B) The animal's height at age 3
C) The age of the animal
D) The number of inches the animal grows in a given year

3

$$S = 0.12M + 1.08$$

The equation above can be used to estimate the speed S, in miles/hour, of a professional adult male runner based on his muscle mass, M, in pounds. What is the meaning of 0.12 in this context?

A) The estimated increase in a professional adult male runner's muscle mass, in pounds, for each one-mile/hour increase in speed.
B) The estimated increase in a professional adult male runner's speed, in miles/hour, for each additional pound of muscle mass.
C) The estimated muscle mass, in pounds, for a professional adult male runner with a speed of 1.08 miles/hour.
D) The estimated increase in a professional adult male runner's muscle mass, in pounds, for each increase of 1.08 to his speed in miles/hour.

4

Which of the following graphs represents the relationship between f and t?

$$f = 68 - 1.5t$$

A)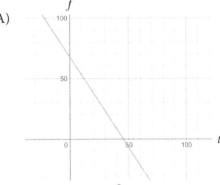

B)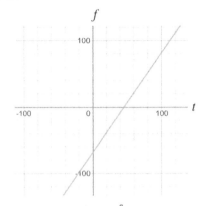

C)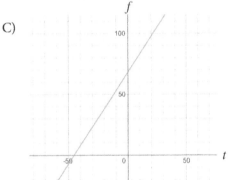

D)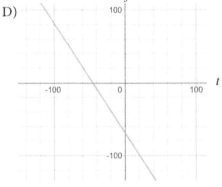

5

x	y
5	13
19	-43

The table above shows some pairs of corresponding x and y values for a linear function. If $x = a$ corresponds with $y = -7$, then what is the value of a?

6

Line A has equation $y = 4x + 2$. Line B has a slope equal to 0.75 times the slope of Line A and a y-intercept equal to the reciprocal of the y-intercept of Line A. If $(5, r)$ is on the graph of Line B in the xy-plane, what is the value of r?

7

The graph of a certain line, Line *L*, in the *xy*-plane contains the point (1, 6) and crosses the *x*-axis at the point (3, 0). Line *L* crosses the *y*-axis at the point (0, *b*). What is the value of *b*?

8

The point (4, *r*) lies on the line that goes through (-2, -3) and (7, 15). What is the value of *r*?

 Questions

1

Price Per "Kitchen-Sink" Sundae with Toppings

Topping Count	Price of Sundae
3	$18.20
6	$20.75
9	$23.30
12	$25.85

The table above shows the price for additional toppings for the grand "Kitchen-Sink" ice cream sundae. Additional toppings are only sold in increments of three. There is a linear relationship between the number of toppings and the price of the kitchen sink sundae. Which function can be used to determine the price of the ice cream sundae, *s*(*x*), in dollars, for a sundae with a topping count of *x*?

A) $s(x) = 0.85x$
B) $s(x) = 0.85x + 15.65$
C) $s(x) = 6.07x$
D) $s(x) = 2.55 + 18.20$

2

Jackie purchased a purse for $2,500. Aware that the purse's value depends on current fashion trends, Jackie estimated her purse's value over the next 10 months in the table below:

Month (*x*) [from date of purchase]	Purse Value (*y*)
2	$2,100
4	$1,700
6	$1,300
8	$900
10	$500

If the above points represent points on a line, which of the following represents the *y*-intercept of this line?

A) The value of the purse when it was purchased
B) The value of the purse after 10 months
C) The value of the purse after 12 months (1 year)
D) The number of months it will take for the purse to have no worth

63

3

Jane's parents are saving up to pay for Jane's college. The total money M, in thousands of dollars, they have in their account t years after Jane was born can be modeled by $M = 4.5t + 2$. What does 4.5 represent in the equation?

A) The number of years the parents have been saving
B) The amount of money, in thousands of dollars, already in the savings account when Jane was born
C) The amount of money, in thousands of dollars, Jane's parents add to the account each year
D) The total amount of money, in thousands of dollars, Jane's parents strive to save in total for Jane's college

4

Line J is displayed below on the xy-plane. If Line J can be modeled with the equation $y = ax + b$ (assuming a and b are both constants), which set of inequalities is true?

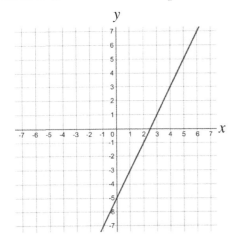

A) $\begin{cases} -1 < a < 0 \\ b > 0 \end{cases}$
B) $\begin{cases} a > 0 \\ b < 0 \end{cases}$
C) $\begin{cases} a < 0 \\ b < 0 \end{cases}$
D) $\begin{cases} a > 0 \\ b > 0 \end{cases}$

5

Jane's parents are saving up to pay for Jane's college. The total money M, in thousands of dollars, they have in their account t years after Jane was born can be modeled by $M = 4.5t + 2$. What does 2 represent in the equation?

A) The number of years the parents have been saving
B) The amount of money, in thousands of dollars, already in the savings account when Jane was born
C) The amount of money, in thousands of dollars, Jane's parents add to the account each year
D) The total amount of money, in thousands of dollars, Jane's parents strive to save in total for Jane's college

6

If the equation of the line going through the points (-0.5, 3) and (7, 9) is written as $y = ax + b$, what is $a + b$?

Answers

For **detailed solutions**, scan the QR code with your phone's camera

or

visit testpreptips.org/lines

Drills (Page 46)

1.

A. $m = 2$
B. $m = -4$
C. $m = 0$

2. $m = -3$

Drills (Page 50)

1. Increases by 5
2. A. Increases by $\frac{2}{7}$
   B. Increases by 2
3. Decreases by 4
4. A. Increases by $\frac{3}{5}$
   B. Increases by 3

Drills (Page 55)

1. $y = 5x - 1$
2. $y = 2x + 1$

Drill (Page 47)

A. $m = -2$
B. $b = 4$
C. $y = -2x + 4$
D. $(0, 4)$

Drill (Page 53)

A. 0.5 represents the <u>slope</u>

<u>Step 1</u>: $y = -0.5x + 20$
<u>Step 2</u>: <u>decreases</u> by <u>0.5</u>
<u>Step 3</u>: <u>decreases</u> by <u>0.5</u>

B. 20 represents the <u>y-intercept</u>
   Before thrown, the height is <u>20</u> feet

C. The *t*-intercept occurs when <u>*h*</u> = 0
   Seconds it takes for height to be <u>0</u>

Drills (Page 58)

1. *y*-intercept = 2
2. *y*-intercept = $\frac{19}{2}$ (or 9.5)

65

Drills (Page 60)

1. y-intercept = 0
2. A

Questions [No Calculator] (Pages 61-63)

1. B
2. B
3. B
4. A
5. 10
6. 15.5 (or $\frac{31}{2}$)
7. 9
8. 9

Questions [Calculator] (Pages 63-64)

1. B
2. A
3. C
4. B
5. B
6. 4.2

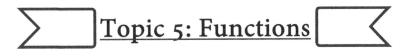

Topic 5: Functions

Function Notation

A function is best thought of in terms of an input and an output.

$$f(\boxed{x}) = \boxed{3x + 5}$$

↑ input   ↑ output

If we want $f(2)$, we will replace every x with 2:

$$f(2) = 3(2) + 5 \rightarrow f(2) = 11$$

If we want $f(10)$, we will replace every x with 10:

$$f(10) = 3(10) + 5 \rightarrow f(10) = 35$$

If we want $f(abc)$, we will replace every x with abc:

$$f(abc) = 3(abc) + 5 \rightarrow f(abc) = 3abc + 5$$

Essentially, we are "copying" the value inside of the parentheses and "pasting" it wherever the variable appears in the output.

$$f(x) = 3x + 5 \xleftrightarrow{\text{equivalent}} y = 3x + 5$$

Whenever you see $f(x)$, you can think of it as y

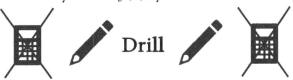

Drill

1

A. For the function $f(x) = 2x + 1$, what is $f(4)$?

B. What is $g(3)$ if $g(y) = -3y - 1$?

C. If $h(k) = 4k^2 - 4$, what is $h(-6)$?

D. If $a(x) = 9x + 6$, what is $a(\star)$?

Table Functions

Interpreting The Table

x	f(x)
0	5
1	8
2	11
3	14
4	17

Remember: x is the input and f(x) is the output

What is f(0)?

f(0) means "0" is the x value. When $x = 0$, $f(x) = 5$.

Therefore, $f(0) = 5$

What is f(3)?

f(3) means "3" is the x value. When $x = 3$, $f(x) = 14$.

Therefore, $f(3) = 14$

Drill

1

x	g(x)
-4	23
-2	15
0	2
2	-1
4	-9

A. What is g(-2)?

B. What is g(2)?

C. What is g(0) – g(-4)?

Graphical Functions

Remember: f(x) can be thought of as y

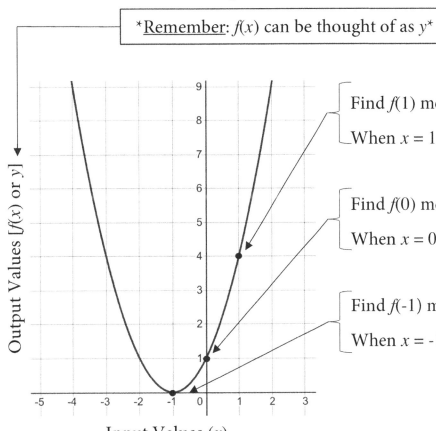

Find f(1) means find f(x) when x = 1
When x = 1, f(x) = 4, so f(1) = 4

Find f(0) means find f(x) when x = 0
When x = 0, f(x) = 1, so f(0) = 1

Find f(-1) means find f(x) when x = -1
When x = -1, f(x) = 0, so f(-1) = 0

  Drill

1

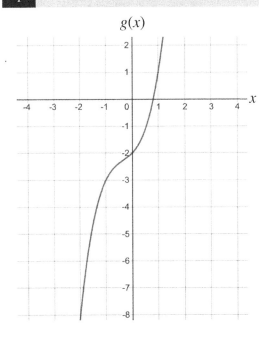

A. What is g(0)?

B. What is g(1)?

C. What is g(-2)?

Characteristics of Functions

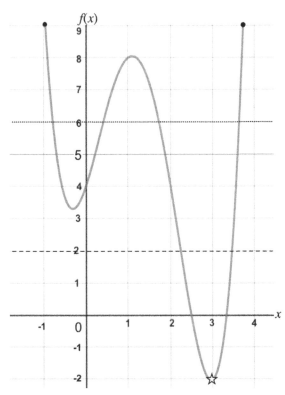

A. What is the **minimum value** of this function?

minimum value = smallest output

The minimum is labeled on the graph with a star: the minimum value is -2.

B. What is the **maximum value** of this function?

maximum value = largest output

The maximum values are labeled on the graph with dots: the maximum value is 9.

C. What is $f(2)$?

$f(2)$ means our input is $x = 2$. At $x = 2$, $f(x) = 4$.

$$f(2) = 4$$

D. What two values of x make $f(x) = 2$?

$f(x)$ is on the vertical axis. There are two values for which $f(x) = 2$: $x = 2.25$ and $x = 3.5$ (shown with the dashed line).

E. For how many values of x does $f(x) = 6$?

$f(x)$ is on the vertical axis. There are 4 values of x that have an output $f(x) = 6$ (shown with the dotted line).

Drill

1

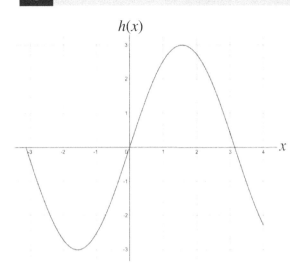

A. What is $h(1)$?

B. What is the minimum value of $h(x)$?

C. What is the maximum value of $h(x)$?

D. For how many values of x does $h(x) = 0$?

E. What two values of x make $h(x) = 2$?

Equations with Functions

$$f(x) = kx^2 + 7$$

Find the value of k given that $(2, 39)$ is a point on the graph of $f(x)$.

If $(2, 39)$ is a point on the graph, then $x = 2$, and $f(x) = 39$. We can plug these points into the equation provided:

$$39 = k(2)^2 + 7$$
$$32 = 4k$$
$$k = 8$$

Drill

1

If $(-2, 36)$ is a point on the graph of $h(x) = 2x^2 + c$, what is the value of c?

Undefined Functions

A function is said to be **undefined** when its denominator = 0

$$f(x) = \frac{9}{x}$$

For what value of x is the above function undefined?

$x = 0$

$$f(x) = \frac{2x}{x-1}$$

For what value of x is the above function undefined?

$x - 1 = 0$
$x = 1$

$$f(x) = \frac{x^2 + 2x + 1}{x^2 - 4}$$

For what values of x is the above function undefined?

$x^2 - 4 = 0$
$x^2 = 4$
$x = \pm 2$

Drills

1

$$f(x) = \frac{x+6}{x-5}$$

For which of the following values of x is $f(x)$ undefined?

A) -6
B) -5
C) 5
D) 6

2

$$k(x) = \frac{14}{x^2 - 9}$$

The function displayed above is undefined at what values of x?

A) 0, 3
B) 0, 9
C) -3, 3
D) -9, 9

Composition of Functions

Sometimes, you will be asked to put one function **INTO** another function. The following notation indicates that this is what you're being asked to do:

$$f(g(x))$$

This notation tells us that we are to **insert** the function $g(x)$ **into** the function $f(x)$.

$$f(x) = 2x^2 + 5$$
$$g(x) = 3x + 1$$

A. What is $f(g(x))$?

*Wherever we see x in $f(x)$ [the outer function], we are going to **insert** $g(x)$ [the inner function]

$$\begin{aligned} f(g(x)) &= 2[g(x)]^2 + 5 \\ &= 2(3x + 1)^2 + 5 \\ &= 2(9x^2 + 6x + 1) + 5 \\ &= 18x^2 + 12x + 2 + 5 \\ &= 18x^2 + 12x + 7 \end{aligned}$$

B. What is $g(f(x))$?

*Wherever we see x in $g(x)$ [now the outer function], we are going to **insert** $f(x)$ [now the inner function]

$$\begin{aligned} g(f(x)) &= 3[f(x)] + 1 \\ &= 3(2x^2 + 5) + 1 \\ &= 6x^2 + 15 + 1 \\ &= 6x^2 + 16 \end{aligned}$$

Drill

1

$$a(x) = 5x - 3$$
$$b(x) = x^2 - 1$$

A. What is $a(b(x))$?

B. What is $b(a(x))$?

Functions in Terms of Another Function

$g(x) = x^2 - 5$
$f(x) = 1 - g(x)$

What is $f(4)$?

$f(x) = 1 - (x^2 - 5) \rightarrow f(x) = -x^2 + 6$

Now that we've defined $f(x)$, we can evaluate the function for a specific value:

$f(4) = -(4)^2 + 6$
$f(4) = -16 + 6 = -10$

$g(x) = x^2 - 5$
$h(x) = 5 - 3g(x)$

What is $h(-1)$?

$h(x) = 5 - 3(x^2 - 5)$
$h(x) = 5 - 3x^2 + 15$
$h(x) = -3x^2 + 20$

Now that we've defined $h(x)$, we can evaluate the function for a specific value:

$h(-1) = -3(-1)^2 + 20$
$h(-1) = -3 + 20 = 17$

Drills

1

$$f(x) = 4x - 2$$
$$g(x) = 2 - 3(f(x))$$

The functions f and g are defined above. What is the value of $g(1)$?

A) -4
B) -2
C) -1
D) 0

2

Function m is defined by $m(x) = 10x$. Function n is defined by $n(x) = 8x - 3$. Which of the following values of x satisfies the functional equation $m(x) - n(x) = 7$?

A) 2
B) 4
C) 7
D) 48

Translation of Functions

We can move functions up or down by manipulating them with constants.

Original Function:
$f(x) = 3x^2 + 7$

Vertical Translation

Up

$f(x) = (3x^2 + 7)\boxed{+1}$

equivalent

$f(x) = 3x^2 + 8$

Function moves **1 unit up**

Down

$f(x) = (3x^2 + 7)\boxed{-1}$

equivalent

$f(x) = 3x^2 + 6$

Function moves **1 unit down**

*__NOTE__: When we move up or down, we do **NOT** touch the *x*-term.

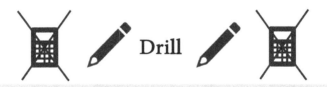
Drill

1

Original Function: $g(x) = x^3 - x + 4$

A. The function $f(x) = (x^3 - x + 4) - 6$ indicates a translation of $g(x)$ by _____ unit(s) up / down / right / left (CIRCLE ONE).

B. The function $f(x) = x^3 - x + 5$ indicates a translation of $g(x)$ by _____ unit(s) up / down / right / left (CIRCLE ONE).

Interpreting Functions in a Linear Context

> $g(x)$ is a linear function such that $g(2) = 20$ and $g(20) = 110$.
> What is the value of $g(10)$?

$$g(2) = 20 \qquad g(20) = 110$$
$$x_1y_1 \qquad x_2y_2$$

All that we need to realize is that we are being told $(2, 20)$ and $(20, 110)$ are two points on the line.

We can now find the equation using the **Slope Formula** and **Point Slope Form** (from Topic 4: Lines). We find that the linear equation is as follows:

$$y = 5x + 10$$

To find $g(10)$, we will just plug in $x = 10$:

$$y = 5(10) + 10$$
$$= 60$$

 Drills

---

1

$g(x)$ is a linear function such that $g(1) = 3$ and $g(5) = 11$. What is the value of the sum of $g(10)$ and $g(11)$?

2

x	$h(x)$
-5	3
3	-21

Some values of the linear function $h(x)$ are displayed in the table above. What is the y-coordinate of the y-intercept of $h(x)$?

A) -12
B) -3
C) $-\dfrac{5}{3}$
D) $-\dfrac{1}{3}$

Interpreting Functions in Real-World Scenarios

The pressure, in pascals (Pa), of an ultra-submarine descending at v meters per second (m/s) can be modeled by the function P, where $P = \frac{7}{4}v^2$. In this context, which of the following best explains the meaning of $P(8) = 112$?

A) When the submarine is descending at a rate of 8m/s, it has a pressure of 112 Pa.
B) When the submarine is descending at a rate of 112m/s, it has a pressure of 8 Pa.
C) When the submarine is descending at a rate of 64m/s, it has a pressure of 112 Pa.
D) When the submarine is descending at a rate of 112m/s, it has a pressure of 64 Pa.

Step 1: Replace variables in the equation with x and y

$$P = \frac{7}{4}v^2 \longrightarrow y = \frac{7}{4}x^2$$

Step 2: Convert function input and output into a point

$$P(8) = 112 \longrightarrow (8, 112)$$

Step 3: Consider meaning of point in context of scenario

When x (the descending velocity) is 8, y (the pressure) is 112 Pa.

Choice A.

Drills

1

The function f below models the mass gained in g/day by a developing fetus in terms of c, the caloric intake of the mother in calories/day. What is the meaning of $(1505.45, c(1505.45))$?

$$f(c) = -0.26(c - 1505.45)^2 + 0.75$$

A) A mass gain of 1505.45 g/day causes a caloric intake of $c(1505.45)$ calories/day
B) A caloric intake of 1505.45 calories/day results in a mass gain of $c(1505.45)$ g/day
C) The mass gained increases by $c(1505.45)$ g/day for every 1505.45 calories/day consumed
D) The number of calories eaten increases by $c(1505.45)$ for every 1505.45 g/day increase in mass gained

2

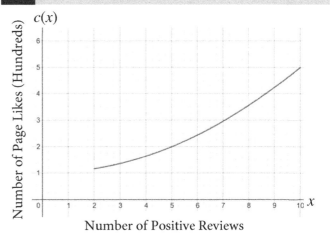

The graph above shows the function c. The number of likes a bakery receives in a day on its social media page, $c(x)$, in hundreds, is based on the number of positive reviews, x, it received the day before. In this context, which of the following is the best interpretation of the equation $c(6) = 2.44$?

A) The vertex of the graph of c is $(6, 2.44)$
B) 2.44 is the y-intercept of c.
C) When the bakery receives 6 positive reviews the day before, it can expect 244 page-likes the next day.
D) When the bakery receives 244 positive reviews the day before, it can expect 6 page-likes the next day.

Changing the Input

For the function g, if $g(4x) = x + 8$, what is the value of $g(8)$?

We want to find the value of $g(8)$.

To find the value of $g(8)$, however, we should **NOT** plug in $x = 8$. As we can see, the input is defined as "$4x$"

Therefore, to find the value of x, we must set $4x = 8$:

$$4x = 8$$
$$x = 2$$

Now we can plug in $x = 2$:

$$g(8) = g(4[2]) = 2 + 8 = 10$$

For the function f, if $f(x - 2) = x + 5$, what is the value of $f(7)$?

We want to find the value of $f(7)$.

To find the value of $f(7)$, however, we should **NOT** plug in $x = 7$. As we can see, the input is defined as "$x - 2$"

Therefore, to find the value of x, we must set $x - 2 = 7$:

$$x - 2 = 7$$
$$x = 9$$

Now we can plug in $x = 9$:

$$f(7) = f(9 - 2) = 9 + 5 = 14$$

 Drills

1

What is the value of $s(12)$ for $s(4x) = 2x - 15$ given that s is a function?

A) -15
B) -9
C) 3
D) 9

2

If for all x-values $g(x + 4) = 5x + 6$, what is the value of $g(9)$?

A) 13
B) 26
C) 31
D) 65

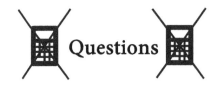

Questions

1

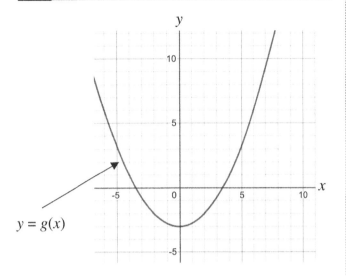

$y = g(x)$

The graph of $y = g(x)$ is shown in the xy-plane. What is the value of $g(0)$?

A) -3.5
B) -3
C) 3
D) 3.5

2

$$g(x) = x^2 - 5$$
$$h(x) = x^2 + 2$$

By how many coordinate units does the graph of g have to be translated to produce the graph of h when both functions are graphed in the xy-plane?

A) 7 units upwards
B) 7 units downwards
C) 2 units upwards
D) 5 units downwards

3

The speed of a plane in meters/second (m/s) after it hits the ground and runs along a friction grip pathway can be modeled by the function a, defined by $a(g) = 80 - \frac{2}{5}g^2$, where g is the number of grips the plane encounters along the pathway. Which of the following statements provides the best interpretation of $a(10) = 40$?

A) If the speed of the plane is 10 m/s as it hits the ground, it will need to run over 40 grips to stop.
B) If the distance traveled by the plane is 40m, it will need to run over 10 grips to stop.
C) Once the plane runs over 40 grips, its speed is 10 m/s.
D) Once the plane runs over 10 grips, its speed is 40 m/s.

4

In the standard xy-coordinate plane, what is the y-intercept of $y = f(x) - 7$ if the coordinates of the y-intercept of $y = f(x)$ are $(0, 5)$?

A) -7
B) -2
C) 5
D) 12

5

What is the minimum value of the function graphed below in the xy-plane for $-2 \leq x \leq 1$?

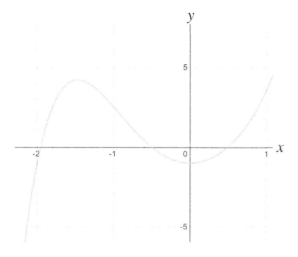

A) -6
B) -1
C) 0
D) 4.2

6

f and h are functions of the variable x. If $f(x) = x^3 - 4$ and $h(x) = x^3 + 3$, which of the following translations, when performed on the graph of h in the xy-plane, produces the graph of f?

A) A translation of 7 units downward
B) A translation of 7 units upward
C) A translation of 7 units to the left
D) A translation of 7 units to the right

7

x	a(x)	b(x)
3	-3	5
5	-1	-6
7	1	-17
9	3	-28

The table above provides values for two unique functions: a and b. For which value of x is $a(x) - b(x) = x$?

A) 3
B) 5
C) 7
D) 9

8

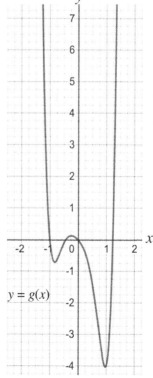

$y = g(x)$

The graph of the function g is shown to the left. For exactly how many values of x does $g(x) = 0$?

A) Less than two
B) Two
C) Three
D) Four

9

$$f(x) = kx^2 - 2x + 12$$

Consider the function above, where k is a constant. If $(-3, 0)$ is a point on the graph of f, what is $f(4)$?

A) -28
B) -2
C) 0
D) 4

10

$y = \dfrac{c}{2x}$ exists in the xy-plane where c is a constant. The point $(5, 8)$ is on the graph. What other point must also be on the graph?

A) (2, 40)
B) (4, 20)
C) (4, 10)
D) (8, 10)

11

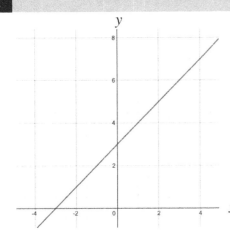

The graph of $y = g(x)$ in the xy-plane is shown to the left. Which of the following is the graph of $y = g(x) - 3$?

A)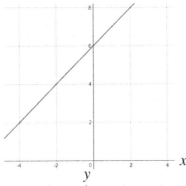

B)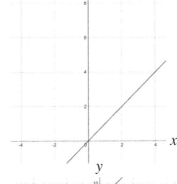

C)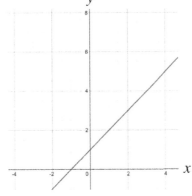

D)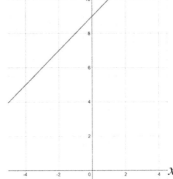

12

The function $h(x) = x^4 + x^3 - 4x^2 + 3$ is graphed in the xy-plane below. If $h(x) = a$ has exactly three unique solutions, which of the following could be the value of a?

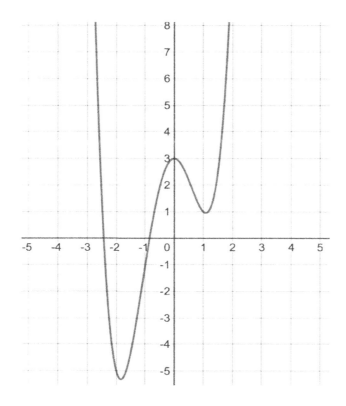

I.   0
II. 2
III. 3
IV. 4

A) II only
B) III only
C) I and III only
D) II and IV only

13

$f(x)$ is a linear function such that $f(-4) = 9$ and $f(11) = 54$. For what value of a is it true that $f(a) = 84$?

Questions

1

Charli is filling up a large empty cup with frozen yogurt. She starts filling it up quickly and then pauses because she spots her friend. Afterwards, she fills it up a bit more, but at a much slower rate than she initially had. Which of the following graphs best models Charli filling up her cup with frozen yogurt?

A)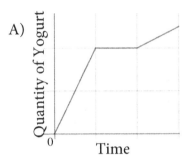

B)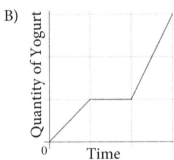

C)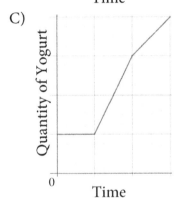

D)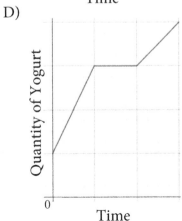

2

The population P of a suburb in Montana t years after 2014 can be modeled using the equation $P = 43,000(1.05)^t$. What is the population of this suburb in 2018?

A) 43,993
B) 52,267
C) 54,880
D) 57,624

3

Yummy Eats calculates the cost of an event based on the number of event attendees. The cost is modeled as follows:

$$f(x) = ax + 350$$

In the model featured, a is a constant and $x > 0$. $f(x)$ represents the cost of the event and x represents the number of attendees. To cater an event for 40 people, the total cost is $950. What is the cost, in dollars, to cater an event consisting of 72 people?

Answers

For **detailed solutions**, scan the QR code with your phone's camera

or

visit **testpreptips.org/functions**

Drill (Page 67)

A. 9
B. -10
C. 140
D. 9★ + 6

Drill (Page 68)

A. 15
B. -1
C. -21

Drill (Page 69)

A. -2
B. 1
C. -8

Drill (Page 71) [No Calculator]

A. 2.5
B. -3
C. 3
D. 3 values
E. $x = 0.75$ and $x = 2.5$

Drill (Page 71) [Calculator]

1. $c = 28$

Drill (Page 72)

A. C
B. C

Drill (Page 74) [Top]

A. $5x^2 - 8$
B. $25x^2 - 30x + 8$

Drills (Page 74) [Bottom]

1. A
2. A

Drill (Page 75)

A. <u>6</u> units <u>down</u>
B. <u>1</u> unit <u>up</u>

Drills (Page 76)

1. 44
2. A

Drills (Page 78)

1. B
2. C

Drills (Page 79)

1. B
2. C

Questions [No Calculator] (Pages 80-83)

1. B
2. A
3. D
4. B
5. B
6. A
7. B
8. D
9. -28
10. C
11. B
12. B
13. 21

Questions [Calculator] (Page 84)

1. A
2. B
3. $1,430

Topic 6: Polynomials

Definitions

A **monomial** consists of a single term

x, $5x^3$, 7, and $-4x^9$ are all examples of monomials.

A **polynomial** is the addition or subtraction of several monomials

$x - 4$, $x^2 - 5x + 6$, $x^3 - 5x + 2$, and $x^5 - 7$ are all examples of polynomials.

A **root** (*x*-intercept) occurs when a function is equal to 0. It is where the graph of a function touches the *x*-axis.

In the graph shown, all roots are circled. The roots indicate that the function equals 0 when $x = -3$, $x = 1$, and $x = 2$.

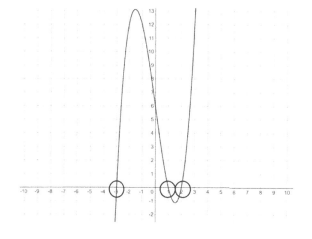

Degree

The **degree** of a polynomial refers to the greatest exponent on any of its monomial terms

$f(x) = 4x^3 - 4$ is a **third**-degree polynomial (greatest exponent = 3)

$f(x) = 6x^6 - 4x^2 + 2x - 1$ is a **sixth**-degree polynomial (greatest exponent = 6)

Factoring Polynomials

The **degree** of a polynomial tells us the number of roots (*x*-intercepts) the polynomial has:

For example, $f(x) = x^4 + 10x^3 + 35x^2 + 50x + 24$ is a **fourth-degree polynomial**. Therefore, it has **4 roots**.

The Relationship Between Roots and Factors

Let's take the equation $y = (x + 2)(x + 3)$

To find the roots (*x*-intercepts), we must set *y* equal to 0 and then set each individual factor equal to 0:

$$0 = (x + 2) \mid (x + 3)$$
$$x + 2 = 0 \mid x + 3 = 0$$
$$x = -2 \mid x = -3$$

Because $y = x^2 + 5x + 6$ is a **second-degree** polynomial, it has **2 roots**: $x = -2$ and $x = -3$.

Let's look at some additional examples:

Factored Form	→ Set Factors = 0	→ Roots
$y = (4x + 7)(x - 2)(x + 9)$	$4x + 7 = 0$ $x - 2 = 0$ $x + 9 = 0$	$x = -\dfrac{7}{4}$ $x = 2$ $x = -9$
$y = x(x + 3)(x - 1)$	$x = 0$ $x + 3 = 0$ $x - 1 = 0$	$x = 0$ $x = -3$ $x = 1$
$y = 3x(x - 4)(x - 8)$	$x = 0$ $x - 4 = 0$ $x - 8 = 0$	$x = 0$ $x = 4$ $x = 8$
$y = 7(x + 5)^2(2x - 5)$	$(x + 5)^2 = 0$ $2x - 5 = 0$	$x = -5$ $x = \dfrac{5}{2}$

***NOTE**: The presence of a constant in front of the factors (like 3 or 7) has **NO** effect on the factors or roots. Therefore, you should **IGNORE** constants when determining the roots.

***NOTE**: The factors and roots always have opposite signs

Factor: $(x - 3)$ ⟷ Root: 3

Factor: $(x + 2)$ ⟷ Root: -2

Factor: $(2x + 1)$ ⟷ Root: $-\dfrac{1}{2}$

 Drills

1

Instructions: Write each root as a factor.

A. $x = 3$

B. $x = -4$

C. $x = 0$

2

Instructions: State the root from each factor.

A. $x - 7$

B. $x + 1$

C. x

D. $4x + 5$

3

Instructions: For each of the following equations, indicate the roots.

A. $y = (x + 1)(x - 4)(3x - 5)$

B. $y = x(3x + 7)(x + 4)$

C. $y = -3x(x - 5)(x + 6)^2$

D. $y = x^2(x - 2)(x - 3)$

Questions Involving Polynomials

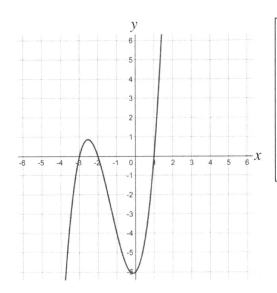

Which of the following represents the equation of the polynomial shown to the left?

A) $(x-3)(x-2)(x+1)$
B) $(x+3)(x+2)(x-1)$
C) $(x-3)(x+2)(x-1)$
D) $(x+3)(x+2)(x+1)$

From Graph:

Root: $x = -3$ ⟷ Factor: $(x+3)$
Root: $x = -2$ ⟷ Factor: $(x+2)$
Root: $x = 1$ ⟷ Factor: $(x-1)$

Answer = Choice B

---

x	$f(x)$
6	-2
4	0
2	8
0	16

Some values of the function $f(x)$ are displayed in the table. Which of the following is a factor of $f(x)$?

A) $x - 4$
B) $x + 4$
C) $x - 16$
D) $x + 16$

Roots (x-intercepts) occur when y [same as $f(x)$] equals 0. Therefore, the root = 4. A factor always has a sign opposite the root, so the appropriate factor is $x - 4$.

Answer = Choice A

Using Factors to Solve Equations

> The function f is defined as $f(x) = x^3 + 5x^2 + ax - 4$. If $x - 2$ is a factor of the polynomial, what is the value of a?

If $x - 2$ is a factor, $x = 2$ is a root. A root occurs when y [$f(x)$] equals 0. Therefore, $(2, 0)$ is a point on the graph of this function. We can plug in $(2, 0)$ to find a:

$$0 = (2)^3 + 5(2)^2 + a(2) - 4$$
$$0 = 8 + 20 + 2a - 4$$
$$0 = 24 + 2a$$
$$-24 = 2a$$
$$a = -12$$

Factoring Polynomials of a Degree Greater Than 2

You will **NEVER** be expected to factor a polynomial of a degree greater than 2. Therefore, if you find yourself trying to do so, you should try another solution (like pulling out common factors):

For example, $f(x) = x^3 + 2x^2 - 3x$ can be broken down into $x(x^2 + 2x - 3)$. Therefore, you only need to factor a **quadratic** to find the roots (discussed in the next chapter, Topic 7: Quadratics).

You would not be expected to find the roots of a function like $f(x) = x^3 - 6x^2 - 8x + 7$ because there is no common factor to be pulled out.

 Drill

1

Find the roots of $f(x) = x^3 + 7x^2 + 10x$.

Graphing Polynomials

Non-Repeated Roots

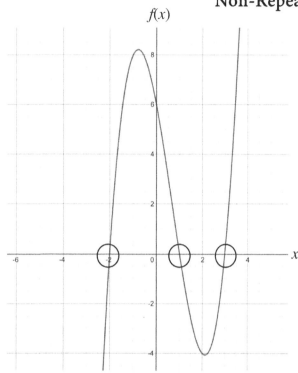

Shown to the left is the graph of the function $f(x) = x^3 - 2x^2 - 5x + 6$. This is a **third-degree** polynomial that has roots of $x = -2$, $x = 1$, and $x = 3$.

None of the roots are repeated, so we will expect to see three different roots on the graph.

Repeated Roots

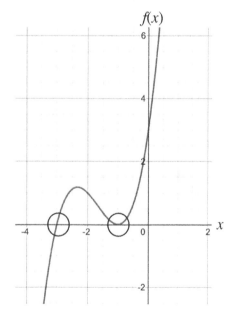

Shown to the left is the graph of the function $f(x) = x^3 + 5x^2 + 7x + 3$. This is a **third-degree** polynomial that has roots of $x = -1$, $x = -1$, and $x = -3$. Notice how we only have two **different** roots: $x = -1$ and $x = -3$. Here, $x = -1$ is a **double** root.

Whenever we have a **double** root, the root will be **tangent** to the x-axis: it will "kiss" the x-axis and then turn back around. Look at the behavior of this function at $x = -1$ on the graph.

Questions

1

The function *f* is defined below. How many distinct roots does the graph of $y = f(x)$ have when graphed in the *xy*-plane if $a > 0$, $b > 0$, and $a \neq b$?

$$y = (x + a)(x - b)^2(x - a)(x + 2a)$$

A) 3
B) 4
C) 5
D) 6

2

The graph of $y = h(x)$ is shown below in the *xy*-plane.

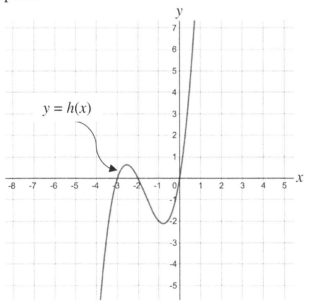

Which of the following equations defines *h*?

A) $h(x) = x^3 + 3x^2 + 2x$
B) $h(x) = x^3 + 3x^2 + 2$
C) $h(x) = x^3 + 5x^2 + 6x$
D) $h(x) = -x^3 + 5x^2 + 6$

3

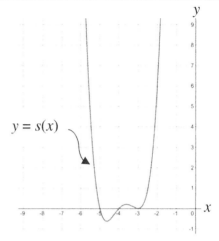

The graph of $y = s(x)$ is shown above in the *xy*-plane. Which of the following functions defines *s*?

A) $s(x) = (x + 5)(x + 4)(x + 3)^2$
B) $s(x) = (x + 5)(x + 4)^2(x + 3)$
C) $s(x) = (x - 5)(x - 4)(x - 3)$
D) $s(x) = (x - 5)(x - 4)(x - 3)^2$

4

The function *h* is defined below. Which of the following is/are *x*-intercepts of the graph of $y = h(x)$ when graphed in the *xy*-plane?

$$h(x) = (4x + 3)(2x - 1)(x + 5)$$

I. $-\dfrac{1}{2}$

II. -2

III. $-\dfrac{3}{4}$

IV. 5

A) I only
B) III only
C) II and III only
D) I, III, and IV only

5

The graph of y = h(x) is graphed below in the xy-plane. Which of the following equations could define h?

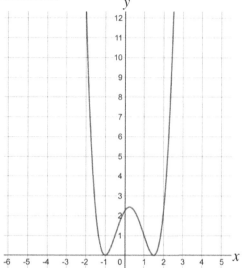

A) $h(x) = (x-1)\left(x+\dfrac{3}{2}\right)$

B) $h(x) = (x+1)\left(x-\dfrac{3}{2}\right)$

C) $h(x) = (x+1)^2\left(x-\dfrac{3}{2}\right)$

D) $h(x) = (x+1)^2\left(x-\dfrac{3}{2}\right)^2$

6

The function h has four distinct x-intercepts when graphed in the xy-plane as y = h(x). The x-intercepts are 0, 2, -7, and -8. Which of the following is a factor of h?

A) $x - 8$
B) $x^2 + 7x$
C) $x^2 - 15x + 56$
D) $2x^2 + 2x$

7

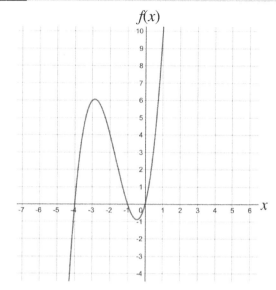

The graph of the function f is shown. Which of the following are factors of f(x)?

I. x
II. x – 4
III. x + 1

A) II only
B) III only
C) I and II only
D) I and III only

8

$$x^3 + ax^2 + bx + c$$

The function f has the following roots: -3, 4, and 6. For function f, as defined above, what is the value of c?

A) -72
B) -7
C) 7
D) 72

9

Which of the following could be the graph of $y = h(x)$ in the xy-plane if h has 4 distinct real roots?

A)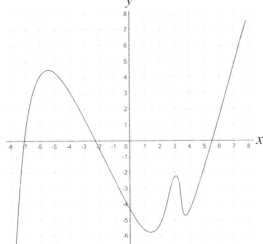

B)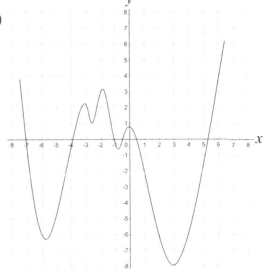

C)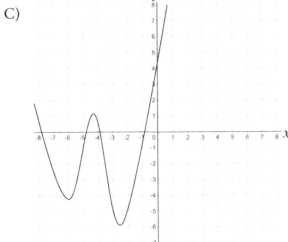

D)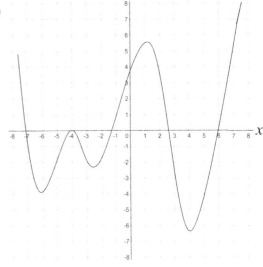

95

10

If $x + 3$ is a factor of the polynomial function g defined as $g(x) = x^3 + kx^2 + 5x - 12$, then what is the value of constant k?

11

$x^3 - 6x^2 + 8x$ can be written in the form $x(x - m)(x - n)$, where m and n are constants. What is the value of $(m)(n)$?

12

$(x - 3)(x + 4)(2x + 3) = 0$

What is the product of all values of x that satisfy the given equation?

Answers

For **detailed solutions**, scan the QR code with your phone's camera

or

visit testpreptips.org/polynomials

Drills (Page 89)

1.

A. $(x - 3)$
B. $(x + 4)$
C. x

2.

A. $x = 7$
B. $x = -1$
C. $x = 0$
D. $x = -\frac{5}{4}$

3.

A. $x = -1$, $x = 4$, and $x = \frac{5}{3}$
B. $x = 0$, $x = -\frac{7}{3}$, and $x = -4$
C. $x = 0$, $x = 5$, and $x = -6$ (double root)
D. $x = 0$, $x = 2$, and $x = 3$

Drill (Page 91)

1. $x = 0$, $x = -5$, and $x = -2$

Questions (Pages 93-96)

1. B
2. C
3. A
4. B
5. D
6. B
7. D
8. D
9. C
10. 6
11. 8
12. 18

Topic 7: Quadratics

Standard Form

$$y = ax^2 + bx + c$$

a tells us the **opening direction** and **width** of the graph

Opening Direction

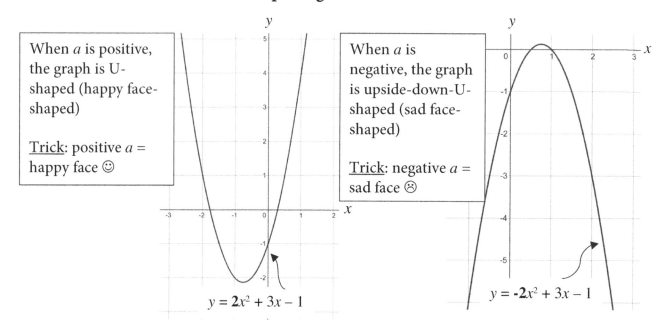

When *a* is positive, the graph is U-shaped (happy face-shaped)

Trick: positive *a* = happy face ☺

$y = 2x^2 + 3x - 1$

When *a* is negative, the graph is upside-down-U-shaped (sad face-shaped)

Trick: negative *a* = sad face ☹

$y = -2x^2 + 3x - 1$

Width

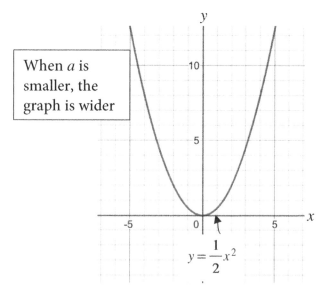

When *a* is smaller, the graph is wider

$y = \frac{1}{2}x^2$

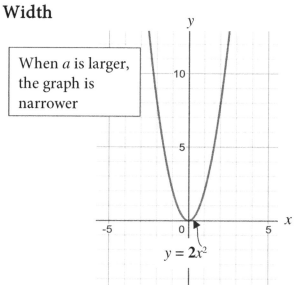

When *a* is larger, the graph is narrower

$y = 2x^2$

c tells us the y-intercept of the graph

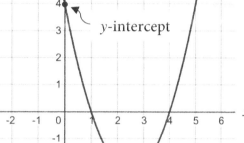

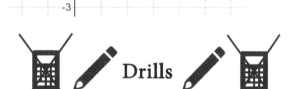 Drills

1

For each of the following quadratics, circle the shape and state the y-intercept.

A. $y = x^2 + 5x - 10$

Shape: U or upside-down-U (circle one)

y-intercept: _____

B. $y = -x^2 + 2x + 1$

Shape: U or upside-down-U (circle one)

y-intercept: _____

C. $y = 5x^2 + 3x$

Shape: U or upside-down-U (circle one)

y-intercept: _____

2

Which quadratic is wider? (Circle one)

A. $y = 3x^2 + 7x - 9$

B. $y = \dfrac{1}{3}x^2 + 7x - 9$

Solving Quadratics in Standard Form

Case 1: $a = 1$

Solve $x^2 - x - 12 = 0$

Step 1: Find all factors that multiply to -12 (the c term).

Factors of -12

(+ / -) 1	(+ / -) 12
(+ / -) 2	(+ / -) 6
(+ / -) 3	(+ / -) 4

Step 2: Determine which factors will add to -1 (the b term). The only combination that adds to -1 is -4 and +3.

Step 3: Write each of the numbers as factors.

$$(x - 4)(x + 3) = 0$$

Step 4: To solve, set each individual factor = 0.

$x - 4 = 0 \qquad x + 3 = 0$
$x = 4 \qquad\quad x = -3$

Instructions: Solve each of the following quadratics where $a = 1$.

1

$x^2 + 7x + 10 = 0$

2

$x^2 - x - 12 = 0$

3

$x^2 + 6x + 9 = 0$

4

$x^2 - 5x + 6 = 0$

5

$x^2 + 2x - 15 = 0$

Case 2: $a \neq 1$

Solve $3x^2 - 5x - 12 = 0$

Step 1: Multiply the *a*-term by the *c*-term: $(3)(-12) = -36$. Find all factors of -36 (*ac*).

Factors of -36

(+ / -) 1	(+ / -) 36
(+ / -) 2	(+ / -) 18
(+ / -) 3	(+ / -) 12
(+ / -) 4	(+ / -) 9
(+ / -) 6	(+ / -) 6

Step 2: Determine which factors will add to -5 (the *b* term). The only combination that adds to -5 is -9 and +4.

Step 3: Write the middle (*b*) term as the sum of the two numbers.

$$3x^2 \boxed{-5x} - 12 = 0 \longrightarrow 3x^2 \boxed{-9x + 4x} - 12 = 0$$

Step 4: Separate the terms into two "groups."

$$3x^2 - 9x + 4x - 12 = 0 \longrightarrow \underbrace{(3x^2 - 9x)}_{\text{Group}} \underbrace{(4x - 12)}_{\text{Group}} = 0$$

Step 5: Pull out the greatest factor from each group. What remains in the parentheses after factoring each of the two groups should be **identical**.

$$(3x^2 - 9x) \mid (4x - 12) = 0 \longrightarrow 3x(x - 3) \mid 4(x - 3) = 0$$

(Identical)

Step 6: Combine the "leftovers" (here, $3x$ and 4) into a single factor. The other factor will be the identical part remaining in the parentheses.

$$3x(x - 3) \mid 4(x - 3) = 0 \longrightarrow (x - 3)(3x + 4) = 0$$

Step 7: To solve, set each individual factor = 0.

$$x - 3 = 0 \qquad 3x + 4 = 0$$
$$x = 3 \qquad x = -\frac{4}{3}$$

Instructions: Solve each of the following quadratics where $a \neq 1$.

1

$3x^2 + 7x + 2 = 0$

2

$3x^2 + 11x - 4 = 0$

3

$2x^2 + 5x - 3 = 0$

4

$5x^2 - 18x - 8 = 0$

5

$3x^2 - 14x + 8 = 0$

Case 3: No c term

Solve $2x^2 + 6x = 0$

Step 1: Pull out the greatest common factor

$$2x^2 + 6x = 0 \longrightarrow 2x(x+3) = 0$$

Step 2: To solve, set each individual factor $= 0$.

$2x = 0 \qquad x + 3 = 0$
$x = 0 \qquad x = -3$

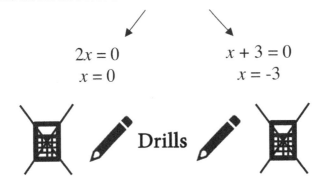 Drills

Instructions: Solve each of the following quadratics that do not have a c-term.

1
$x^2 + 7x = 0$

3
$x^2 - 3x = 0$

2
$2x^2 - 4x = 0$

4
$4x^2 - 12x = 0$

Case 4: No b term

***NOTE**: When there is no b term, we do **NOT** need to factor

Solve $x^2 - 9 = 0$

<u>Step 1</u>: Move the number to other side of the equation

$$x^2 - 9 = 0 \longrightarrow x^2 = 9$$

<u>Step 2</u>: Solve the equation (do not forget to take both the **positive** and **negative** solution when taking the square root)

$$\sqrt{x^2} = \pm \sqrt{9}$$
$$x = \pm 3$$

Solve $7x^2 - 28 = 0$

$$7x^2 = 28$$

Divide both sides by 7

$$x^2 = 4$$

$$x = \pm 2$$

Instructions: Solve each of the following quadratics that do not have a *b*-term.

1

$x^2 = 25$

2

$5x^2 - 45 = 0$

3

$x^2 - 20 = 0$

4

$x^2 - 9 = 0$

5

$2x^2 = 72$

6

$5x^2 = 35$

The Quadratic Formula

If you are unable to factor the quadratic you're given, you can always use the **Quadratic Formula**.

$$x = \frac{-b \pm \sqrt{b^2 - 4ac}}{2a}$$

Solve $3x^2 - 16x + 7 = 0$

Step 1: Multiply a and c: $(3)(7) = 21$. Find all factors of 21 (ac).

Factors of 21

$(+/-)\ 1$	$(+/-)\ 21$
$(+/-)\ 3$	$(+/-)\ 7$

There is **NO** combination that adds up to -16 (the b term). Therefore, we must use the Quadratic Formula:

$$3x^2 - 16x + 7 = 0$$

$$a = 3$$
$$b = -16$$
$$c = 7$$

$$x = \frac{-(-16) \pm \sqrt{(-16)^2 - 4(3)(7)}}{2(3)}$$

$$\frac{16 \pm \sqrt{172}}{6}$$

$$\frac{16 \pm \sqrt{4}\sqrt{43}}{6}$$

$$\frac{16 \pm 2\sqrt{43}}{6} \quad \leftarrow \text{Use the "Heart Method" to simplify this fraction}$$

$$\frac{8 \pm \sqrt{43}}{3}$$

Rearranging Equations

*__NOTE__: Sometimes we will need to rearrange an equation to solve it.

$$\boxed{\text{Solve } x^2 + 7x = -10}$$

Before we can solve this quadratic, we must set it equal to 0. We can do so by adding 10 to both sides.

$$x^2 + 7x + 10 = 0$$

Now we are good to go!

$$\boxed{\text{Solve } x^2 + 2x - 5 = 3x}$$

Before we can solve this quadratic, we must set it equal to 0. We can do so by moving the $3x$ to the left-hand side of the equation.

$$x^2 - x - 5 = 0$$

Now we are good to go!

Instructions: Solve each of the following quadratics by using **the Quadratic Formula**.

1

$x^2 + 5x + 2 = 0$

2

$2x^2 = x + 5$

3

What are the solutions to the equation shown below?

$$x^2 - 6x = -4$$

A) $x = 3 \pm \sqrt{5}$
B) $x = 3 \pm \sqrt{10}$
C) $x = 3 \pm \sqrt{20}$
D) $x = 6 \pm \sqrt{20}$

4

What are the solutions to the equation shown below?

$$3x^2 + 6x = -1$$

A) $x = -1 \pm \dfrac{\sqrt{6}}{3}$
B) $x = -1 \pm 4\sqrt{6}$
C) $x = 1 \pm 2\sqrt{6}$
D) $x = 1 \pm 4\sqrt{6}$

Factored Form

$$y = a(x - \text{root}_1)(x - \text{root}_2)$$

a tells us the **opening direction** and **width** of the graph (as in Standard Form)

The **roots** (also called <u>zeroes</u> or <u>x-intercepts</u>) are where the parabola hits the *x*-axis

If…
$a = 3$
Roots: $x = 2$ and $x = -4$

↓

<u>Factored Form</u>: $y = 3(x - 2)(x + 4)$

Drill

1

For each of the following quadratics, find the roots and state whether the quadratic has a U or upside-down-U shape.

A. $y = (x + 3)(x - 1)$ Roots: _____ Shape: _____

B. $y = -(x - 6)(x + 2)$ Roots: _____ Shape: _____

C. $y = 3(x + 1)(x + 4)$ Roots: _____ Shape: _____

D. $y = x(x - 5)$ Roots: _____ Shape: _____

E. $y = -2x(x - 5)$ Roots: _____ Shape: _____

Vertex Form

$$y = a(x - h)^2 + k$$

a tells us the **opening direction** and **width** of the graph (as in Standard Form)

The vertex refers to the **minimum** or **maximum** point of the quadratic

(h, k) is the vertex point

$$y = 3(x + 1)^2 - 5$$

$a = 3$
$h = -1$
$k = -5$

Vertex Point = $(h, k) = (-1, -5)$

$$y = -3(x + 1)^2 - 5$$

$a = -3$
$h = -1$
$k = -5$

Vertex Point = $(h, k) = (-1, -5)$

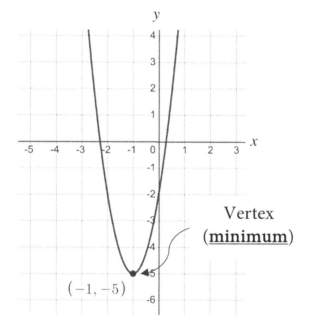

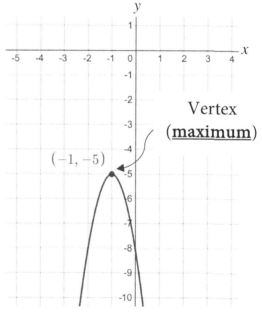

Because *a* is positive (the graph is U-shaped), the vertex represents a **minimum**

Because *a* is negative (the graph is upside-down-U-shaped), the vertex represents a **maximum**

1

For each of the following quadratics, identify the vertex and whether it is a maximum or minimum.

A. $y = (x + 3)^2 - 5$ Vertex: (____ , ____) Max or Min? _____

B. $y = 4(x - 2)^2 - 3$ Vertex: (____ , ____) Max or Min? _____

C. $y = -5(x + 1)^2 + 9$ Vertex: (____ , ____) Max or Min? _____

D. $y = -(x - 4)^2 + 1$ Vertex: (____ , ____) Max or Min? _____

Converting Between the Forms

Standard → Factored

Use Factoring Techniques discussed under "Solving Quadratics in Standard Form"

> Write $y = x^2 + 5x + 4$ in Factored Form

This is a Case 1 ($a = 1$) Quadratic

Factors of 4

(+ / -) 1	(+ / -) 4
(+ / -) 2	(+ / -) 2

The only factors that add to 5 are +1 and +4

Factored Form: $y = (x + 1)(x + 4)$

*__NOTE__: We were asked to **factor** (NOT solve) the equation, so we should **STOP** after creating our two factors.

Standard → Vertex

$$h = \frac{-b}{2a}$$

Write $y = 2x^2 - 20x + 18$ in Vertex Form

Step 1: Find the *x*-coordinate of the vertex (*h*) by using the formula shown above.

$$a = 2$$
$$b = -20$$

$$h = \frac{-(-20)}{2(2)} = \frac{20}{4} = 5$$

Step 2: Find the *y*-coordinate of the vertex (*k*) by plugging "*x* = 5" back into the original equation

$$y = 2(5)^2 - 20(5) + 18$$
$$y = 50 - 100 + 18$$
$$y = -32$$
$$(k = -32)$$

Step 3: Plug $a = 2$, $h = 5$, and $k = -32$ into Vertex Form.

$$y = 2(x - 5)^2 - 32$$

Instructions: For each of the following quadratics, indicate the vertex and whether it is a maximum or minimum for the quadratic. Then, write the equation in Vertex Form.

1

$y = x^2 + 6x + 1$

Vertex? (____ , ____)

Max or Min? _____

Vertex Form: _____

2

$y = x^2 - 2x + 3$

Vertex? (____ , ____)

Max or Min? _____

Vertex Form: _____

3

$y = -2x^2 + 20x + 3$

Vertex? (____ , ____)

Max or Min? _____

Vertex Form: _____

4

$y = -3x^2 - 12x + 5$

Vertex? (____ , ____)

Max or Min? _____

Vertex Form: _____

Factored → Vertex

> Write $y = -2(x + 3)(x - 1)$ in Factored Form

*NOTE: The *x*-coordinate of the vertex (h) is halfway between the two roots*

Because the roots of the above quadratic are -3 and 1, $h = -1$

To find the *y*-coordinate, we can plug "$x = -1$" back into the original equation:

$$y = -2(-1 + 3)(-1 - 1) = -2(2)(-2) = 8 \ [k = 8]$$

$$\text{Vertex} = (-1, 8)$$

Now we can plug $a = -2$, $h = -1$, and $k = 8$ into Vertex Form: $y = -2(x + 1)^2 + 8$

> What is the *x*-coordinate of the vertex of the parabola shown below?

We can also find the vertex if we are given a graph.

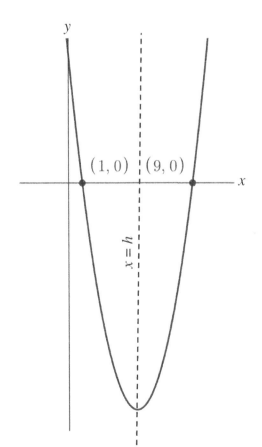

Because the *x*-coordinate of the vertex (h) is halfway between the two roots, $h = 5$.

All parabolas exhibit symmetry

$x = h$ is the line of symmetry for any parabola

For this parabola, $x = 5$ represents the line of symmetry

 Drill

1

For each of the following quadratics, identify the coordinates of the vertex.

A. $y = (x + 3)(x - 1)$ Vertex? (____ , ____)

B. $y = -(x - 6)(x + 2)$ Vertex? (____ , ____)

C. $y = 3(x + 1)(x + 4)$ Vertex? (____ , ____)

D. $y = x(x - 5)$ Vertex? (____ , ____)

E. $y = -2x(x - 5)$ Vertex? (____ , ____)

Summary of the Three Forms

Conversions

STANDARD FORM
$$y = ax^2 + bx + c$$

Find the *x*-coordinate of the vertex (*h*) by using $h = \frac{-b}{2a}$. Then plug in to find *y* (*k*).

Factor the equation

VERTEX FORM
$$y = a(x - h)^2 + k$$

Vertex: (*h*, *k*)

Axis of Symmetry: *x* = *h*

Find the *x*-coordinate of the vertex (*h*) by identifying the number halfway between the two roots. Then plug in to find *y* (*k*).

FACTORED FORM
$$y = a(x - r_1)(x - r_2)$$

Meaning of the Constants

Standard Form $y = ax^2 + bx + c$	*a* tells us: -U-shape/upside-down U-shape -Wide/Skinny	*c* = *y*-intercept	
Vertex Form $y = a(x - h)^2 + k$	*a* tells us: -U-shape/upside-down U-shape -Wide/Skinny	*h* = *x*-coordinate of vertex	*k* = *y*-coordinate of vertex
Factored Form $y = a(x - r_1)(x - r_2)$	*a* tells us: -U-shape/upside-down U-shape -Wide/Skinny	r_1 = root r_2 = root	

Benefit of Form

Standard Form $y = ax^2 + bx + c$	*y*-intercept is visible ("*c*")
Vertex Form $y = a(x - h)^2 + k$	Vertex point is visible (*h*, *k*)
Factored Form $y = a(x - r_1)(x - r_2)$	Roots are visible (r_1 and r_2)
All 3 Forms	Shape is visible (*a* tells us whether the graph is shaped like a U or an upside-down-U)

Sum and Product of Roots

Sum of Roots	Product of Roots
$\dfrac{-b}{a}$	$\dfrac{c}{a}$

To find the sum and product of the roots, we can either…

1. Pull the constants from <u>Standard Form</u> and use the **equations above**
2. Find the roots (from <u>Factored Form</u>) and add or multiply them

 Drill

1

Without solving each quadratic, find the sum and product of its solutions.

A. $3x^2 + 12x + 6 = 0$ Sum of Solutions: _____

Product of Solutions: _____

B. $x^2 = 10x - 4$ Sum of Solutions: _____

Product of Solutions: _____

The Discriminant

$$x = \frac{-b \pm \sqrt{\boxed{b^2 - 4ac}}}{2a}$$

The boxed expression is called **The Discriminant**. It's the most important part of the Quadratic Formula.

Using the discriminant, we can learn a lot about the roots **without having to actually calculate them**.

Discriminant is…	Root Characteristics
Less than 0	2 imaginary (complex) roots → graph never touches the x-axis
Greater than 0	2 real roots
Exactly 0	1 real root

> How many x-intercepts does the equation $y = x^2 + 6x + 9$ have?

$$a = 1$$
$$b = 6$$
$$c = 9$$

$$b^2 - 4ac = (6)^2 - 4(1)(9) = 36 - 36 = 0$$

Because the discriminant is exactly 0, we know that there is **one** real root (one x-intercept)

*<u>NOTE</u>: This question asked us to determine the **number** of roots – not the actual roots themselves. Therefore, there is no need to solve the equation – we just need to use the discriminant.

1

Using the discriminant, determine if each of the following quadratics has 2 imaginary (complex) solutions, 1 real solution, or 2 real solutions.

A. $x^2 - x + \dfrac{1}{4} = 0$

B. $x^2 + 5x + 6 = -4$

C. $3x^2 + 12x + 8 = 0$

2

Label each graph as being a representation of either A) $b^2 - 4ac = 0$
B) $b^2 - 4ac > 0$
C) $b^2 - 4ac < 0$

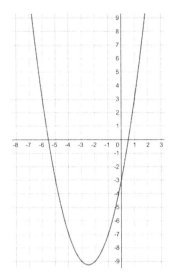

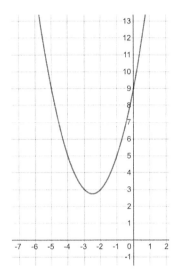

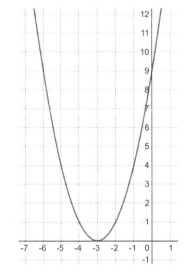

_____   _____   _____

3

For what value of k does the equation $x^2 - 10x + k = 0$ have exactly one real solution?

4

$$7x^2 + cx + 2 = 0$$

For the quadratic equation shown, c is a constant. If the equation has 2 real solutions, which of the following must be true?

A) $c^2 > 0$
B) $c^2 < 0$
C) $c^2 > 56$
D) $c^2 < 56$

Real-Life Applications

> A projectile is launched from a building. The height h of the projectile in feet can be modeled by the following equation: $h = -t^2 - 5t + 40$, where t is the time in seconds since the projectile was launched. What does 40 indicate in this context?

The equation above is in Standard Form, so 40 is the c-term (the y-intercept). In a physical context, the y-intercept represents the starting point. In this situation, then, 40 feet is the initial height of the projectile.

> A jewelry company sells beaded pearl necklaces. Its total revenue r, in thousands of dollars, can be modeled by the following equation: $r(x) = -0.5x^2 + 5x$, where x represents the number of necklaces sold in thousands.
>
> A. How many necklaces must the company sell to generate maximum revenue?
> B. What is the company's maximum revenue?

A. To find the number of necklaces (x) the company will need to sell to generate maximum revenue, we must find the x-coordinate (h) of the vertex.

$$h = \frac{-b}{2a} = \frac{-5}{2(-0.5)} = \frac{-5}{-1} = 5$$

Therefore, the company must sell 5,000 necklaces (x is in thousands) to generate maximum revenue.

B. To find the maximum revenue, we will need to find the y-coordinate (k) of the vertex.

To find the y-coordinate, plug "$x = 5$" back into the original equation.

$$y = -0.5(5)^2 + 5(5) = 12.5$$
$$k = 12.5$$

The company's maximum revenue is $12,500 (the revenue is in thousands of dollars)

Drills

1

$$p(t) = -(t-3)^2 + 50$$

The function above models the height p in feet of a projectile launched from the top of a house after t seconds have passed. Which of the following is the best interpretation of the point $(3, 50)$ in this context?

A) The projectile was launched from a point 50 feet above ground level
B) 3 seconds after the projectile was launched, the projectile reaches its maximum speed of 50 feet/second
C) 3 seconds after the projectile was launched, the projectile reaches its minimum height of 50 feet
D) 3 seconds after the projectile was launched, the projectile reaches its maximum height of 50 feet

2

$P(x) = -\dfrac{1}{2}x^2 + 10x - 30$ models the hourly profit, $P(x)$, of a local bakery from selling customized cakes for a price of x dollars. Based on this equation, what is the maximum profit, in dollars, the bakery can earn in a single hour?

Questions

1

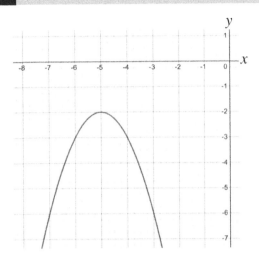

Which of the following provides the appropriate equation for the quadratic shown above in the xy-plane?

A) $y = (x - 5)^2 - 2$
B) $y = (x + 5)^2 - 2$
C) $y = -(x - 5)^2 - 2$
D) $y = -(x + 5)^2 - 2$

2

What is the minimum value of the function d defined as $d(x) = (x - 3)^2 - 5$?

A) 0
B) -5
C) -3
D) 3

3

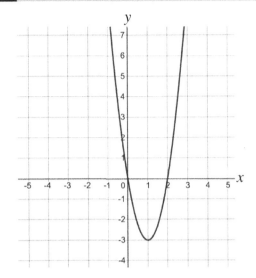

Which of the following provides the appropriate equation for the quadratic shown above in the xy-plane?

A) $y = 3x(x + 2)$
B) $y = 3x(x - 2)$
C) $y = \frac{1}{3}x(x - 2)$
D) $y = \frac{1}{3}x(x + 2)$

4

$(x + 5)(x - 3) = 0$

What is the product of the solutions to the equation shown above?

A) -15
B) -2
C) 8
D) 15

5

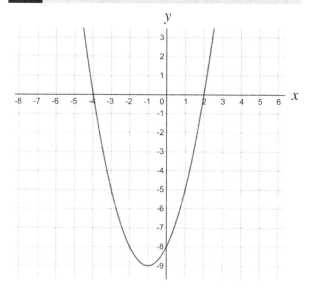

Which of the following is the equation of the parabola graphed in the xy-plane above?

A) $y = (x + 4)(x - 2)$
B) $y = (x - 4)(x - 2)$
C) $y = -(x + 4)(x - 2)$
D) $y = -(x - 4)(x - 2)$

6

$$3x^2 + 11x + 6$$

If the expression shown above is written as $(3x + z)(x + 3)$ where z is a constant, what is the value of z?

7

Shown below is the graph of g in the xy-plane.

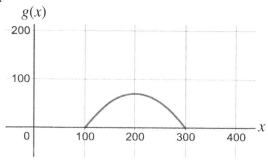

Which of the following is a factor of $g(x)$?

A) $x + 100$
B) $x - 300$
C) $x - 70$
D) $x + 70$

8

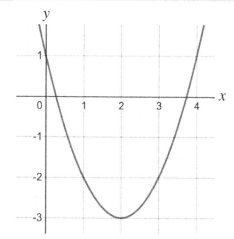

Which of the following provides the appropriate equation for the quadratic shown above in the xy-plane?

A) $y = (x - 2)^2 - 3$
B) $y = (x - 2)^2 + 1$
C) $y = (x + 2)^2- 3$
D) $y = (x + 2)^2 + 1$

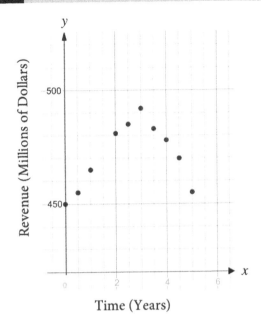

The scatterplot to the left shows the revenue generated, in millions of dollars, by a technology start-up company during its first five years of business.

Which equation below best models the data?

A) $y = 5.54x^2 + 30.36x + 450$
B) $y = 5.54x^2 + 30.36x - 450$
C) $y = -5.54x^2 + 30.36x + 450$
D) $y = -5.54x^2 + 30.36x - 450$

Answers

For **detailed solutions**, scan the QR code with your phone's camera

or

visit testpreptips.org/quadratics

Drills (Page 99)

1.

A. <u>Shape</u>: U
   <u>y-intercept</u> = -10

B. <u>Shape</u>: upside-down-U
   <u>y-intercept</u> = 1

C. <u>Shape</u>: U
   <u>y-intercept</u> = 0

2. B

Drills (Page 101)

1. $x = -5$ and $x = -2$
2. $x = 4$ and $x = -3$
3. $x = -3$
4. $x = 3$ and $x = 2$
5. $x = -5$ and $x = 3$

Drills (Page 103)

1. $x = -\frac{1}{3}$ and $x = -2$
2. $x = -4$ and $x = \frac{1}{3}$
3. $x = -3$ and $x = \frac{1}{2}$
4. $x = 4$ and $x = -\frac{2}{5}$
5. $x = 4$ and $x = \frac{2}{3}$

Drills (Page 104)

1. $x = 0$ and $x = -7$
2. $x = 0$ and $x = 2$
3. $x = 0$ and $x = 3$
4. $x = 0$ and $x = 3$

Drills (Page 106)

1. $x = \pm 5$
2. $x = \pm 3$
3. $x = \pm 2\sqrt{5}$
4. $x = \pm 3$
5. $x = \pm 6$
6. $x = \pm \sqrt{7}$

Drills (Page 109)

1. $x = \dfrac{-5 \pm \sqrt{17}}{2}$
2. $x = \dfrac{1 \pm \sqrt{41}}{4}$
3. A
4. A

Drills (Page 110)

A. Roots: $x = -3$ and $x = 1$
   Shape: U

B. Roots: $x = 6$ and $x = -2$
   Shape: upside-down-U

C. Roots: $x = -1$ and $x = -4$
   Shape: U

D. Roots: $x = 0$ and $x = 5$
   Shape: U

E. Roots: $x = 0$ and $x = 5$
   Shape: upside-down-U

Drills (Page 112)

A. Vertex: (-3, -5)
   Min or Max: Minimum

B. Vertex: (2, -3)
   Min or Max: Minimum

C. Vertex: (-1, 9)
   Min or Max: Maximum

D. Vertex: (4, 1)
   Min or Max: Maximum

Drills (Page 114)

1. Vertex: (-3, -8)
   Max or Min: Minimum
   Vertex Form: $y = (x + 3)^2 - 8$

2. Vertex: (1, 2)
   Max or Min: Minimum
   Vertex Form: $y = (x - 1)^2 + 2$

3. Vertex: (5, 53)
   Max or Min: Maximum
   Vertex Form: $y = -2(x - 5)^2 + 53$

4. Vertex: (-2, 17)
   Max or Min: Maximum
   Vertex Form: $y = -3(x + 2)^2 + 17$

Drills (Page 116)

A. Vertex: (-1, -4)

B. Vertex: (2, 16)

C. Vertex: (-2.5, -6.75)

D. Vertex: (2.5, -6.25)

E. Vertex: (2.5, 12.5)

Drills (Page 118)

A. Sum: -4
   Product: 2

B. Sum: 10
   Product: 4

Drills (Pages 120-121)

1.

A. 1 Real Solution
B. 2 Imaginary (Complex) Solutions
C. 2 Real Solutions

2. First Graph (left): B) $b^2 - 4ac > 0$
   Second Graph (center): C) $b^2 - 4ac < 0$
   Third Graph (right): A) $b^2 - 4ac = 0$

3. $k = 25$

4. C

Drills (Page 123)

1. D

2. $20

Questions (Pages 124-126)

1. D
2. B
3. B
4. A
5. A
6. $z = 2$
7. B
8. A
9. C

Topic 8: Factoring

Finding the Greatest Common Factor (GCF)

The **Greatest Common Factor (GCF)** is the greatest combination of numbers and variables that all terms of an expression are divisible by.

<u>Find the Greatest Common Factor (GCF) One Step at a Time:</u>

1. Determine the greatest **number** that can be pulled out from all terms
2. Determine the highest power of each **variable** that can be pulled out from all terms

Once we determine the GCF, we will **divide (factor)** it out of **each term** of the original expression.

<u>Goal</u>: Find the GCF for each expression. Then, write the expression in factored form.

$$3xy + 12y^3$$

1. The greatest number that can be pulled out is 3.
2. The greatest variable that can be pulled out is y.

⟶ **GCF**: $3y$ ⟶ **Factored Form**: $3y(x + 4y^2)$

$$4x^3 + 6x^2 + 8x$$

1. The greatest number that can be pulled out is 2.
2. The greatest variable that can be pulled out is x.

⟶ **GCF**: $2x$ ⟶ **Factored Form**: $2x(2x^2 + 3x + 4)$

$$8xy^2 - 20xy^3$$

1. The greatest number that can be pulled out is 4.
2. The greatest variables that can be pulled out are xy^2.

⟶ **GCF**: $4xy^2$ ⟶ **Factored Form**: $4xy^2(2 - 5y)$

131

$$5a^5 + 10a^6 + 15a^7$$

1. The greatest number that can be pulled out is 5.
2. The greatest variable that can be pulled out is a^5.

⟶ **GCF**: $5a^5$ ⟶ **Factored Form**: $5a^5(1 + 2a + 3a^2)$

***NOTE**: Whenever the entire term of an expression is itself the GCF (like $5a^5$ in the above example), it is written as "1" in factored form.

Drills

Instructions: First, state the GCF. Then, factor the GCF out of the expression.

1

$$x^3 - 2x^2$$

GCF: _____

Factored Expression:

_____

2

$$10x^5 + 20x^3 - 15x^2$$

GCF: _____

Factored Expression:

_____

3

$$8xy^2 + 12x^2y$$

GCF: _____

Factored Expression:

_____

4

$$6x^5y^3 - 4x^2y^4$$

GCF: _____

Factored Expression:

_____

5

$$3xy + 9x^4y^2$$

GCF: _____

Factored Expression:

_____

The Three Must-Know Factored Forms

$$\boxed{\textbf{Form 1}: a^2 + 2ab + b^2 = (a+b)^2}$$

Recall from Topic 3 (Exponents) that we **CANNOT** distribute a power to terms that are being **added**. Therefore…

$(a+b)^2$ **DOES NOT EQUAL** $a^2 + b^2$

$(a+b)^2 = (a+b)(a+b)$. We can use FOIL to get $a^2 + 2ab + b^2$.

$$\boxed{\textbf{Form 2}: a^2 - 2ab + b^2 = (a-b)^2}$$

Recall from Topic 3 (Exponents) that we **CANNOT** distribute a power to terms that are being **subtracted**. Therefore…

$(a-b)^2$ **DOES NOT EQUAL** $a^2 - b^2$

$(a-b)^2 = (a-b)(a-b)$. We can use FOIL to get $a^2 - 2ab + b^2$.

$$\boxed{\begin{array}{c}\textbf{Form 3}: a^2 - b^2 = (a+b)(a-b) \\ \text{``The Difference of Perfect Squares''}\end{array}}$$

This factoring form is used when one perfect square is subtracted from another perfect square.

This expression does **NOT** contain an "ab" term because the "b" term is of opposite signs in each factor:

$(a+b)(a-b) = a^2 \; \cancel{+ ab - ab} \; - b^2 = a^2 - b^2$

Recognizing Direct Versions of the Three Factored Forms

> Which of the following is equivalent to $x^2 + 4x + 4$?
>
> A) $(x - 2)^2$
> B) $(x + 2)^2$
> C) $(x - 4)^2$
> D) $(x + 4)^2$

We can find a by taking the square root of the first term: $a = \sqrt{x^2} = x$

We can find b by taking the square root of the last term: $b = \sqrt{4} = 2$

Because the middle term is positive, this is a **Type 1** Factored Form:
$$a^2 + 2ab + b^2 = (a + b)^2$$

Choice B: $(a + b)^2$ → $(x + 2)^2$

> Which of the following is equivalent to $y^2 - 8y + 16$?
>
> A) $(y - 4)^2$
> B) $(y + 4)^2$
> C) $(y + 4)(y - 4)$
> D) $2(y - 4)(y + 4)$

We can find a by taking the square root of the first term: $a = \sqrt{y^2} = y$

We can find b by taking the square root of the last term: $b = \sqrt{16} = 4$

Because the middle term is negative, this is a **Type 2** Factored Form:
$$a^2 - 2ab + b^2 = (a - b)^2$$

Choice A: $(a - b)^2$ → $(y - 4)^2$

> Which of the following is equivalent to $x^2 - 9$?
> A) $(x - 3)^2$
> B) $(x + 3)^2$
> C) $(x + 3)(x - 3)$
> D) $(x - 9)^2$

Both x^2 and 9 are perfect squares. The above expression contains no middle term. Therefore, we are working with the **"Difference of Perfect Squares."**

This is a **Type 3** Factored Form: $a^2 - b^2 = (a + b)(a - b)$

We can find *a* by taking the square root of the first term: $a = \sqrt{x^2} = x$

We can find *b* by taking the square root of the last term: $b = \sqrt{9} = 3$

Choice C: $a^2 - b^2 = (a + b)(a - b) \rightarrow (x + 3)(x - 3)$

> Which of the following is equivalent to $x^2 - y^2$?
> A) $(x - y)^2$
> B) $(x + y)^2$
> C) $(x + y)(x - y)$
> D) $2(x - y)$

Both x^2 and y^2 are perfect squares. The above expression contains no middle term. Therefore, we are working with the **"Difference of Perfect Squares."**

This is a **Type 3** Factored Form: $a^2 - b^2 = (a + b)(a - b)$

We can find *a* by taking the square root of the first term: $a = \sqrt{x^2} = x$

We can find *b* by taking the square root of the last term: $b = \sqrt{y^2} = y$

Choice C: $a^2 - b^2 = (a + b)(a - b) \rightarrow (x + y)(x - y)$

 Drills

Instructions: First, state the values of *a* (by taking the square root of the first term) and *b* (by taking the square root of the last term). Then, write the equation in factored form.

1

$$x^2 - 25$$

a: _____   *b*: _____

Type of Factored Form (1, 2, or 3): _____

Equation in Factored Form:

_____

2

$$x^2 + 10x + 25$$

a: _____   *b*: _____

Type of Factored Form (1, 2, or 3): _____

Equation in Factored Form:

_____

3

$$x^2 - 6x + 9$$

a: _____   *b*: _____

Type of Factored Form (1, 2, or 3): _____

Equation in Factored Form:

_____

4

$$m^2 - n^2$$

a: _____   *b*: _____

Type of Factored Form (1, 2, or 3): _____

Equation in Factored Form:

_____

Recognizing Less-Direct Versions of the Three Factored Forms

> Which of the following is equivalent to $9x^2 + 6xy + y^2$?
>
> A) $(3x + y)^2$
> B) $(3x - y)^2$
> C) $(3x + y)(3x - y)$
> D) $(9x + y)^2$

We can find a by taking the square root of the first term: $a = \sqrt{9x^2} = 3x$

We can find b by taking the square root of the last term: $b = \sqrt{y^2} = y$

Because the middle term is positive, this is a **Type 1** Factored Form:
$$a^2 + 2ab + b^2 = (a + b)^2$$

Choice A: $(a + b)^2 \rightarrow (3x + y)^2$.

> Which of the following is equivalent to $9x^2 - 12xy + 4y^2$?
>
> A) $(3x - 2y)^2$
> B) $(3x + 2y)^2$
> C) $(3x - 2y)(3x + 2y)$
> D) $(9x - 4y)^2$

We can find a by taking the square root of the first term: $a = \sqrt{9x^2} = 3x$

We can find b by taking the square root of the last term: $b = \sqrt{4y^2} = 2y$

Because the middle term is negative, this is a **Type 2** Factored Form:
$$a^2 - 2ab + b^2 = (a - b)^2$$

Choice A: $(a - b)^2 \rightarrow (3x - 2y)^2$.

> Which of the following is equivalent to $16m^2 - 49n^2$?
>
> A) $(4m + 7n)^2$
> B) $(4m - 7n)^2$
> C) $4(m - 7n)^2$
> D) $(4m - 7n)(4m + 7n)$

Both $16m^2$ and $49n^2$ are perfect squares. The above expression contains no middle term. Therefore, we are working with the **"Difference of Perfect Squares."**

This is a **Type 3** Factored Form: $a^2 - b^2 = (a + b)(a - b)$

We can find a by taking the square root of the first term: $a = \sqrt{16m^2} = 4m$

We can find b by taking the square root of the last term: $b = \sqrt{49n^2} = 7n$

Choice D: $a^2 - b^2 = (a + b)(a - b)$ → $(4m + 7n)(4m - 7m)$

> Which of the following is equivalent to $x^4 - 16$?
>
> A) $(x + 2)^4$
> B) $(x - 2)^4$
> C) $(x + 2)(x - 2)^3$
> D) $(x^2 + 4)(x^2 - 4)$

Both x^4 and 16 are perfect squares. The above expression contains no middle term. Therefore, we are working with the **"Difference of Perfect Squares."**

This is a **Type 3** Factored Form: $a^2 - b^2 = (a + b)(a - b)$

We can find a by taking the square root of the first term: $a = \sqrt{x^4} = x^2$

We can find b by taking the square root of the last term: $b = \sqrt{16} = 4$

Choice D: $a^2 - b^2 = (a + b)(a - b)$ → $(x^2 + 4)(x^2 - 4)$

 Drills

Instructions for Drills 1-4: First, state the values of a (by taking the square root of the first term) and b (by taking the square root of the last term). Then, write the equation in factored form.

1

$$x^4 - 25$$

a: _____ b: _____

Type of Factored Form (1, 2, or 3): _____

Equation in Factored Form:

_____

2

$$4x^2 - 4x + 1$$

a: _____ b: _____

Type of Factored Form (1, 2, or 3): _____

Equation in Factored Form:

_____

3

$$x^4 + 6x^2 + 9$$

a: _____ b: _____

Type of Factored Form (1, 2, or 3): _____

Equation in Factored Form:

_____

4

$$9x^2 + 6xy + y^2$$

a: _____ b: _____

Type of Factored Form (1, 2, or 3): _____

Equation in Factored Form:

_____

5

Which of the following is equivalent to the expression $x^4 - 16$?

I. $(x^2 + 4)(x^2 - 4)$
II. $(x^2 + 4)(x + 2)(x - 2)$

A) I
B) II
C) I and II
D) Neither I nor II

Solving for Entire Expressions

You must be able to recognize identical factors with different multipliers.

<u>Examples:</u>

$5a + 10b \rightarrow 5(a + 2b)$

$6x - 4y \rightarrow 2(3x - 2y)$

> If $3x + 3y - 7 = 11$, what is the value of $x + y$?

We want to first isolate $3x + 3y$, so we must add 7 to both sides

$$3x + 3y = 18$$

$$3(x + y) = 18$$

$$\frac{3(x + y)}{3} = \frac{18}{3}$$

$$x + y = 6$$

> What is the value of $4a + 5b - 7c$ if $16a + 20b - 28c = 20$?

$$16a + 20b - 28c = 20 \rightarrow 4(4a + 5b - 7c) = 20$$

$$\frac{4(4a + 5b - 7c)}{4} = \frac{20}{4}$$

$$4a + 5b - 7c = 5$$

Drills

1

What is the value of $a + b - c$ if $10a + 10b - 10c = 70$?

2

What is the value of $x - 5y$ if $4x - 20y = 24$?

Answers

For **detailed solutions**, scan the QR code with your phone's camera

or

visit testpreptips.org/factoring

Drills (Page 133)

1. <u>GCF</u>: x^2
   <u>Factored Expression</u>: $x^2(x - 2)$

2. <u>GCF</u>: $5x^2$
   <u>Factored Expression</u>: $5x^2(2x^3 + 4x - 3)$

3. <u>GCF</u>: $4xy$
   <u>Factored Expression</u>: $4xy(2y + 3x)$

4. <u>GCF</u>: $2x^2y^3$
   <u>Factored Expression</u>: $2x^2y^3(3x^3 - 2y)$

5. <u>GCF</u>: $3xy$
   <u>Factored Expression</u>: $3xy(1 + 3x^3y)$

Drills (Page 137)

1. <u>*a*</u>: x
   <u>*b*</u>: 5
   <u>Type of Factored Form</u>: 3
   <u>Equation in Factored Form</u>: $(x + 5)(x - 5)$

2. <u>*a*</u>: x
   <u>*b*</u>: 5
   <u>Type of Factored Form</u>: 1
   <u>Equation in Factored Form</u>: $(x + 5)^2$

3. <u>*a*</u>: x
   <u>*b*</u>: 3
   <u>Type of Factored Form</u>: 2
   <u>Equation in Factored Form</u>: $(x - 3)^2$

4. <u>*a*</u>: m
   <u>*b*</u>: n
   <u>Type of Factored Form</u>: 3
   <u>Equation in Factored Form</u>: $(m + n)(m - n)$

Drills (Page 140)

1. $\underline{a}$: x^2
   $\underline{b}$: 5
   Type of Factored Form: 3
   Equation in Factored Form: $(x^2 + 5)(x^2 - 5)$

2. $\underline{a}$: $2x$
   $\underline{b}$: 1
   Type of Factored Form: 2
   Equation in Factored Form: $(2x - 1)^2$

3. $\underline{a}$: x^2
   $\underline{b}$: 3
   Type of Factored Form: 1
   Equation in Factored Form: $(x^2 + 3)^2$

4. $\underline{a}$: $3x$
   $\underline{b}$: y
   Type of Factored Form: 1
   Equation in Factored Form: $(3x + y)^2$

5. C

Drills (Page 141)

1. 7
2. 6

Topic 9: Fractions

A <u>fraction</u> represents the number of parts of a whole.

Fractions are written in terms of a **numerator** (top number) and a **denominator** (bottom number). The **numerator** tells us how many "parts" we have, and the **denominator** tells us what the "whole" is.

$$\frac{\text{numerator}}{\text{denominator}}$$

Fractions Without Variables

Addition and Subtraction

We can only add or subtract fractions with **identical denominators**.

<u>Can be Added in Current Form:</u>

$$\frac{5}{7} + \frac{3}{7}$$

<u>**CANNOT** be Added in Current Form:</u>

$$\frac{5}{7} + \frac{3}{4}$$

We only add or subtract the numerators – **NOT** the denominators.

$$\frac{4}{5} - \frac{3}{5} = \frac{4-3}{5} = \frac{1}{5} \qquad \frac{5}{19} + \frac{11}{19} = \frac{5+11}{19} = \frac{16}{19}$$

Finding the Least Common Denominator (LCD)

If the denominators of two fractions are **NOT** identical, we must make them identical before we can add or subtract them. To do this, we will find the Least Common Denominator (LCD) – the smallest number that both denominators fully divide into.

<u>Goal:</u> Find the LCD for each of the following fraction pairs.

$$\boxed{\frac{1}{4} \text{ and } \frac{1}{8}} \quad \underline{LCD = 8}$$

8 is the smallest number that both 4 and 8 fully divide into.

$$\boxed{\frac{5}{7} \text{ and } \frac{3}{5}} \quad \underline{LCD = 35}$$

35 is the smallest number that both 5 and 7 fully divide into.

$$\boxed{\frac{1}{12} \text{ and } \frac{7}{18}} \quad \underline{LCD = 36}$$

36 is the smallest number that both 12 and 18 fully divide into.

Now that we know how to find the LCD, we can use it to add and subtract fractions with different denominators.

$$\boxed{\frac{1}{4} - \frac{1}{8}} \quad \underline{LCD = 8}$$

$\frac{1}{8}$ already contains the LCD of 8, so we only need to modify $\frac{1}{4}$. To get the denominator of 4 to be 8, we must multiply the denominator by 2.

*<u>NOTE</u>: Any operation applied to the denominator must also be applied to the numerator to keep the fraction <u>balanced</u>.

Therefore, both the numerator and denominator must be multiplied by 2:

$$\left(\frac{1}{4}\right)\left(\frac{2}{2}\right) = \frac{2}{8}$$

Now that both of our denominators are identical, we can finally subtract the numerators:

$$\frac{2}{8} - \frac{1}{8} = \frac{1}{8}$$

Drill

Instructions: First, indicate the LCD of both fractions. Then, add or subtract the fractions.

A. $\dfrac{1}{6} + \dfrac{3}{4}$

LCD = _____

B. $\dfrac{5}{9} - \dfrac{6}{7}$

LCD = _____

C. $\dfrac{6}{20} + \dfrac{40}{100}$

LCD = _____

Reducing (Simplifying) Fractions

For multiple choice questions, fractions will be presented in simplest form.

$$\boxed{\dfrac{5}{6} + \dfrac{11}{3}} \qquad \underline{LCD = 6}$$

$\dfrac{5}{6}$ already contains the LCD of 6, so we only need to modify $\dfrac{11}{3}$. To get the denominator of 3 to be 6, we must multiply the denominator by 2.

$$\left(\dfrac{11}{3}\right)\left(\dfrac{2}{2}\right) = \dfrac{22}{6}$$

$$\dfrac{5}{6} + \dfrac{22}{6} = \dfrac{27}{6} \quad \longleftarrow \quad \text{Our fraction is \textbf{NOT} in simplest form.}$$

To get a fraction in simplest form, we want to find the **largest** number that divides completely into both the numerator and denominator. This is also called the Greatest Common Factor (GCF). We then divide the numerator and denominator by the GCF.

The largest number that divides completely into both 27 and 6 is 3.

$\dfrac{27}{6} \rightarrow$ GCF = 3

$27 \div 3 = 9$
$6 \div 3 = 2$

Reduced Fraction: $\dfrac{9}{2}$

Drill

1

Instructions: First, identify the GCF of the numerator and denominator. Then, simplify each of the following fractions.

A. $\dfrac{10}{15}$ GCF = _____   B. $\dfrac{8}{20}$ GCF = _____   C. $\dfrac{18}{4}$ GCF = _____

Multiplication and Division

When multiplying or dividing fractions (unlike adding or subtracting fractions) the denominators do **NOT** have to be identical.

Multiplication

To **multiply** two fractions, we multiply **BOTH** the numerator **AND** the denominator:

$$\left(\dfrac{6}{5}\right)\left(\dfrac{7}{8}\right) = \dfrac{42}{40} \xrightarrow{\text{reduce}} \dfrac{21}{20}$$

Division

Before we discuss **dividing** fractions, let's talk about **reciprocals**. The reciprocal of any fraction is found by flipping its numerator and denominator.

$\dfrac{4}{5} \xrightarrow{\text{reciprocal}} \dfrac{5}{4}$

$-\dfrac{5}{3} \xrightarrow{\text{reciprocal}} -\dfrac{3}{5}$

Any number, variable, or expression that does not contain a fraction can be written as a fraction by putting it over "1."

$8 = \dfrac{8}{1} \xrightarrow{\text{reciprocal}} \dfrac{1}{8}$

$x + 3 = \dfrac{x+3}{1} \xrightarrow{\text{reciprocal}} \dfrac{1}{x+3}$

To **divide** fractions, we multiply by the reciprocal of the **second fraction**.

$$\dfrac{9}{17} \div \dfrac{2}{3} \longrightarrow \left(\dfrac{9}{17}\right)\left(\dfrac{3}{2}\right) = \dfrac{27}{34}$$

$$\dfrac{2}{3} \div 5 = \dfrac{2}{3} \div \dfrac{5}{1} \longrightarrow \left(\dfrac{2}{3}\right)\left(\dfrac{1}{5}\right) = \dfrac{2}{15}$$

Drill

Instructions: Multiply or divide each of the following pairs of fractions. Simplify your answer if possible.

A. $\dfrac{1}{2}\left(\dfrac{2}{5}\right)$

B. $3\left(\dfrac{1}{18}\right)$

C. $\left(\dfrac{5}{3}\right)\left(\dfrac{6}{5}\right)$

D. $\dfrac{5}{6} \div \dfrac{1}{2}$

E. $\dfrac{2}{5} \div 3$

Fractions with Variables

Addition and Subtraction

Find the Least Common Denominator (LCD) One Step at a Time:

1. Find the LCD of the **numbers**
2. Take the highest power of each **variable**
3. Take the highest power of each **expression**

Goal: Find the LCD. Then, add or subtract the fractions.

$\boxed{\dfrac{3}{8} + \dfrac{2}{x}}$ → Get Common Denominators $\left(\dfrac{3}{8}\right)\left(\dfrac{x}{x}\right) = \dfrac{3x}{8x}$ $\left(\dfrac{2}{x}\right)\left(\dfrac{8}{8}\right) = \dfrac{16}{8x}$ → Add Fractions $\dfrac{3x}{8x} + \dfrac{16}{8x} = \dfrac{3x+16}{8x}$

LCD = $8x$

$\boxed{\dfrac{3}{10x^2} - \dfrac{1}{2x^2}}$ → Get Common Denominator $\left(\dfrac{1}{2x^2}\right)\left(\dfrac{5}{5}\right) = \dfrac{5}{10x^2}$ → Subtract Fractions $\dfrac{3}{10x^2} - \dfrac{5}{10x^2} = -\dfrac{2}{10x^2} = -\dfrac{1}{5x^2}$

LCD = $10x^2$

$\boxed{\dfrac{2}{x-5} + \dfrac{6}{x+4}}$ → Get Common Denominators $\left(\dfrac{2}{x-5}\right)\left(\dfrac{x+4}{x+4}\right) = \dfrac{2x+8}{(x-5)(x+4)}$ $\left(\dfrac{6}{x+4}\right)\left(\dfrac{x-5}{x-5}\right) = \dfrac{6x-30}{(x-5)(x+4)}$

LCD = $(x-5)(x+4)$

↓ Add Fractions

$\dfrac{2x+8}{(x-5)(x+4)} + \dfrac{6x-30}{(x-5)(x+4)} = \dfrac{8x-22}{(x-5)(x+4)}$

$\boxed{\dfrac{2}{5x} - 3x}$ → Get Common Denominator $\left(\dfrac{3x}{1}\right)\left(\dfrac{5x}{5x}\right) = \dfrac{15x^2}{5x}$ → Subtract Fractions $\dfrac{2}{5x} - \dfrac{15x^2}{5x} = \dfrac{2-15x^2}{5x}$

LCD = $5x$

$\boxed{\dfrac{2}{(x-2)^2} - \dfrac{4}{x-2}}$ → Get Common Denominator $\left(\dfrac{4}{x-2}\right)\left(\dfrac{x-2}{x-2}\right) = \dfrac{4x-8}{(x-2)^2}$ → Subtract Fractions $\dfrac{2}{(x-2)^2} - \dfrac{4x-8}{(x-2)^2} = \dfrac{2-(4x-8)}{(x-2)^2} = \dfrac{-4x+10}{(x-2)^2}$

LCD = $(x-2)^2$

149

Drill

Instructions: First, find the LCD. Then, add or subtract each of the following examples.

A. $\dfrac{3}{2x} + \dfrac{1}{4x}$

LCD = _____

B. $\dfrac{5}{2x^2} - \dfrac{1}{3x^2}$

LCD = _____

C. $\dfrac{3}{x} - \dfrac{1}{x^2}$

LCD = _____

D. $\dfrac{4}{x+2} - \dfrac{1}{x-5}$

LCD = _____

E. $\dfrac{10}{x} + \dfrac{3}{x-2}$

LCD = _____

F. $\dfrac{1}{2x} + 5x$

LCD = _____

G. $\dfrac{7}{(x-1)^2} + \dfrac{1}{x-1}$

LCD = _____

150

Multiplication and Division
Multiplication

Again, to **multiply** two fractions, we multiply **BOTH** the numerator **AND** the denominator. The denominators do **NOT** need to be identical:

$$\left(\frac{1}{2x}\right)\left(\frac{6}{x^2}\right) = \frac{6}{2x^3} = \frac{3}{x^3}$$

$$\left(\frac{x}{5}\right)\left(\frac{x}{3}\right) = \frac{x^2}{15}$$

$$3\left(\frac{x}{2}\right) \rightarrow \left(\frac{3}{1}\right)\left(\frac{x}{2}\right) = \frac{3x}{2}$$

To simplify a fraction, we must **cross out** any variables or expressions that are common to both the numerator and denominator:

$$(x+4)\frac{1}{(x+4)^2} \rightarrow \left(\frac{(x+4)}{1}\right)\left(\frac{1}{(x+4)^2}\right) \rightarrow \frac{x+4}{(x+4)^2} \rightarrow \frac{\cancel{x+4}}{\cancel{(x+4)}(x+4)} = \frac{1}{x+4}$$

Division

Again, to **divide** two fractions, we multiply by the reciprocal of the second fraction.

$$\frac{3}{5x} \div \frac{1}{x} \rightarrow \left(\frac{3}{5x}\right)\left(\frac{x}{1}\right) = \frac{3\cancel{x}}{5\cancel{x}} = \frac{3}{5}$$

# Drill

1

Instructions: Multiply or divide each of the following pairs of fractions. Simplify your answer if possible.

A. $\left(\dfrac{7}{x}\right)\left(\dfrac{3x}{14}\right)$

B. $\dfrac{2x}{7}(5)$

C. $\dfrac{(x-3)}{5} \cdot \dfrac{5}{(x-3)^2}$

D. $\dfrac{x^3}{2} \div x$

E. $2(x+4)^2 \div \dfrac{x+4}{6}$

Splitting Fractions

To simplify fractions with expressions that are being added or subtracted, we use the **Heart Method**.

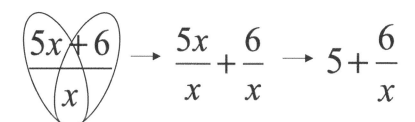

With the **Heart Method**, we divide each term in the numerator by the singular term in the denominator.

Instructions: Use the Heart Method to rewrite each of the following expressions.

1

$$\frac{6x + 10}{2}$$

2

$$\frac{9x - 12}{3x}$$

Solving Equations with Fractions
Method 1: Cross-Multiplication

When two fractions are set equal, we can cross multiply them to solve for a variable. To cross multiply, we multiply each of the diagonals and then set them equal.

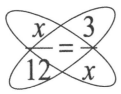

$x^2 = 36$
$x = \pm 6$

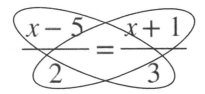

$3(x-5) = 2(x+1)$
$3x - 15 = 2x + 2$
$x = 17$

  Drills

1

$$\frac{2x-3}{2} = \frac{x+4}{5}$$

What value of x solves the above equation?

A) -4
B) 7
C) $\frac{23}{8}$
D) $\frac{19}{9}$

2

$$\frac{2}{x+1} = -\frac{1}{x-3}$$

What is the value of x that solves the above equation?

Method 2: Clearing Denominators

When cross multiplication is not an option, we should use the method of **Clearing Denominators** to remove all fractions from the equation.

$$4 = \frac{3}{5}x + 2$$

To clear the denominator, we can multiply both sides by 5 (denominator of $\frac{3}{5}$)

$$5(4) = 5\left(\frac{3}{5}x + 2\right)$$

$$20 = 5\left(\frac{3}{5}\right) + 5(2)$$

$$20 = 3x + 10$$

$$x = \frac{10}{3}$$

$$-x = \frac{3x}{5} - \frac{8}{10}$$

To clear the denominator, we can multiply both sides by 10 (the LCD of the two fractions)

$$10(-x) = 10\left(\frac{3x}{5} - \frac{8}{10}\right)$$

$$-10x = 10\left(\frac{3x}{5}\right) - 10\left(\frac{8}{10}\right)$$

$$-10x = 6x - 8$$

$$-16x = -8$$

$$x = \frac{1}{2}$$

Factoring to Clear Denominators

$$\frac{-1}{x^2 - 3x} + \frac{1}{x} = 1$$

A) 0
B) 1
C) 2
D) 3

Step 1: Before finding x by Clearing Denominators, we should **eliminate** all choices that would make either fraction **undefined** (denominator = 0)

Here, both 0 and 3 would make at least one fraction undefined, so we can eliminate Choices A and D.

Step 2: Find the LCD

To clearly see the LCD, we must first factor $x^2 - 3x$:

$$\frac{-1}{(x-3)(x)} + \frac{1}{x} = \frac{1}{1}$$

The LCD, then, is $(x-3)(x)$

Step 3: To remove all fractions, we can multiply both sides by $(x-3)(x)$ [the LCD]. We should cross out all terms that appear in both the numerator and denominator.

$$(x-3)(x)\left(\frac{-1}{(x-3)(x)} + \frac{1}{x}\right) = 1(x-3)(x)$$

$$\cancel{(x-3)(x)}\left(\frac{-1}{\cancel{(x-3)(x)}}\right) + (x-3)\cancel{(x)}\left(\frac{1}{\cancel{x}}\right) = 1(x-3)(x)$$

$$-1 + (x-3) = (x-3)(x)$$
$$x - 4 = x^2 - 3x$$
$$x^2 - 4x + 4 = 0$$
$$(x-2)(x-2) = 0$$
$$x = 2 \text{ (\textbf{Choice C})}$$

Drills

1

What is the value of x if $\frac{1}{5}x + 2 = 6$?

2

If $1 - \frac{1}{x+4} = \frac{3(x-1)}{x+4}$, what is the value of x?

3

What is the value of a if $\frac{3}{5} - \frac{1}{8} = \frac{3}{10}a - \frac{1}{5}a$?

4

What is the set of all solutions to the equation below?

$$\frac{12}{(x-1)(x+3)} - \frac{x}{x+3} = 2$$

A) {-3, -2}
B) {-2}
C) {-3, 2}
D) {2}

157

5

In the equation shown below, what is the value of x?

$$\frac{4x^2}{x^2-4} + \frac{8}{x-2} = \frac{4x}{x+2}$$

A) -1
B) $-\frac{1}{4}$
C) $\frac{1}{4}$
D) 1

6

If $\dfrac{bx+c}{x^2-3x} = \dfrac{4}{x} + \dfrac{5}{x-3}$, what is $b-c$?

Answers

For **detailed solutions**, scan the QR code with your phone's camera

or

visit testpreptips.org/fractions

Drill (Page 146)

A. LCD = 12
   Answer = $\frac{11}{12}$

B. LCD = 63
   Answer = $-\frac{19}{63}$

C. LCD = 100
   Answer = $\frac{70}{100}$

Drill (Page 147)

A. GCF = 5
   Simplified Fraction = $\frac{2}{3}$

B. GCF = 4
   Simplified Fraction = $\frac{2}{5}$

C. GCF = 2
   Simplified Fraction = $\frac{9}{2}$

Drill (Page 148)

A. $\frac{1}{5}$

B. $\frac{1}{6}$

C. 2

D. $\frac{5}{3}$

E. $\frac{2}{15}$

Drill (Page 150)

A. LCD = $4x$
   Answer = $\dfrac{7}{4x}$

B. LCD = $6x^2$
   Answer = $\dfrac{13}{6x^2}$

C. LCD = x^2
   Answer = $\dfrac{3x-1}{x^2}$

D. LCD = $(x+2)(x-5)$
   Answer = $\dfrac{3x-22}{(x+2)(x-5)}$

E. LCD = $x(x-2)$
   Answer = $\dfrac{13x-20}{x(x-2)}$

F. LCD = $2x$
   Answer = $\dfrac{10x^2+1}{2x}$

G. LCD = $(x-1)^2$
   Answer = $\dfrac{x+6}{(x-1)^2}$

Drill (Page 152)

A. $\dfrac{3}{2}$

B. $\dfrac{10x}{7}$

C. $\dfrac{1}{x-3}$

D. $\dfrac{x^2}{2}$

E. $12x + 48$

Drills (Page 153)

1. $3x + 5$
2. $3 - \dfrac{4}{x}$

Drills (Page 154)

1. C
2. $x = \dfrac{5}{3}$

Drills (Pages 157-158)

1. $x = 20$
2. $x = 3$
3. $a = \dfrac{19}{4}$
4. D
5. A
6. 21

Topic 10: Systems of Equations

Methods of Solving Systems

Elimination

Elimination should be used when we have two **linear** equations written in **Standard Form** ($ax + by = c$ Form).

Example
$5x + 3y = 6$
$2x - y = 8$

With Elimination, our goal is to **eliminate** (cancel out) one of the variables.

Level: Easy
What is the solution (x, y) to the system of equations below?

$x + 2y = 7$
$4x - 2y = -2$

$$\begin{array}{r} x + 2y = 7 \\ + \ 4x - 2y = -2 \\ \hline 5x = 5 \end{array}$$

$x = 1$

↓ Now find y

$x + 2y = 7$
$(1) + 2y = 7$
$2y = 6$
$y = 3$

When we add the two equations, the y variable is eliminated. The new equation ($5x = 5$) only contains x, which we can easily solve.

We can then use the x-value to find the y-value by plugging $x = 1$ into either of the two original equations.

The solution to this system is $(1, 3)$.

> **Level**: Medium
>
> What is the solution (x, y) to the system of equations below?
>
> $$3x + 4y = 26$$
> $$x + 2y = 12$$

$$3x + 4y = 26$$
$$-2(x + 2y = 12)$$

Multiply bottom equation

$$+\begin{array}{r} 3x + 4y = 26 \\ -2x - 4y = -24 \end{array}$$
$$x = 2$$

Now find y

$$x + 2y = 12$$
$$(2) + 2y = 12$$
$$2y = 10$$
$$y = 5$$

To eliminate a variable, we must **multiply** the entire bottom equation by a constant. We can eliminate y by multiplying the bottom equation by -2. This way, the "$2y$" becomes "$-4y$," so when we add the equations together, y will be eliminated.

We can then use the x-value to find the y-value by plugging $x = 2$ into either of the two original equations.

The solution to this system is $(2, 5)$.

> Level: Hard
> What is the solution (x, y) to the system of equations below?
> $$5x + 4y = 13$$
> $$-2x + 3y = 4$$

$2(5x + 4y = 13)$
$5(-2x + 3y = 4)$

↓ Multiply both equations

$+\begin{array}{r} \cancel{10x} + 8y = 26 \\ \cancel{-10x} + 15y = 20 \end{array}$
$23y = 46$
$y = 2$

↓ Now find x

$-2x + 3y = 4$
$-2x + 3(2) = 4$
$-2x + 6 = 4$
$-2x = -2$
$x = 1$

To eliminate a variable, we must multiply **both** equations by a constant. We can eliminate x by multiplying the top equation by 2 and the bottom equation by 5. This way, the "$5x$" becomes "$10x$" and the "$-2x$" becomes "$-10x$" so when we add the equations together, x will be eliminated.

We can then use the y-value to find the x-value by plugging $y = 2$ into either of the two original equations.

The solution to this system is $(1, 2)$.

Drill

1

What is the solution (x, y) to the system of equations below?

$-2(4x - 3y = 9)$
$7x - 6y = 15$

$-8x + 6y = -18$
$\underline{7x - 6y = 15}$
$\dfrac{-x = -3}{-1}$ $\quad x = 3$

$7(3) - 6y = 15$
$-6y = -6$
$y = 1$

$\overset{11}{\cancel{21}}$
$\underline{15}$
06

Substitution

Substitution should be used in all cases where Elimination is not appropriate (when we do not have two linear equations in Standard Form).

With Substitution, our goal is to **isolate** a variable in one equation and then **substitute** (plug) it into the other equation.

> What is the solution (x, y) to the system of equations below?
>
> $$y = 5$$
> $$x + 2y = 13$$

$x + 2y = 13$
$x + 2(5) = 13$
$x + 10 = 13$
$x = 3$

Because y is already isolated, we can take $y = 5$ and plug it in for y in the equation "$x + 2y = 13$."

The solution to this system is $(3, 5)$.

> What is the solution (x, y) to the system of equations below?
>
> $$x = 4y + 3$$
> $$2x - y = 13$$

$2x - y = 13$
$2(4y + 3) - y = 13$
$8y + 6 - y = 13$
$7y + 6 = 13$
$7y = 7$
$y = 1$

Because x is already isolated, we can take $x = 4y + 3$ and plug it in for y in the equation "$2x - y = 13$."

We can then use the y-value to find the x-value by plugging $y = 1$ into either of the two original equations.

The solution to this system is $(7, 1)$.

↓ Now find x

$2x - y = 13$
$2x - (1) = 13$
$2x = 14$
$x = 7$

> What is the solution (x, y) to the system of equations below?
>
> $$y = x + 5$$
> $$y = -2x + 14$$

$x + 5 = -2x + 14$
$3x = 9$
$x = 3$

Because both equations equal y, we can set the two equations equal to find x.

↓ Now find y

We can then use the x-value to find the y-value by plugging $x = 3$ into either of the two original equations.

$y = x + 5$
$y = 3 + 5$
$y = 8$

The solution to this system is $(3, 8)$.

> What is the solution (x, y) to the system of equations below?
>
> $$y - x^2 = 7$$
> $$x^2 + 3x - y = 11$$

$y - x^2 = 7$
$y = x^2 + 7$

We do not have any variables isolated, so we first must isolate a variable. We can get "y" alone in the top equation by adding "x^2" to both sides.

↓ Substitute y

$x^2 + 3x - (x^2 + 7) = 11$
$x^2 + 3x - x^2 - 7 = 11$
$3x - 7 = 11$
$3x = 18$
$x = 6$

Now that y is isolated, we can take $y = x^2 + 7$ and plug it in for y in the equation "$x^2 + 3x - y = 11$."

We can then use the x-value to find the y-value by plugging $x = 6$ into either of the two original equations.

↓ Now find y

The solution to this system is $(6, 43)$.

$y - x^2 = 7$
$y - (6)^2 = 7$
$y - 36 = 7$
$y = 43$

Drills

1

What is the solution (x, y) to the system of equations below?

$$3x - 4y = 33$$
$$x = 5y$$

$3(5y) - 4y = 33$
$15y$ $11y = 33$
     $y = 3$
     $x = 15$

2

What are the solutions (x, y) to the system of equations below?

$5(y = x^2 + 2x + 11)$
$y = -5x + 1$

$5x^2 + 10x + 55$
$\underline{ -5x + 1}$
$5x$

$x = -5, -2$
$y = 11, 26$

3

What are the solutions (x, y) to the system of equations below?

$$y + 4x = 3x^2 - 5$$
$$y - 2x^2 + 17 = 3x$$

$y - 2x^2 - 3x = -17$
$(-1)(y + 3x^2 + 4x = -5)$ ← crossed through
$-y + 3x^2 + 4x = -5$

$x^2 + x = -25$

$-11 = x^2 + 2x - y$
$-1(-1 = -5x - y)$
$1 = 5x + y$

$0 = x^2 + 7x + 10$
$(x+5)(x+2)$
$x = -5, -2$

$-5(-5) + 1 = 26$
$-5(-2) + 1 \cdot$ $y = 26$
       $y = 11$

Clever Combination

Sometimes, you will be asked for the value of an expression (say, $x + y$ or $2y - 2x$) rather than of an isolated variable. Oftentimes, there is a much faster way to solve the system than by using Elimination or Substitution.

> What is the value of $8x + 8y$?
>
> $5x + 2y = 10$
> $3x + 6y = 9$

$$+\begin{array}{r} 5x + 2y = 10 \\ 3x + 6y = 9 \\ \hline 8x + 8x = 19 \end{array}$$

By adding up the two equations, we directly found the value of the desired expression.

> ***NOTE**: When you are asked to solve for **an expression**, you should try adding or subtracting the two equations. In most cases, you will obtain the desired expression.

1

$2x + y = 12$
$+\ x + 3y = 15$

Based on the system of equations above, what is the value of $3x + 4y$?

$3x + 4y = 27$

$3(4.5) + 4(3) =$
$13.5 + 12 = \boxed{25.5}$

$-2(x + 3y = 15)$
$-2x - 6y = -30$
$2x + y = 12$
$\overline{}$
$\dfrac{-5y = -18}{-5}$
$y = 3$

$2(x) + 3 = 12$
$\dfrac{2x = 9}{2}$
$x = 9/2$

$9 + 4.5$

$\begin{array}{r} 4.5 \\ 3.0 \\ \hline 15.0 \end{array}$

167

Word Problems

> Bulldog High School is selling tickets to its annual school play. Tickets for children sell for $8 a piece, and tickets for adults sell for $12 a piece. If 75 total individuals attend the play and the event raises $732, how many attendees were adults?

Let c = # children attending
Let a = # adults attending

We will want to set up two equations: one that accounts for the total number of attendees and one that accounts for the total money raised.

Attendees: $c + a = 75$
Money: $8c + 12a = 732$

Because we have two linear equations in Standard Form, we can use Elimination to solve the system.

$$-8\,(c + a = 75)$$
$$8c + 12a = 732$$

Multiply top equation

$$\boxed{-8c} - 8a = -600$$
$$+\ \boxed{8c} + 12a = 732$$
$$4a = 132$$
$$a = 33 \longrightarrow 33 \text{ adults}$$

Drill

1

Shirts x
Pants y

ABC Clothes Company sells shirts and pants. Shirts are sold for $7 each and pants are sold for $12 each. On a given day, the company in total sold 150 shirts and pants for $1,350. How many pants did the company sell that day?

$$7x + 12y = 1350$$
$$-7(\,x + y = 150\,)$$
$$-7x - 7y = -1050$$

$$5x = 300$$
$$\boxed{y = 60}$$

$\begin{array}{r} 150 \\ \times\ 7 \\ \hline 1050 \end{array}$

Meaning of the Solutions

| Solutions to a System = Intersection Points of Graphs |

$y = x^2 + 4x + 11$
$y = -3x + 1$

<u>Solutions</u>: (-2, 7) and (-5, 16)

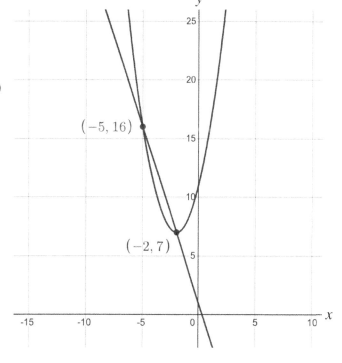

We can tell how many solutions two equations have by observing the number of times their graphs intersect in the *xy*-plane.

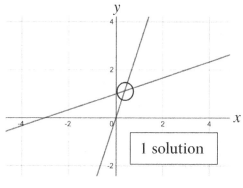

1 solution

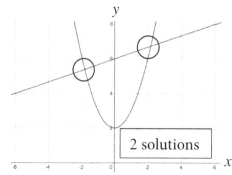

2 solutions

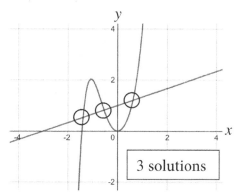

3 solutions

169

 Drill

1

The graphs of $y = 3x + 5$ and $y = 7x - 3$ intersect at one point in the xy-plane. Which of the following is the x-coordinate of the intersection point?

A) 2
B) 3
C) 4
D) 5

$y = 3x + 5$
$(-1)\ y = -7x + 3$
$0 = -4x + 8$
$-8 = -4x$
$x = 2$

 Questions

1

What is the solution (x, y) to the system of equations below?

$$7x - 2y = 22$$
$$y = 3$$

$7x - 2(3) = 22$
$7x = 28$
$x = 4$

$(4, 3)$

2

What is the solution (x, y) to the system of equations below?

$$-x + y = 4$$
$$x + y = 2$$

$0 + y$

$2y = 6$
$y = 3$

$x + 3 = 2$
$x = -1$

3

What is the solution (x, y) to the system of equations below?

$$3y - x = 17$$
$$\frac{x}{2} = 4y - 1 \quad (2)$$

$x = 8y - 2$

$3y - 8y + 2 = 17$
$-5y = 15$
$\boxed{y = -3}$

$3(-3) - x = 17$

$x = 8(-3) - 2 = (-26, -3)$

4

What is the solution (x, y) to the system of equations below?

$2(8x + 5y = 31)$
$5(3x - 2y = 0)$

$16x + 10y = 62$
$15x - 10y = 0$

$(2, 3)$

$31x = 62$
$x = 2$

$3(2) - 2y = 0$
$6 - 2y = 0$
$-2y = -6$
$\overline{-2}$
$y = 3$

5

What is the solution (x, y) to the system of equations below?

$$3x - 4y = 11$$
$$-2(5x - 2y = 23)$$

$-10x + 4y = -46$
$3x - 4y = 11$
$\overline{-7x = -35}$
$x = 5$

$3(5) - 4y = 11$
$15 - 4y = 11$
$-4y = -4$
$y = 1$

$(5, 1)$

6

What are the solutions (x, y) to the system of equations below?

$$y = -x^2 + 2$$
$$2x - y = 1$$

$2x - (-x^2 + 2) = 1$
$2x + x^2 - 2 = 1$
$x^2 + 2x = 3$

$y = -(-3)^2 + 2$ $x^2 + 2x - 3$
$y = -9 + 2$ $(x+3)(x-1)$
$y = -7$
$y = -(1)^2 + 2$ $x = 1, -3$
$y = 1$ $y = 1, -7$

171

7

Based on the system of equations shown below, what is the value of $5x - 2y$?

$-3 \mid 2x - 8y = -2$
$2 \mid 3x + 6y = 20$

$-6x + 24y = 6$
$6x + 12y = 40$

$36y = 46$
$y = $

$\boxed{5x - 2y = 18}$

8

When $y = x^2 - 7x + 8$ and $y = -3x + 5$ are graphed in the xy-plane, they intersect at the points (x_1, y_1) and (x_2, y_2). What is the value of $|y_1 + y_2|$?

$y = x^2 - 7x + 8$
$y = -3x + 5$

$-3x + 5 = x^2 - 7x + 8$

$x^2 - 4x + 3 = 0$
$(x-3)(x-1)$

$-3(3) + 5 = -4$
$-3(1) + 5 = 2$ $x = 3, 1$

$|-4 + 2| = 6$
$|-2| = 2$

9

A dog training for an agility competition is rewarded with treats for each task he performs. He earns 2 treats for performing a task he already knows and earns 5 treats for mastering a new task. The dog performs 10 tasks and earns 29 treats. If x represents the number of tasks performed that he already knows and y represents the number of new tasks performed, which of the following systems models this situation?

A) $x + y = 29$
   $2x + 5y = 10$
B) $x + y = 10$
   $2x + 5y = 29$
C) $x - y = 29$
   $2x + 5y = 10$
D) $x - y = 10$
   $2x + 5y = 29$

Answers

For **detailed solutions**, scan the QR code with your phone's camera

or

visit testpreptips.org/systems

Drill (Page 163)

1. (3, 1)

Drills (Page 166)

1. (15, 3)
2. (-5, 26) and (-2, 11)
3. (4, 27) and (3, 10)

Drill (Page 167)

1. 27

Drill (Page 168)

1. 60 pants

Drill (Page 170)

1. A

Questions (Pages 170-172)

1. (4, 3)
2. (-1, 3)
3. (-26, -3)
4. (2, 3)
5. (5, 1)
6. (-3, -7) and (1, 1)
7. 18
8. 2
9. B

Topic 11: Types of Solutions – Two Lines

No Solutions

If a system of linear equations has **no solutions**, it means that the lines are

PARALLEL

Same slope   Different *y*-intercept

System Version

$$y = 3x + 1$$
$$y = 3x + 2$$

Because the two lines are parallel, they will **never** intersect; therefore, they have no solutions.

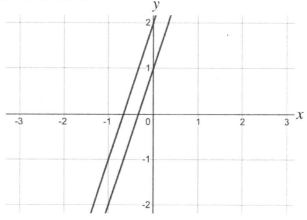

> In the system of equations shown below, *a* is a constant. If the system has **no** solutions, what is the value of *a*?
>
> $$y = \frac{1}{4}x - 4$$
> $$y = ax - 8$$

No Solutions = parallel lines (same slope, different *y*-intercept)

The "different *y*-intercept" part is already covered (-4 ≠ -8)

Now, we must make the slopes identical: $a = \dfrac{1}{4}$

Equation Version

System	Equation
$y = 3x + 1$	
$y = 3x + 2$	$3x + 1 = 3x + 2$

This equation is the same as the system: the equation has no solutions because the slopes are the same, but the *y*-intercepts are different.

> In the equation below, a is a constant. If the equation has **no** solutions, what is the value of a?
>
> $$ax - 7 = 4x - 10$$

No Solutions = parallel lines (same slope, different *y*-intercept)

The "different *y*-intercept" part is already covered (-7 ≠ -10)

Now, we must make the slopes identical: $a = 4$

Infinitely Many Solutions

If a system of linear equations has <u>**infinitely many solutions**</u>, it means that the lines are IDENTICAL

Same slope   Same *y*-intercept

System Version

$$\boxed{\begin{array}{l} y = 3x + 1 \\ y = 3x + 1 \end{array}}$$

If the two lines have infinitely many solutions, it means they sit **exactly** on top of one another in the *xy*-plane and intersect at **every** point.

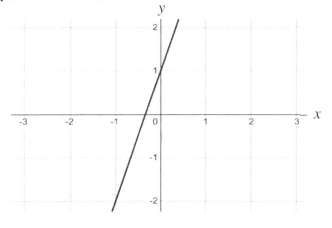

> In the system of equations shown below, b is a constant. If the system has **infinitely many** solutions, what is the value of b?
> $$y = 2x + 5$$
> $$y = bx + 5$$

Infinitely Many Solutions = lines are identical (same slope, same y-intercept)

The "same y-intercept" part is already covered ($5 = 5$)

Now, we must make the slopes identical: $b = 2$

Equation Version

System		Equation
$y = 3x + 1$	$\longrightarrow$	$3x + 1 = 3x + 1$
$y = 3x + 1$		

This equation is the same as the system: the equation has infinitely many solutions because the slopes and the y-intercepts are the same.

> In the equation below, b is a constant. If the equation has **infinitely many** solutions, what is the value of b?
> $$5x - 15 = bx - 15$$

Infinitely Many Solutions = lines are identical (same slope, same y-intercept)

The "same y-intercept" part is already covered ($-15 = -15$)

Now, we must make the slopes identical: $b = 5$

One Solution

If a system of linear equations has **one solution**, it means that the lines intersect ONCE

Different slope y-intercept is irrelevant
(could be same, could be different)

System Version

$$\begin{array}{|l|} \hline y = 3x + 1 \\ y = 9x + 1 \\ \hline \end{array}$$

If the two lines have One Solution, they must have different slopes. It does not matter if their y-intercepts are the same or different. Here, the y-intercepts happen to be the same.

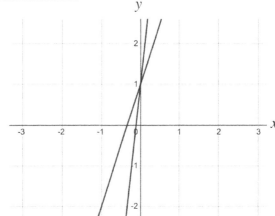

$$\begin{array}{|l|} \hline y = 3x + 1 \\ y = 9x - 2 \\ \hline \end{array}$$

If the two lines have One Solution, they must have different slopes. It does not matter if their y-intercepts are the same or different. Here, the y-intercepts happen to be different.

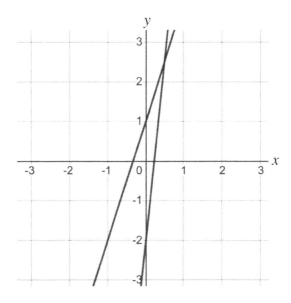

> In the system of equations shown below, c is a constant. If the system has **exactly one** solution, which of the following could **NOT** be the value of c?
>
> $$y = 8x + 5$$
> $$y = cx + 4$$

c **CANNOT** equal 8. For the system to have exactly one solution, the lines CANNOT have the same slope.

Equation Version

System		Equation
$y = 3x + 1$ $y = 9x - 2$	$\longrightarrow$	$3x + 1 = 9x - 2$

This equation is the same as the system: the equation has **one** solution because the slopes are different.

> In the equation below, c is a constant. If the equation has **exactly one** solution, which of the following could **NOT** be the value of c?
>
> $$cx - 8 = 4x - 8$$

c **CANNOT** equal 4. For the equation to have exactly one solution, the lines CANNOT have the same slope.

Solving More Advanced Examples

> Type 1: Systems **NOT** in $y = mx + b$ Form

In the system of equations shown below, a is a constant. If the system has **no** solutions, what is the value of a?

$$2x + 3y = 6$$
$$ax + 6y = 10$$

Step 1: Put both equations into $y = mx + b$ form

$$2x + 3y = 6 \rightarrow y = -\frac{2}{3}x + 2$$

$$ax + 6y = 10 \rightarrow y = -\frac{a}{6}x + \frac{5}{3}$$

Step 2: Now that the slopes are visible, we can match them up

$$-\frac{2}{3} = -\frac{a}{6} \rightarrow a = 4$$

> Type 2: Matching Required [Equation]

In the equation below, k is a constant. If the system has **infinitely many** solutions, what is the value of k?

$$5kx + 10 = 15x + 10$$

Step 1: Match up the slopes to find k

$$5k = 15$$
$$k = 3$$

> Type 3: Matching and Distributing Required [Equation]

In the equation below, b is a constant. If the system has **no** solutions, what is the value of b?

$$4b(x - 5) = 8x - 42$$

Step 1: Distribute

$$4bx - 20b = 8x - 42$$

Step 2: Match up the slopes to find b

$$4b = 8$$
$$b = 2$$

> Type 4: Matching, Distributing, and Combining Like Terms Required [Equation]

In the equation below, k is a constant. If the system has **infinitely many** solutions, what is the value of k?

$$5(2kx + 3) - 14x = 16x + 15$$

Step 1: Distribute

$$10kx + 15 - 14x = 16x + 15$$

Step 2: Combine Like Terms (by adding "$14x$" to both sides)

$$10kx - 14x + 15 = 16x + 15$$
$$10kx + 15 = 30x + 15$$

Step 3: Match up the slopes to find k

$$10k = 30$$
$$k = 3$$

If Asked for the Number of Intersection Points of Two Lines…

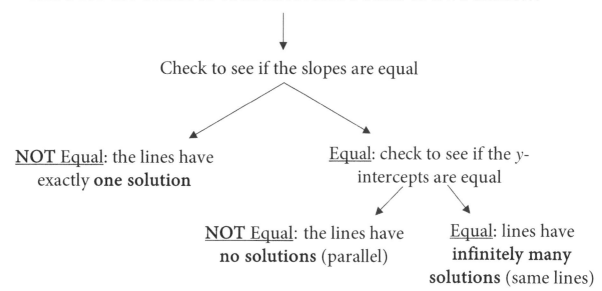

Check to see if the slopes are equal

NOT Equal: the lines have exactly **one solution**

Equal: check to see if the *y*-intercepts are equal

NOT Equal: the lines have **no solutions** (parallel)

Equal: lines have **infinitely many solutions** (same lines)

Questions
No Solutions

1

$$y = \frac{1}{2}x + 5$$
$$y = kx + 8$$

In the system of equations above, k is a constant. If the system has no solutions, what is the value of k?

2

Which of the following systems of equations has no solution?

A) $y = 3x + 7$
   $y = 7x + 2$
B) $y = 3x + 7$
   $y = 3x + 7$
C) $y = 3x + 7$
   $y = 3x + 2$
D) $y = 3x + 7$
   $y = 2x + 7$

3

The equation $2x - 8y = 12$ is one of two equations in a linear system. The system has no solution. Which of the following could be the other equation in the system?

A) $x + 4y = -6$
B) $x + 4y = 6$
C) $x - 4y = 6$
D) $x - 4y = 2$

4

$$4x + 10y = 5$$
$$6x + ky = 13$$

The system of equations above has no solution and k is a constant. What is the value of k?

A) $\dfrac{5}{2}$
B) 5
C) 13
D) 15

Infinitely Many Solutions

5

$$cx - 10 = 3x - 10$$

In the given equation, c is a constant. The equation has infinitely many solutions. What is the value of c?

A) -10
B) 1
C) 3 ✓
D) 10

6

$$2(5 + 3kx) = 42x + 10$$

In the given equation, k is a constant. The equation has infinitely many solutions. What is the value of k?

What makes infinite solutions?

$10 + 6kx = 42x + 10$

$42/6 = 7$

$7 = k$

7

$$18x - 5 = k(3x - 1) + 6x - 1$$

In the given equation, k is a constant. The equation has infinitely many solutions. What is the value of k?

A) 3
B) 4 ✓
C) 5
D) 6
E) 2

Same m
Same b

$18x - 5 = 3kx - k + 6x - 1$

Slope = $18x$

$18x = 9kx$

$-5 = -k - 1$

$k = 4$

8

$$2x - 8y = 12$$
$$ax - 14y = 21$$

The system of equations above has infinitely many solutions and a is a constant. What is the value of a?

A) $\frac{1}{4}$ ✓
B) $\frac{4}{7}$
C) $\frac{7}{4}$
D) $\frac{7}{2}$

$2x - 8y = 12$
$2x - 14y = 21$

$-8y = -2x + 12$ over -8

$y = \frac{1}{4}x +$

One Solution

9

$$7x - 5 = ax - 5$$

In the given equation, *a* is a constant. If the equation has exactly one solution, which of the following could NOT be the value of *a*?

A) -5
B) 0
C) 1
D) 7

10

$$18d - 4 = k(3d + 4) - 3d$$

In the given equation, *k* is a constant. If the equation has exactly one solution, which of the following could NOT be the value of *k*?

A) -4
B) 3
C) 4
D) 7

11

Which of the following systems of equations has exactly one solution?

(Circle all correct choices)

A) $y = 2x + 7$
   $y = 2x + 7$

B) $y = -2x + 1$
   $y = 6x + 1$

C) $y = -3x - 10$
   $y = -3x + 4$

D) $y = x + 5$
   $y = -x + 9$

Answers

For **detailed solutions**, scan the QR code with your phone's camera

or

visit testpreptips.org/typesofsolutions

Questions (Pages 182-184)

No Solutions [Page 182]

1. $k = \dfrac{1}{2}$
2. C
3. D
4. D

Infinitely Many Solutions [Page 183]

5. C
6. $k = 7$
7. B
8. D

One Solution [Page 184]

9. D
10. D
11. B and D

Topic 12: Inequalities

Symbols

Sign	Meaning
$x > 5$	x is greater than 5
$x < 5$	x is less than 5
$x \geq 5$	x is greater than or equal to 5 OR x is at least 5
$x \leq 5$	x is less than or equal to 5 OR x is at most 5

Solving Inequalities

In **most** cases, we solve inequalities just as we solve equations.

$$2x + 7 > 5$$
$$\underline{\ -7\ \ -7}$$
$$\frac{2x}{2} > \frac{-2}{2}$$
$$x > -1$$

The **only** time solving an inequality differs from solving an equation is when we **multiply** or **divide** both sides of the inequality by a **negative value**.

When we **multiply** or **divide** by a **negative**, we must <u>**FLIP**</u> the sign of the inequality.

$$-x > 5$$
$$\frac{-x}{-1} < \frac{5}{-1}$$
$$x < -5$$

Compound Inequalities

A **compound inequality** "sandwiches" a variable between two values.

We solve a compound inequality by performing the desired operation (whether it be addition, subtraction, multiplication, or division) on all **three** parts of the inequality.

*<u>NOTE</u>: Remember, though, that if we multiply or divide by a negative, we must flip the signs of **BOTH** inequalities.

$$-18 < 2x - 6 < 16$$
$$+6 \qquad +6 \quad +6$$
$$\overline{\frac{-12}{2} < \frac{2x}{2} < \frac{22}{2}}$$
$$-6 < x < 11$$

Inequalities on a Number Line

An **open circle** indicates that the listed value (here, 3) is **NOT** included in the solution set.

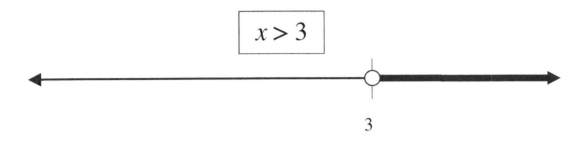

A **closed circle** indicates that the listed value (here, 3) is included in the solution set.

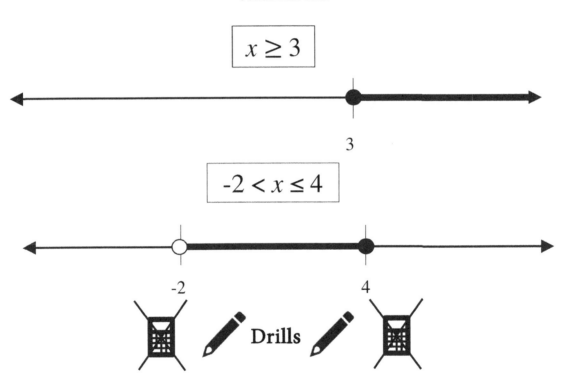

Instructions: Graph the solution to each of the following inequalities on the number line.

1

$5 \leq 2x + 1 < 12$

2

$4x - 2(x + 3) < 22$

Graphing Inequalities

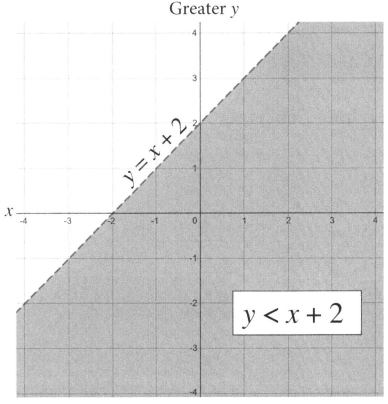

Goal: Graph $y < x + 2$

Understanding the Shading

The **line** $y = x + 2$ is simply all the (x, y) coordinates where y equals **exactly** $x + 2$.

Because the inequality states that we want all points where y is **less than** $x + 2$, we will shade directly **below** the line itself.

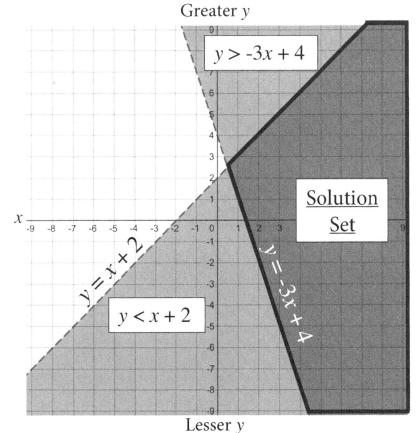

Goal: Graph the solution set of $y < x + 2$ and $y > -3x + 4$

Understanding the Shading

$y < x + 2$ represents all the points **below** the line $y = x + 2$.

$y > -3x + 4$ represents all the points **above** the line $y = -3x + 4$.

The **Solution Set** is the **darkly-shaded** region. This is where the shadings for both inequalities cross.

***NOTE**: If an inequality is **NOT** written in $y > mx + b$ or $y < mx + b$ form, rearrange the inequality. Once rearranged, we will know whether to shade above or below.

$$3x + 4 > y \longrightarrow y < 3x + 4$$

Graphing Constants

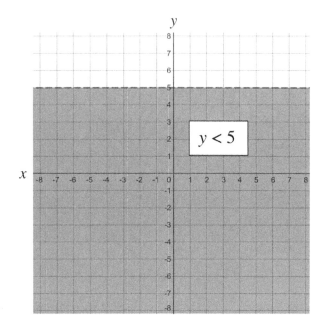
$y < 5$

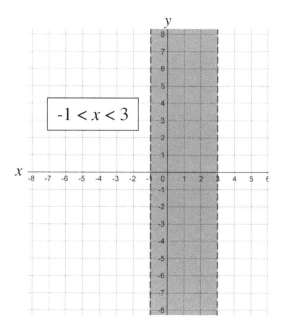
$-1 < x < 3$

Drills

1

Graph $y > 4x - 1$.

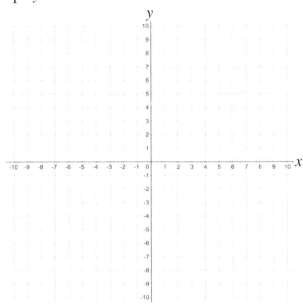

2

Graph $x > -2$.

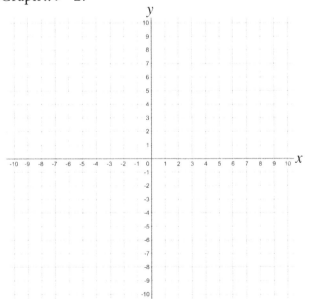

3

Graph the solution set of $y > 4x - 1$ and $x + 2 > y$.

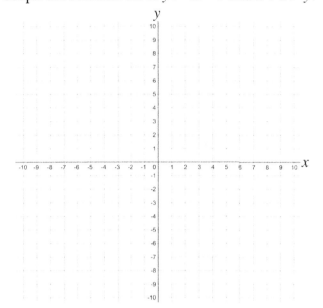

4

Graph $y < 3$.

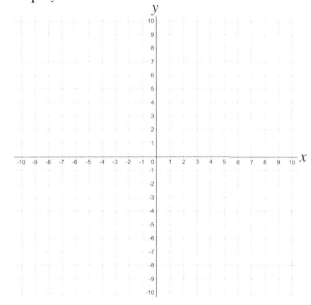

5

Graph $0 < x < 4$.

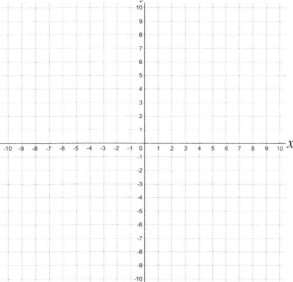

6

Graph $-1 < y < 2$.

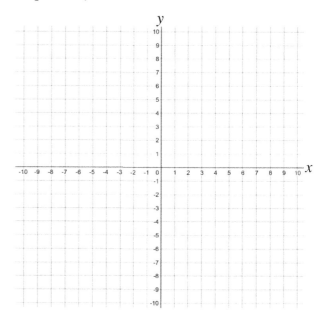

Decoding Word Problems

Pranoy plans to buy s pounds of steak and r pounds of ribs. Each pound of steak costs $60, and each pound of ribs costs $45. If he expects to spend at least $350, which of the following inequalities most accurately models this situation?

    A) $60s + 45r \geq 350$
    B) $s + r \geq 350$
    C) $45s + 60r \geq 350$
    D) $60s + 45r \leq 350$

s represents the **number** of pounds of steak, so to find the total cost of the steak, we must multiply s (the number of pounds) by the price **per** pound of steak, giving us $60s$.

r represents the **number** of pounds of ribs, so to find the total cost of the ribs, we must multiply r (the number of pounds) by the price **per** pound of ribs, giving us $45r$.

Pranoy will spend **at least** $350, so $60s + 45r$ must be **greater than or equal to** $350, leaving us with **Choice A**.

*<u>NOTE</u>: Choice B is a very commonly picked answer, but this answer cannot possibly be correct, as it is NOT accounting for the price of the steak or ribs. s and r simply represent the **number** of pounds – not the price per pound.

George works for Brian's tutoring company. Within the company, George has two primary tasks: performing administrative work, which pays $35 per hour, and tutoring students, which pays $60 per hour. George can work no more than 65 hours each week, but he wants to make a minimum of $2,800 each week. Which of the following systems of inequalities represents this situation if x is the number of hours spent performing administrative work and y is the number of hours spent tutoring students?

A) $35x + 60y \leq 2,800$
$x + y \geq 65$

B) $35x + 60y \leq 2,800$
$x + y \leq 65$

C) $35x + 60y \geq 2,800$
$x + y \leq 65$

D) $35x + 60y \geq 2,800$
$x + y \geq 65$

There are two separate inequalities we must set up: hours worked and money.

It's easiest to begin with the number of hours worked. Because x represents the number of hours spent on administrative work and y represents the number of hours spent tutoring students, $x + y$ must be less than or equal to 65 ("George can work no more than 65 hours each week"). Therefore, Choices A and D are out, as they state George is working more than 65 hours each week.

Now for the money inequality: George wants to make **at least** $2,800 each week, so when we multiply the number of hours spent on administrative work, x, by 35 (the pay per hour of administrative work) and the number of hours spent tutoring, y, by 60 (the pay per hour of tutoring), the sum must be greater than or equal to 2,800, leaving us with **Choice C**.

Drills

1

To cover her rent, Sally must earn at least $1,100 per month. Sally is able to allot 80 hours maximum to working. At her on-campus job, she earns $18 per hour, and, at her retail job, she earns $12 per hour. If Sally works c hours at her on-campus job and r hours at her retail job, which of the following systems of inequalities best represents this situation?

A) $18c + 12r \geq 1,100$
$c + r \geq 80$

B) $18c + 12r \geq 1,100$
$c + r \leq 80$

C) $18c + 12r \leq 1,100$
$c + r \leq 80$

D) $18c + 12r \leq 1,100$
$c + r \geq 80$

2

Farah is applying to graduate philosophy programs. She is applying to two types of programs: MS and PhD. All MS program applications cost $270, and all PhD program applications cost $425. Her total graduate school application budget is $2,500. She wants to apply to at least 5 MS programs and no more than 2 PhD programs. Which of the following systems of inequalities represents the situation described above if m represents the number of MS programs applied to and p represents the number of PhD programs applied to?

A) $270m + 425p \leq 2,500$
$m \geq 5$
$p \geq 2$

B) $270m + 425p \geq 2,500$
$m \geq 5$
$p \geq 2$

C) $270m + 425p \leq 2,500$
$m \geq 5$
$p \leq 2$

D) $270m + 425p \geq 2,500$
$m \geq 5$
$p \leq 2$

Questions

1

Which of the following ordered pairs satisfies the inequality shown below?

$$6y - 4x \leq 16$$

I. $(5, 6)$
II. $(-8, -7)$
III. $(4, 6)$

A) I only
B) III only
C) I and II only
D) II and III only

2

Which of the following number lines represents the solution set of $4x + 1 > 5$?

A)
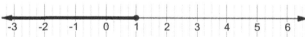

B)

C)
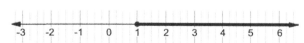

D)
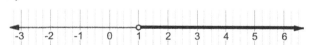

3

Megan needs to complete a project for school. She decides to order glitter beads and plain beads, each sold in packs. Due to high demand, the maximum number of beads she can order is 17,000. Each pack of glitter beads contains 300 beads, and each pack of regular beads contains 500 beads. Megan wants to order three times as many packs of glitter beads as packs of regular beads. If g represents the number of packs of glitter beads and r represents the number of packs of regular beads, which of the following inequalities best models this situation?

A) $300g + 500r \leq 17,000$
$g = 3r$

B) $300g + 500r \leq 17,000$
$3g = r$

C) $900g + 500r \leq 17,000$
$g = 3r$

D) $900g + 500r \leq 17,000$
$3g = r$

4

$$y > 2x - 2$$
$$y \geq -3x + 5$$

The two inequalities shown above are graphed in the xy-plane. Point J is included in the solution set of the two inequalities. Which of the following could be coordinates of Point J?

A) $(1, 10)$
B) $(3, 2)$
C) $(-5, 5)$
D) $(0, 0)$

$$y \geq x + 3$$
$$x + 2y \leq -5$$

Which of the following represents the solution set of the two inequalities shown above when graphed in the *xy*-plane?

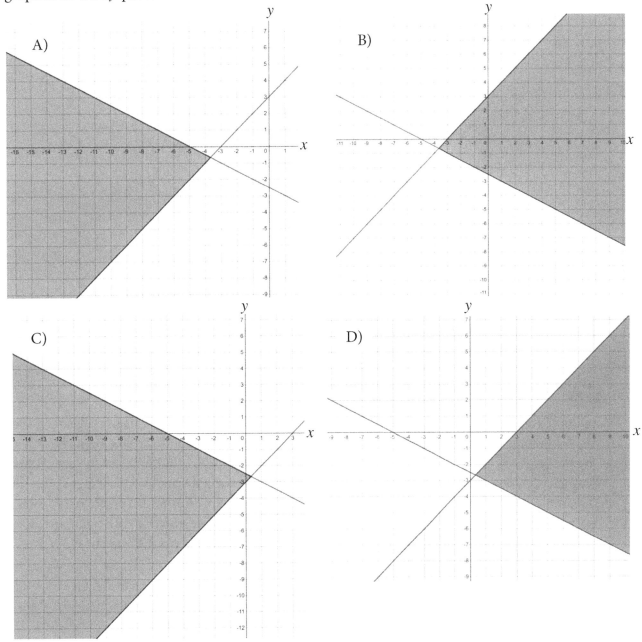

6

The graph below shows the coordinates of four points in the *xy*-plane. Which inequality contains each of these four points in its solution region?

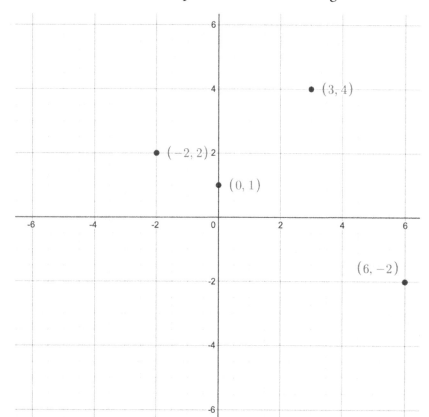

A) $y \geq -x + 2$

B) $y \geq x - 4$

C) $y \leq x + 3$

D) $y \geq -2x - 2$

7

In 2000, researchers estimated that there were approximately 14 billion pounds of garbage in the ocean. Each year, humans dump 1.4 billion pounds of additional garbage into the ocean. If the amount of garbage in the ocean *x* years after 2000 was between 22.4 and 37.8 billion pounds, which of the following must be true?

A) $16 < x < 27$
B) $6 < x < 17$
C) $10 < x < 17$
D) $10 < x < 27$

8

Terrence, who invests in real estate, increases the number of homes he owns by at least 4 but no more than 6 homes each year. Which of the following inequalities represents the number of possible homes *h* Terrence will own after 6 consecutive years of real-estate investment if he initially owns 3 properties?

A) $24 \leq h \leq 36$
B) $27 \leq h \leq 39$
C) $12 \leq h \leq 18$
D) $72 \leq h \leq 108$

9

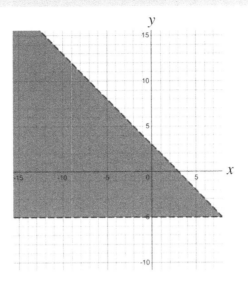

Which of the following systems of inequalities represents the shaded region of the graph?

A) $y > -x + 3$
$y > -5$
B) $y > -x + 3$
$y < -5$
C) $y < -x + 3$
$y > -5$
D) $y < -x + 3$
$y < -5$

Answers

For **detailed solutions**, scan the QR code with your phone's camera

or

visit testpreptips.org/inequalities

Drills (Page 188)

1. $2 \leq x < 5.5$

2. $x < 14$

Drills (Pages 191-192)

1.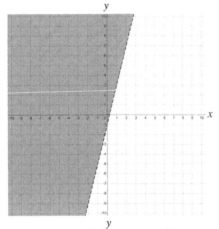

2.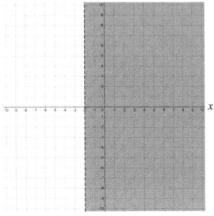

3.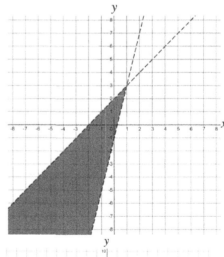

4.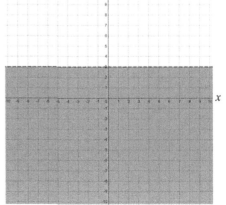

5.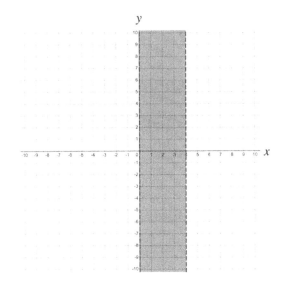

6.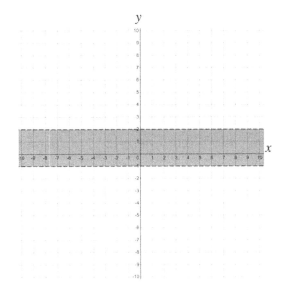

Drills (Page 195)

1. B
2. C

Questions (Pages 196-199)

1. C
2. D
3. A
4. A
5. A
6. D
7. B
8. B
9. C

201

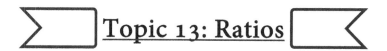

"Recipe" Ratios – A Simple Explanation

The recipe on a box of cake mix states that the cake is intended to feed 12 people. You only have 6 people at your party. If the box recipe calls for 8 eggs, how many eggs should your modified recipe contain?

This problem is particularly simple in that the number of people at your party is exactly $\frac{1}{2}$ the number of people the box recipe of cake feeds. We can just halve the number of eggs needed to get that your recipe requires 4 eggs.

However, for more difficult questions we will want to think of ratios in terms of proportions:

Keep the units consistent across the numerator and denominator $\longrightarrow \dfrac{8 \text{ eggs}}{12 \text{ people}} = \dfrac{x \text{ eggs}}{6 \text{ people}}$ → cross-multiply → $12x = 48$ → $x = 4$ eggs

1

The recipe for a standard container of cold brew coffee requires 15 tablespoons of ground coffee beans to produce 6 cups of coffee. Jenna only wants to brew 2 cups of coffee. How many tablespoons of ground coffee beans should Jenna use?

$$\frac{15 \text{ tbs}}{6 \text{ cups}} = \frac{x}{2 \text{ cups}} \qquad \boxed{5 \text{ tbs}}$$

Explicit Ratios

A ratio shows the relationship between the **quantity** of two or more things.

Ratios can be expressed by using either a colon or a fraction.

A ratio will remain the same when it is **scaled** (the ratio quantities are multiplied or divided by a constant):

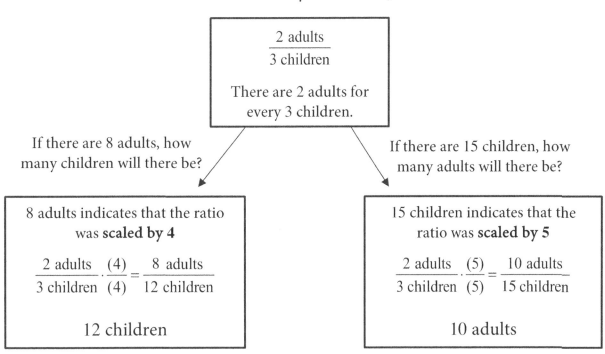

Order is Important

If the ratio of toys to books is 1 : 5, it means that the first item (toys) pairs with the first number in the ratio (1), and the second item (books) pairs with the second number in the ratio (5).

If 2 : 5 : 7 is the ratio of whales to sharks to dolphins at a local aquarium, it means that the first animal (whales) pairs with the first number in the ratio (2), the second animal (sharks) pairs with the second number in the ratio (5), and the third animal (dolphins) pairs with the third number in the ratio (7).

3+ Ratios

Ratios with more than two values work just as ratios with two values do.

> If the ratio of whales to sharks to dolphins is 2:5:7, how many whales are there if there are 28 dolphins?

Step 1: Pull out the desired ratio (whales to dolphins). Ignore the non-essential part of the ratio (here, sharks):

$$2 \text{ whales} : 7 \text{ dolphins}$$

Step 2: Set up a proportion as usual

$$\frac{2 \text{ whales}}{7 \text{ dolphins}} = \frac{x \text{ whales}}{28 \text{ dolphins}} \rightarrow 7x = 56 \rightarrow x = 8 \text{ whales}$$

  Drills

1

The ratio of juice bottles to soda bottles is 3:7. If there are 21 soda bottles, how many juice bottles are there?

$$3 : 7$$
$$9 : 21$$

2

The ratio of apples to oranges to bananas is 6:9:14.

a o b

A. If there are 45 oranges, how many bananas are there? __70__ bananas.

$$\frac{9}{14} = \frac{45}{x}$$

B. If there are 12 apples, how many oranges are there? __18__ oranges.

$$\frac{6}{9} = \frac{12}{x}$$

C. If there are 42 bananas, how many apples are there? __18__ apples.

$$\frac{6}{14} = \frac{x}{42}$$

Standard vs. Total Ratios

Standard

> A group of boys and girls gathers in an auditorium for an assembly. The ratio of boys to girls is 5:3. If there are 75 boys, how many girls are there?

$$\frac{\text{ratio boys}}{\text{ratio girls}} = \frac{\text{number of boys}}{\text{number of girls}} \rightarrow \frac{5}{3} = \frac{75}{x} \rightarrow 5x = 225 \rightarrow x = 45 \text{ girls}$$

Total

> A group of boys and girls gathers in an auditorium for an assembly. The ratio of boys to girls is 5:3. If there are 240 students in all, how many girls are there?

Notice that we are only given the <u>total</u> number of students. Therefore, we need to find the ratio quantity associated with the <u>total</u>.

To find the ratio quantity of the **total**, we need to **add both ratio values (5 + 3)**, in which case we'd get 8. Now, we can use the 240 and its associated ratio quantity of 8 to find the number of girls:

$$\frac{\text{ratio girls}}{\text{ratio total}} = \frac{\text{number of girls}}{\text{total number of students}} \rightarrow \frac{3}{8} = \frac{x}{240} \rightarrow 8x = 720 \rightarrow x = 90 \text{ girls}$$

Questions

1

Ursula makes various types of pottery, which she sells to community members. The dimensions of some of her most recent pieces are summarized in the table below:

	Width	Length	Height
Coffee cup	5 in.	5 in.	6 in.
Plate	8 in.	8 in.	0.5 in.
Sculpture	7 in.	6.25 in.	4 in.

Of the following, which ratio most accurately represents the ratio of the length of the sculpture to the length of the coffee cup?

A) 0.8 : 1
B) 1.25 : 1
C) 1 : 0.85
D) 1 : 1.25

2

At a pizzeria, the ratio of regular slices sold to specialty slices sold is 7:4. If 84 regular slices are sold in a day, how many specialty slices are sold in a day?

3

To create her traditional chocolate cake, Kathleen mixes 3 eggs with 4 cups of flour and 2 tablespoons of cocoa powder. Kathleen, however, is planning on hosting a very large dinner party in the next few weeks. To ensure that her cake tastes the same as it usually does, she decides to maintain her usual proportion of ingredients. If she uses 9 cups of flour, how many eggs will she need?

A) Four times as many eggs as she traditionally uses to make her cake.

B) $\frac{4}{9}$ times as many eggs as she traditionally uses to make her cake.

C) 3.75 more eggs than she traditionally uses to make her cake.

D) 9.5 more eggs than she traditionally uses to make her cake.

4

On a college debate team, there are 36 upperclassmen for every 10 lowerclassmen. If there are 368 total members on the debate team, how many of them are upperclassmen?

5

A birding company called all of its 500 current customers and asked whether or not they would be interested in a new pair of birding binoculars. 200 birders said they would be interested. Suppose these responses are indicative of the national birder population of 16,000. How many birders would want the new binoculars?

$\frac{200}{500}$ $\frac{2}{5} \cdot 16000$

$\boxed{6400}$

7

The ratio of students who were accepted to a local university to students who applied to the university is 7:8. If 720 students applied, how many students were NOT accepted?

$\frac{1}{8} = \frac{x}{720}$

$\boxed{90}$

6

56,600 New Yorkers were polled asking for their current feelings towards the state's anti-pollution programs: 31,130 expressed approval, 14,150 expressed neutrality, and 11,320 expressed disapproval. Assuming that this was a representative sample, how many of the 19.54 million New Yorkers would express neutrality? Express your answer to the nearest million.

?
19540000 14150
2

$\frac{7}{28300} \cdot \overline{19.540000}$

~~4833 mil?~~

8

A snack vending machine sells only chips and pretzels. The ratio of bags of chips to bags of pretzels is 14:9. If there are 253 snacks in total in the vending machine, how many of those snacks are bags of pretzels?

14:9

$\boxed{99}$

$\frac{9}{23} = \frac{x}{253}$

9

The student to faculty ratio in an introductory biology class is 57:2. If there are 513 students in the class, how many faculty members are there?

$$\frac{57}{2} = \frac{513}{x}$$

$$\boxed{18}$$

10

Amanda is making two batches of cookies from the same container of dough. The width and baking time per batch are displayed in the table below.

	Width	Baking Time
Batch 1	5 cm	10 minutes
Batch 2	8 cm	?

Batch 2's ratio of width to baking time is 5:9. How long will it take to bake Batch 2 cookies, in minutes?

$$\frac{5}{9} = \frac{8}{x} \qquad \boxed{14 \text{ min}}$$

Unit Conversions

Example 1: How many feet are in 20 miles?
(1 mile = 5,280 feet)

Conversion Factor

Miles → $\frac{20 \text{ miles}}{x \text{ feet}} = \frac{1 \text{ mile}}{5,280 \text{ feet}}$
Feet →

cross-multiply

$x = 105,600$ feet

Example 2: How many cups are in 36 fluid ounces?
(1 cup = 8 fluid ounces)

Conversion Factor

Fluid ounces → $\frac{36 \text{ fluid ounces}}{x \text{ cups}} = \frac{8 \text{ fluid ounces}}{1 \text{ cup}}$
Cups →

cross-multiply

$x = 4.5$ cups

 Drill

1

A. Convert 110 minutes to hours (round your answer to the nearest tenth).

$$\frac{110}{60} = \quad 1.8 \text{ hr}$$

B. Convert 17 kilograms to pounds.
(1 kilogram ≈ 2.2 pounds)

$$\frac{1}{2.2} = \frac{17}{x} \quad = 37.4 \text{ lbs}$$

C. Convert 20 pounds to kilograms (round your answer to the nearest tenth).
(1 kilogram ≈ 2.2 pounds)

$$\frac{1}{2.2} = \frac{x}{20} \quad 9.1 \text{ kg}$$

D. Convert 12 miles to kilometers (round your answer to the nearest tenth).
(1 kilometer ≈ 0.621 miles)

$$\frac{1}{.621} = \frac{}{12} \quad = 19.3 \text{ km}$$

E. Convert 27 kilometers to miles (round your answer to the nearest tenth).
(1 kilometer ≈ 0.621 miles)

$$\frac{1}{.621} = \frac{27}{x} \quad \boxed{16.8}$$

Rates

Case 1: Units are Identical

A dog barks 10 times every 4 days. How many times does the dog bark in 6 days?

In this instance, the units match up (days = days, barks = barks), so we will NOT need to perform any unit conversions

Step 1: Set up a proportion

$$\text{Barks} \longrightarrow \frac{10 \text{ barks}}{4 \text{ days}} = \frac{x \text{ barks}}{6 \text{ days}} \longleftarrow \text{Days}$$

cross-multiply

$x = 15$ barks

Case 2: One Unit Differs

A horse travels 7 miles in 40 minutes. How many miles does it travel in 3 hours?

Step 1: Set up the **initial** proportion

Distance units ⟶ $\dfrac{7 \text{ miles}}{40 \text{ minutes}} = \dfrac{x \text{ miles}}{3 \text{ hours}}$ ⟵ Time units

We cannot yet cross-multiply because the units do not match
(minutes ≠ hours)

Step 2: Perform necessary unit conversions (here, we will have **one**)

Convert 3 hours to minutes:

$$\dfrac{3 \text{ hours}}{x \text{ hours}} = \dfrac{1 \text{ hour}}{60 \text{ minutes}}$$

or

3 hours · 60 minutes **per** hour

= 180 minutes

Step 3: Write out the **final** proportion by swapping in the converted unit

3 hours = 180 minutes

$\dfrac{7 \text{ miles}}{40 \text{ minutes}} = \dfrac{x \text{ miles}}{\boxed{3 \text{ hours}}}$ ⟶ $\dfrac{7 \text{ miles}}{40 \text{ minutes}} = \dfrac{x \text{ miles}}{\boxed{180 \text{ minutes}}}$

cross-multiply

$x = 31.5$ miles

Case 3: Two Units Differ

> An ant travels 20 meters in 12 minutes. At this rate, how many inches does it travel in 50 seconds, rounded to the nearest inch?
>
> (1 meter ≈ 39.37 inches)

Step 1: Set up the **initial** proportion

$$\text{Distance units} \longrightarrow \frac{20 \text{ meters}}{12 \text{ minutes}} = \frac{x \text{ inches}}{50 \text{ seconds}} \longleftarrow \text{Time units}$$

We cannot yet cross-multiply because the units do not match
(**meters** ≠ **inches** ; **minutes** ≠ **seconds**)

Step 2: Perform necessary unit conversions (here, we will have **two**)

Distance Unit Conversion
Convert 20 meters to inches:

$$\frac{20 \text{ meters}}{x \text{ inches}} = \frac{1 \text{ meter}}{39.37 \text{ inches}}$$

cross-multiply

= 787.4 inches

Time Unit Conversion
Convert 12 minutes to seconds:

$$\frac{12 \text{ minutes}}{x \text{ seconds}} = \frac{1 \text{ minute}}{60 \text{ seconds}}$$

or

12 minutes · 60 seconds **per** minute

= 720 seconds

Step 3: Write out the **final** proportion by swapping in the converted units

20 meters = 787.4 inches
12 minutes = 720 seconds

$$\frac{\boxed{20 \text{ meters}}}{\enclose{circle}{12 \text{ minutes}}} = \frac{x \text{ inches}}{50 \text{ seconds}} \longrightarrow \frac{\boxed{787.4 \text{ inches}}}{\enclose{circle}{720 \text{ seconds}}} = \frac{x \text{ inches}}{50 \text{ seconds}}$$

cross-multiply

$x = 55$ inches

Drills

Units are Identical

1

Jen writes 2 books every 3.75 years. How many years will it take for her to write 18 books?

$$\frac{2 \text{ books}}{3.75 \text{ years}} = \frac{18}{\boxed{67.5 \text{ years}}}$$

One Unit Differs

2

If a car is moving at 40 miles per hour, how many minutes would it take the car to cover 28 miles?

~~40mph~~

$$\frac{40 \text{ miles}}{1 \text{ hr}} = \frac{28 \text{ miles}}{x \text{ min}}$$

$$\frac{40}{60} = \frac{28}{x}$$

$$\boxed{x = 42}$$

Two Units Differ

3

Sharon can stack 10 pounds of bricks in 75 minutes. If she continues at this rate, how many hours will it take Sharon to stack 2.5 tons of bricks?

(1 ton = 2,000 pounds)

$$\frac{10 \text{ lbs}}{75 \text{ min}} \quad \frac{2.5 \text{ tons}}{x \text{?}}$$

$$\frac{10}{75} = \frac{5000}{x}$$

$$x = 37500 \text{ min}$$

$$\frac{37500}{60} = \boxed{625 \text{ hrs}}$$

Questions

1

A dentist sees 9 patients every 1.5 hours. How many hours does it take for the dentist to see 63 patients?

$$\frac{9}{1.5} = \frac{63}{x}$$

10.5 hrs

2

If a car is moving at 30 miles per hour, how many seconds would it take the car to cover a distance of 2 miles?

$$\frac{30}{1} = \frac{2}{x}$$

.0$\overline{66}$ hrs
4 minutes
240 sec.

3

A car drives 60 miles in 2 hours. How many miles does the car travel in 5 hours?

$$\frac{60}{2} = \frac{x}{50}$$

150 mi.

4

The flying distance from New York to Los Angeles is 3,983 kilometers. Avi is a pilot and wants to complete the flight in 6 hours. What average speed, in yards/hour, would Avi have to maintain to accomplish this goal, rounded to the nearest whole number?

(1 kilometer ≈ 1,094 yards)

$$\frac{1 \text{ km}}{1094 \text{ y}} = \frac{3983 \text{ km}}{} \quad 72 ?$$

$$\frac{4357402 \text{ km·y}}{6} = \frac{}{1}$$

726234 y/hr

5

A clock chimes 3 times every 14 seconds. How many times will this clock chime in 4 days, rounded to the nearest chime?

A) 8,229
B) 18,514
C) 74,057
D) 907,200

$$\frac{3}{14 \text{ seconds}} = \frac{x}{60}$$

$$\frac{12.86}{60 \text{ sec in } 60 \text{ min}} = \frac{}{60 \text{ min}}$$

$$\frac{771.4}{1 \text{ hr}} = \frac{}{24 \text{ hrs}}$$

6

A horse trotting down a graveled path travels 27 miles in 34 minutes without stopping. The same horse trotting down a smooth path travels 35 miles in 38 minutes without stopping. Find the difference between the speed, in miles/hour, of the horse trotting on gravel and the horse trotting on a smooth path. Round your answer to the nearest tenth.

$$\frac{27 \text{ mi}}{34 \text{ min}} = \frac{35 \text{ mi}}{38 \text{ min}} = \frac{}{60}$$

$$\frac{27}{34} = \frac{\frac{810}{17}}{60}$$

$$\frac{\frac{810}{17}}{60} \qquad \frac{\frac{1050}{19}}{60}$$

7

The trip from Linda's house to the airport is 4.5 kilometers. If her drive took 12 minutes, which of the following is closest to her average speed in miles/hour?

1 mile ≈ 1.6 kilometers

A) 1.4 miles/hour
B) 14 miles/hour
C) 18 miles/hour
D) 24 miles/hour

$$\frac{2.8125 \text{ mi}}{12 \text{ min}} = \frac{}{60}$$

8

57 pounds per liter is equivalent to how many kilograms per fluid ounce? Round your answer to the nearest hundredth.

(1 kilogram = 2.2 pounds)
(1 liter = 33.8 fluid ounces)

$$\frac{57 \text{ lbs}}{1 \text{ L}} \qquad \frac{25.9 \text{ kg}}{1 \text{ L}}$$

$$\frac{1 k}{57 \text{ lbs}} = \frac{25.9 k}{2.2 \text{ lbs}}$$

$$\frac{25.9 \text{ kg}}{33.8 \text{ fl oz}} = .77$$

Degrees ⟷ Radians

Going from Degrees to Radians or from Radians to Degrees requires a Unit Conversion

Conversion Factor: π radians = 180°

*You must **MEMORIZE** this Conversion Factor*

Example 1: The arc of a circle is $\frac{4}{3}\pi$ radians. How many degrees is this arc?

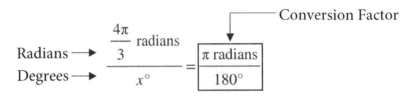

cross-multiply

$$x = 240°$$

Example 2: How many radians are in 120°?

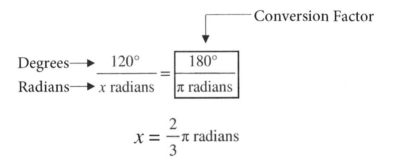

$$x = \frac{2}{3}\pi \text{ radians}$$

Questions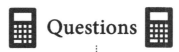

1

A circle consists of two angles: *x* and *y*. Angle *y* is 330°. What is the measure of Angle *x* in radians?

*Note: There are 360° total in a circle.

A) $\dfrac{\pi}{6}$

B) $\dfrac{6\pi}{11}$

C) $\dfrac{11\pi}{6}$ ← circled

D) 6π

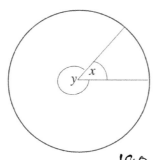

$\dfrac{330\pi}{180}$

$\dfrac{180}{\pi} = \dfrac{330}{}$

2

What is 270° in radians?

$\dfrac{180°}{\pi} = \dfrac{270°}{}$

$\dfrac{3\pi}{2}$

3

How many degrees is $\dfrac{5\pi}{6}$ radians?

$\dfrac{5\pi}{6} = \dfrac{\pi}{180}$

$\dfrac{\dfrac{5\pi}{6}}{x} = \dfrac{\pi}{180}$ $\dfrac{900\pi}{6\pi} = \dfrac{900\pi}{900\pi}$

$\dfrac{x\pi}{150\pi}$ $\boxed{150°}$

4

An angle measuring 300° can be expressed as measuring $b\pi$ radians. What is the value of *b*?

$\dfrac{}{300} = \dfrac{\pi}{180}$

$\dfrac{300\pi}{180}$

$5/3$

5

A circle's arc measures 3.5 radians. To the nearest degree, what is the degree measure of the arc?

$$\frac{\pi}{180} = \frac{3.5}{x}$$

$$\frac{630}{x\pi}$$

1.11

$$630 = \pi x$$

200.5

6

A certain angle is 0.81π radians. How many degrees is this angle?

$$\frac{\pi}{180} = \frac{.81\pi}{x}$$

$$\frac{145.8\pi}{x\pi}$$

Map Unit Conversions

On a pocket map, $\frac{3}{5}$ inch represents 12 actual miles. On the pocket map, the distance between the gas station and the grocery store is $4\frac{1}{5}$ inches. How far apart are the actual two locations in miles?

$$\text{Inches} \longrightarrow \quad \frac{\frac{3}{5} \text{ inches}}{12 \text{ miles}} = \frac{4\frac{1}{5} \text{ inches}}{x \text{ miles}}$$
$$\text{Miles} \longrightarrow$$

cross-multiply

$$\frac{3}{5}x = 50\frac{2}{5}$$

$$x = 84 \text{ miles}$$

Drills

1

On a house blueprint, $\frac{3}{2}$ cm represents 20 feet. How many feet are between the kitchen and the dining room if they're $\frac{9}{5}$ cm apart on the blueprint?

A) 15 feet
B) 22 feet
C) 24 feet ✓
D) 25 feet

$$\frac{\frac{3}{2}}{20} = \frac{\frac{9}{5}}{x}$$

$$\frac{3}{2}x = 36$$

2

On a map, $\frac{3}{4}$ inch represents 48 actual feet. Two car garbage cans that are $3\frac{3}{4}$ inches apart on the map are how many actual feet apart?

$$\frac{\frac{3}{4}}{48} = \frac{3\frac{3}{4}}{x}$$

$$\frac{3}{4}x = 180$$

240

Answers

For **detailed solutions**, scan the QR code with your phone's camera

or

visit testpreptips.org/ratios

Drill (Page 202)

1. 5 tablespoons

Drills (Page 204)

1. 9 juice bottles

2.
A. 70 bananas
B. 18 oranges
C. 18 apples

Questions (Pages 206-208)

1. B
2. 48 specialty slices
3. C
4. 288 upperclassmen
5. 6,400 birders
6. 5 million New Yorkers
7. 90 students NOT accepted
8. 99 bags of pretzels
9. 18 faculty members
10. 14.4 minutes

Drill (Page 209)

A. 1.8 hours
B. 37.4 pounds
C. 9.1 kilograms
D. 19.3 kilometers
E. 16.8 miles

Drills (Page 213)

1. 33.75 years
2. 42 minutes
3. 625 hours

Questions (Pages 214-215)

1. 10.5 hours
2. 240 seconds
3. 150 miles
4. 726,234 yards/hour
5. C
6. 7.6 miles
7. B
8. 0.77

Questions (Pages 217-218)

1. A
2. $x = \dfrac{3}{2}\pi$ radians
3. 150°
4. $b = \dfrac{5}{3}$
5. 201°
6. 145.8°

Drills (Page 219)

1. C
2. 240 feet

Topic 14: Percentages

"School" Way
(not so helpful)

$$\frac{\text{part}}{\text{whole}} = \frac{\%}{100}$$

⟹

Our Way
(**very** helpful)

$$(\text{pre})(\text{decimal }\%) = \text{post}$$

Taking a Percent

To go from % to **decimal %**, move the decimal 2 places to the left:

<u>Ex</u>: 42% = 0.42, 56% = 0.56, 250% = 2.5

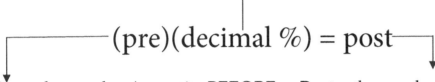

<u>Pre</u> – the number / quantity **BEFORE** the percent has been applied

<u>Post</u> – the number / quantity **AFTER** the percent has been applied (the "result")

Basic Examples

What is 25% of 40? <u>Pre</u>: 40 (percent was **NOT** yet applied) <u>Decimal %</u>: 25% → 0.25 <u>Post</u>: x $(40)(0.25) = x$ $x = 10$	25% of a number x equals 10. What is this number? <u>Pre</u>: x <u>Decimal %</u>: 25% → 0.25 <u>Post</u>: 10 (10 is the **result** of already having taken 25% of x) $(x)(0.25) = 10$ $x = 40$
What is 125% of 90? <u>Pre</u>: 90 (percent was **NOT** yet applied) <u>Decimal %</u>: 125% → 1.25 <u>Post</u>: x $(90)(1.25) = x$ $x = 112.5$	125% of a number x equals 112.5. What is this number? <u>Pre</u>: x <u>Decimal %</u>: 125% → 1.25 <u>Post</u>: 112.5 (112.5 is the **result** of already having taken 125% of x) $(x)(1.25) = 112.5$ $x = 90$

Word Problems

A designer purse at a department store originally costs $580, but it is on sale for only 75% of its original price. What is the price of the discounted purse? Pre: $580 (we have **NOT** yet applied the sale) Decimal %: 75% → 0.75 Post: x ($580)(0.75) = x x = $435	Due to a spring clearance sale, Jessica was able to purchase a pair of expensive shoes for $90 – only 30% of the original price. What was the original price of the shoes? Pre: x Decimal %: 30% → 0.30 Post: $90 ($90 is the **result** of having already taken the percent) (x)(0.30) = $90 x = $300

Questions

1

What is 65% of 800?

2

20% of a number is 60. What is the value of this number?

3

What percent of 45 is 36?

4

Ben is eating dinner at the local diner with his daughter. His daughter's meal is 40% of the original price of the meal. If her meal originally costs $12.50, what is the discounted price of her meal?

5

45% of c equals 18. What is the value of c?

6

What is 300% of 6?

7

900% of a number is 90. What is this number?

8

After removing change, Silvia's wallet weighs 12 ounces. If her wallet now weighs 75% of what it originally weighed, what was the original weight of the wallet, in ounces?

Fractions as Percentages

For certain types of questions, you'll need to be able to think of percentages in terms of not only decimals but also fractions. These types of problems can stretch across multiple topics: geometry, probability, etc. Let's look at a few examples:

Probability Example

A bag contains 25 marbles. 8 of the marbles are blue, 7 are green, 5 are yellow, and 5 are red. What is the probability of drawing a green marble?

Depending on how our answer choices are written, the correct answer to this question is either a…

Fraction — $\frac{7}{25}$

Decimal — 0.28

Percent — 28%

Geometry Example

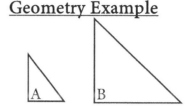

Triangle A has an area of 3 inches². Triangle B has an area of 12 inches². Triangle A is what percent of Triangle B?

$$\frac{\text{Triangle A}}{\text{Triangle B}} \rightarrow \frac{3 \text{ inches}^2}{12 \text{ inches}^2} \rightarrow \frac{3}{12} \rightarrow 0.25 \rightarrow 25\%$$

Drill

1

Michael has an arrangement of gift cards in his drawer: 5 Coffee Hut, 1 Hotdog Harry, 6 Wingz, and 4 Burger Palace. What is the probability that when he randomly picks a gift card, he draws a Coffee Hut gift card?

A. Express your answer as a fraction.

B. Express your answer as a decimal.

C. Express your answer as a percent.

Percentages from Tables and Graphs

Tables

Julie made a video entitled "What I Spend in a Month Living in NYC." After seeing multiple comments that said she spends too much money, Julie decided to make a chart of her expenses:

Category	Associated Expense
Food	$550
Rent	$1,370
Gas	$125
Car Insurance	$300
Designer Clothes	$765

What percent of Julie's monthly expenses are being allocated to designer clothes? Round to the nearest 1%.

To find the percent of Julie's monthly expenses spent on designer clothes, we want to create a fraction just as we did for the probability and geometry examples on the previous page:

$$\frac{\text{designer clothes}}{\text{total monthly expenses}}$$

To find Julie's total monthly expenses, we will have to add up each expense:

$$\$550 + \$1{,}370 + \$125 + \$300 + \$765 = \$3{,}110$$

$$\frac{\$765}{\$3{,}110} = 0.24598\ldots = 0.25 = 25\%$$

Graphs

A survey was conducted to determine how many weekdays per week a group of 20 gym-goers exercised at a gym. What percent of gym-goers who were surveyed exercise exactly 4 times per week?

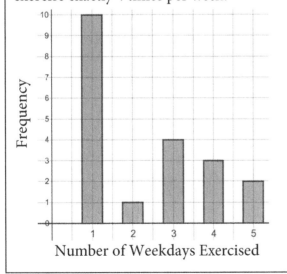

The *y*-axis (the **Frequency**) tells us **how many** people exercised for each number of weekdays:

10 gym-goers exercised 1 weekday per week
1 gym-goer exercised 2 weekdays per week
4 gym-goers exercised 3 weekdays per week
3 gym-goers exercised 4 weekdays per week
2 gym-goers exercised 5 weekdays per week

We again want to create a fraction to find out what percent of gym-goers exercised 4 times per week:

$$\frac{\text{\#4-weekday exercisers}}{\text{\# total exercisers}} \rightarrow \frac{3}{20} \rightarrow 0.15 \rightarrow 15\%$$

Drills

1

105 students registered to take a standardized test at a local high school. All 105 students guessed on which subject they thought they would perform best. Listed below are their predictions:

Subject	Number of Students
English	45
Math	10
Reading	30
Social Studies	20

What percent of students predicted that reading would be their best section, rounded to the nearest 1%?

- A) 10%
- B) 19%
- C) 29%
- D) 43%

2

33 students were asked how many hours they had spent on extracurricular activities within the last month. The 33 responses are shown in the graph below.

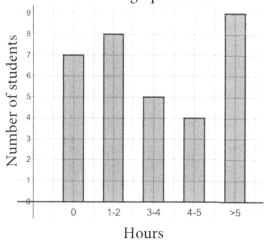

What percent of students spent >5 hours on extracurricular activities in the last month, rounded to the nearest percent?

Percent Increase / Decrease

Percent Increase

"30% increase"

⇩ equals

(100% + 30%) = **130%**

130% is the **true percent**
30% increase = taking 130%

The number of homeruns Louis hit last year was 50. If he hits **20% more** homeruns this year than he did last year, how many homeruns will he hit this year?

"20% more" means "20% increase," so we will take **120%**:

120% = 1.2

(50)(1.2) = **60 homeruns**

Percent Decrease

"30% decrease"

⇩ equals

(100% − 30%) = **70%**

70% is the **true percent**
30% decrease = taking 70%

The number of homeruns Louis hit last year was 50. If he hits **20% less** homeruns this year than he did last year, how many homeruns will he hit this year?

"20% less" means "20% decrease," so we will take **80%**:

80% = 0.80
(50)(.8) = **40 homeruns**

Drills

1

Instructions: Convert each percent increase / decrease into the **true** percentage and then into the percent decimal.

[Ex: 5% decrease → 95% → 0.95]

A. 25% increase → _____ → _____

B. 40% decrease → _____ → _____

C. 2% increase → _____ → _____

D. 3% decrease → _____ → _____

E. 4.72% increase → _____ → _____

F. 7.81% decrease → _____ → _____

G. 200% increase → _____ → _____

2

In the third quarter, a restaurant profited $130,000. In the fourth quarter, the restaurant's profit increased by 35%. What was the restaurant's fourth quarter profit?

3

Penelope used 340 plastic straws in 2018. In an effort to reduce her plastic waste, Penelope used 35% fewer plastic straws in 2019 than she did in 2018. How many plastic straws did she use in 2019?

4

Billy scored 15% higher on his second science test than he did on his first test. If he scored a 92 on his second test, what did he score on his first test?

Consecutive Percentages

Going Forward (Pre → Post)

> In 2017, a new store opened and charged $50 for boots. In an effort to increase sales, the owners decided to offer a 20% discount in 2018. After deeply regretting their decision, the owners decided to increase the discounted price of the boots by 20% in 2019. What was the price of the boots in 2019?

The temptation here is to think "wouldn't the answer just be $50…?" **NO!**

<u>Step 1</u>: Consecutive Percentages

Convert each percent increase / decrease into a decimal percent:

<u>2018</u>: 20% decrease → 80% → 0.8
<u>2019</u>: 20% increase → 120% → 1.2

To get the overall percent, multiply the decimal percentages:

<u>Overall Percent</u>: (0.8)(1.2) = **0.96**

This multiplication tells us that a 20% decrease in price followed by a 20% increase in price is the same as simply taking 96% of the price in one-shot. This means that the boots have decreased in value by 4% from 2017 to 2019.

<u>Step 2</u>: (pre)(decimal %) = post

To find the value of the boots in 2019, we must multiply the overall percent by the starting cost ("pre" value) of the boots:

($50)(0.96) = **$48**

Going Backward (Post → Pre)

The kangaroo population in an area of Australia decreased by 35% from 2016 to 2017 due to the introduction of a natural predator – the dingo. This predator was then removed in 2017, and the kangaroo population then increased by 85% from 2017 to 2018. If the kangaroo population was 20,000 in 2018, what was the population in 2016?

Step 1: Consecutive Percentages

2016 to 2017: Decrease of 35% → 65% → 0.65
2017 to 2018: Increase of 85% → 185% → 1.85

Overall Percent: $(0.65)(1.85) = \mathbf{1.2025}$

Step 2: (pre)(decimal %) = post

The value of 20,000 that we were given is the value **after** the percentages were applied. Therefore, it is our "post" value.

Let x = number of kangaroos in 2016 ("pre")

$(x)(1.2025) = 20{,}000$
$x = \mathbf{16{,}632 \text{ kangaroos}}$

1

5,400 unique algae were introduced to a lake in the beginning of June. The population decreased by 60% in June, increased by 80% in July, and increased by 25% in August. How many algae were in the lake at the end of August?

2

A professional MMA fighter put on weight over a year to enter a higher weight class. If his weight increased by 5% over the first 3 months, accidentally decreased by 1% over the next 3 months, increased by 2% over the next 3 months, and increased by 3% over the final three months of the year, what was his weight at the beginning of the year if his weight at the end of the year was 205 pounds? Round your answer to the nearest whole number.

What is the Percent Increase / Decrease?

We use the formula below to determine the percent increase or decrease:

$$\frac{|\text{New Value} - \text{Original Value}|}{\text{Original Value}} \cdot 100\%$$

> A coffee cost $3.00 last year. This year, it costs $4.50. By what percent did the price of coffee increase over the last year?

$3.00 = $ original value
$4.50 = $ new value

$$\frac{|\$4.50 - \$3.00|}{\$3.00} \cdot 100\%$$

$$0.5(100\%)$$

50% increase

  Drills

1

A shirt originally priced at $45 is discounted to $36. What is the percent by which the shirt was discounted?

A) 15%
B) 20%
C) 25%
D) 30%

2

Shares of stock in ABC Company increased from $50 to $80. By what percent did the price of the stock increase?

Questions

1

Ilana lives in a very desirable area in San Diego, California. When she first moved into her apartment complex, her monthly rent was $2,340. Two years later, her monthly rent was increased to $2,565. By what percent did Ilana's monthly rent increase, rounded to the nearest tenth of a percent?

A) 6.5%
B) 8.8%
C) 9.1%
D) 9.6%

2

Paul and his wife decide that they want to go into the restaurant industry. They have a budget of $95,000. Rattling off items that they need, Paul and his wife come up with the following expense table:

Category	Budget Expense
Ovens	$12,500
Microwaves	$580
Venue	$56,320
Ingredients	$3,500
Labor	Unknown
Electricity	Unknown

They are unsure how much labor and electricity will cost. What percent of their total budget do they have remaining to allocate to these unknown expenses (rounded to the nearest 1%)?

A) 23%
B) 25%
C) 59%
D) 77%

3

Justin purchased a brand-new tablet with an original value of $550 at a 30% discount. He was also required to pay a local sales tax of 8.25% on the discounted price of the tablet. What is the total price that Justin paid for the tablet, rounded to the nearest cent?

A) $31.76
B) $178.61
C) $416.76
D) $453.76

4

In a virtual reality game, a player's "ultimate score," U, is calculated by subtracting the number of losses, L, from 70% of the player's cash value, C. Which of the following equations expresses the relationship between "ultimate score," the number of losses, and cash value in this virtual reality game?

A) $U = \dfrac{70}{100}C - L$

B) $U = \dfrac{70}{100}L - C$

C) $U = L - \dfrac{70}{100}C$

D) $U = 70C - L$

5

Displayed below is the blueprint layout for a new apartment building complex.

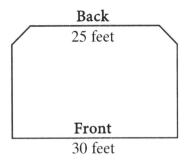

The length of the front of the complex is what percent of the length of the back of the complex?

A) 25%

B) 30%

C) 83.3%

D) 120%

6

If 60% of a given number is 15, then what is 25% of the given number?

A) 1.5
B) 2.25
C) 6.25
D) 6.5

7

A coffee machine consists of a water chamber, coffee-loading sleeve, and a coffee pot. When the machine is turned on, the machine begins making coffee, and the amount of water in the water chamber decreases. In the first minute, the amount of water decreases by 15%. In the second and third minutes, the amount of water decreases by 20% and 25%, respectively. If the initial volume of water in the water chamber was 200mL, what is the volume of water, in mL, after the third minute the coffee pot was on?

A) 13.5
B) 80
C) 102
D) 120

8

A yellow blouse is on clearance for $30. If the blouse was discounted by 40%, then what was its original price?

A) $42
B) $48
C) $50
D) $75

9

Mario purchased a meal subscription plan for *d* dollars. He received a 35% discount on the original price, paid a 9% sales tax on the discounted price, and paid a 6% shipping fee on the after-tax price. Which of the following represents the non-discounted price of the meal plan before tax and fees?

A) $d(0.65)(1.06)(1.09)$
B) $d(0.35)(.06)(.09)$
C) $\dfrac{d}{(0.35)(0.06)(0.09)}$
D) $\dfrac{d}{(0.65)(1.06)(1.09)}$

10

A population of *S. pyogenes*, the bacteria that causes strep throat, multiplies quickly. In a petri dish, the population increases by 350% the first day. The subsequent day, the population increases by an additional 45%. The following day, the dish experiences contamination, and the population decreases in size by 28%. After removing the contaminant, on Day 4, the population grows again by 74%. Which of the following expressions represents the overall growth of this *S. pyogenes* population?

A) $(3.5)(0.45)(0.28)(0.74)$
B) $(4.5)(1.45)(0.28)(1.74)$
C) $(4.5)(1.45)(0.72)(1.74)$
D) $(3.5)(1.45)(0.72)(1.74)$

11

Number of Candies Sold at a Convenience Store by Age in January 2020

Age	Sour Candies	Chocolates	Gummies	Caramels
Young adult (11-18)	25	18	15	4
Adult (18-64)	7	30	1	12
Senior (65+)	3	23	3	35

At this particularly busy convenience store, each individual is only allowed to purchase a single item in a given month.

Unaccounted for in the store's monthly sales' figures was the number of children (5-10) who purchased candy. If the adults accounted for 40% of the number of chocolates sold in January 2020, how many chocolates were purchased by children?

A) 4
B) 12
C) 59
D) 75

12

A $60 shirt is on sale for 50% off. What is the cost of the discounted shirt?

13

A $70 pair of leggings is sold for 150% of its original price. What is the new, increased price of the leggings?

14

The owners of a furniture store increased the price of their couches by 50%, making them cost $500. What is the price of their couches before the price increase was implemented, to the nearest dollar?

15

When a vacuum cleaner is sold at 25% of its original price, it is sold for $100. What is the original price of the vacuum?

16

During a food shortage, rice, which usually costs $5 per bag, is priced at 400% of its usual cost. What is the price of a bag of rice during a food shortage?

17

Last year, Jackie ate 780 bars of candy. This year, she decreased her candy consumption by 80%. How many bars of candy did Jackie eat this year?

18

An appliance is currently sold for $50. If the appliance is increased by x% to make it $80, what is the value of x?

19

Rob purchased a limited-edition couch valued at $750 from a furniture store. Each year, the value of the couch is anticipated to increase 20% from the previous year's value. The estimated value of the couch, in dollars, 2 years after its initial purchase can be modeled using the expression $750c$, where c is a constant. What is the value of c?

20

There are 363 freshmen students in Awesome High School. This represents 22% of the students that attend Awesome High School. How many students attend Awesome High School in total?

21

Last month, Scott solved 40 math equations. If he solved 30% more problems this month than he did last month, how many problems did he solve this month?

22

XYZ Car Dealership is selling a car for 85% of its original price. All buyers who pay with cash receive 10% off the discounted price. If Adam purchases the car for $6,500 using cash, what was the original price of the car, to the nearest dollar?

Answers

For **detailed solutions**, scan the QR code with your phone's camera

or

visit **testpreptips.org/percentages**

Questions (Page 224)

1. 520
2. 300
3. 80%
4. $5.00
5. 40
6. 18
7. 10
8. 16 ounces

Drill (Page 225)

A. $\frac{5}{16}$

B. 0.3125

C. 31.25%

Drills (Page 227)

1. C
2. 27%

Drills (Page 229)

1.

A. 125% → 1.25
B. 60% → 0.60
C. 102% → 1.02
D. 97% → 0.97
E. 104.72% → 1.0472
F. 92.19% → 0.9219
G. 300% → 3

2. $175,500
3. 221 straws
4. 80

Drills (Page 231)

1. 4,860 algae
2. 188 pounds

Questions (Pages 233-237)

1. D
2. A
3. C
4. A
5. D
6. C
7. C
8. C
9. D
10. C
11. A
12. $30
13. $105
14. $333
15. $400
16. $20
17. 156 bars of candy
18. 60
19. 1.44
20. 1,650 students
21. 52 math problems
22. $8,497

Drills (Page 232)

1. B
2. 60%

Topic 15: Exponentials

Linear vs. Exponential Functions

Linear

For a **linear** function, we take $f(x)$ and **add / subtract** the same number each time x increases by 1.

x	$f(x)$
1	1
2	3
3	5
4	7

add 2
add 2
add 2

This table represents a **linear** function because we add the same number (2) to $f(x)$ each time x increases by 1.

Exponential

For an **exponential** function, we take $f(x)$ and **multiply / divide** by the same number each time x increases by 1.

x	$f(x)$
1	1
2	2
3	4
4	8

multiply by 2
multiply by 2
multiply by 2

This table represents an **exponential** function because we **multiply** $f(x)$ by the same number (2) each time x increases by 1.

---

x	$f(x)$
0	5
1	25
2	k

The table to the left shows certain values of the function f.

A. If $f(x)$ were a linear function, what is k?
B. If $f(x)$ were an exponential function, what is k?

A. Linear

x	$f(x)$
0	5
1	25
2	k

add 20
add 20

Each increase in x results in **adding** 20 to $f(x)$.

Therefore, if $f(x)$ were a linear function, we would add 20 to 25 to find that $k = 45$.

B. Exponential

x	$f(x)$
0	5
1	25
2	k

multiply by 5
multiply by 5

Each increase in x results in **multiplying** $f(x)$ by 5.

Therefore, if $f(x)$ were an exponential function, we would multiply 25 by 5 to find that $k = 125$.

Linear vs. Exponential Situations

Situation	Linear or Exponential?
A population of rabbits increases by 22 rabbits each year.	<u>Linear</u> – each year, 22 rabbits are **added** to the overall population
Once every 55 years, the number of dandelions halves in a California valley.	<u>Exponential</u> – every 55 years, the number of dandelions is **divided** by 2 *<u>**NOTE**</u>: Multiplication and division words (doubles, triples, halves, etc.) indicate exponential growth
Each year, a mutual fund increases its current value by 6%.	<u>Exponential</u> – each year, the value of the mutual fund is **multiplied** by 1.06 (6% increase → 106% → 1.06)

Questions

1

Which of the following situations establishes an exponential relationship amongst the two variables described?

A) Every millisecond, a sprinter's speed S increases by a constant rate of 0.025 miles / hour.
B) For every 5-pound increase in the weight w of a developing pelican, its body length l increases by 10 centimeters.
C) The amount of ice cream A exiting an ice cream machine, in ounces, decreases by 2 ounces each second.
D) For every 30-second increase in pace p, the calories burned by a runner c increase by 15%.

2

Species J, an endangered population, halves in size every 2 years. Which of the following statements best describes how Species J changes over time?

A) Linear - the population of Species J decreases by a constant amount every 2 years.
B) Linear - the population of Species J decreases by the same percentage every 2 years.
C) Exponential– the population of Species J decreases by a constant amount every 2 years.
D) Exponential– the population of Species J decreases by the same percentage every 2 years.

3

Natasha baked brownies for a school fundraiser to raise money for her senior class trip. For every additional 2 brownies she baked, Natasha added an extra half cup of flour to her batter. If $f(b)$ models the amount of flour Natasha adds to her batter for b brownies, which of the following statements best describes the function f?

A) The function f decreases in a linear fashion.
B) The function f increases in a linear fashion.
C) The function f decreases in an exponential fashion.
D) The function f increases in an exponential fashion.

4

The weight of a professional wrestler preparing for an upcoming fight is shown in the table below.

Time (months)	Weight (pounds)
1	188.4
2	169.6
3	152.6
4	137.3
5	123.6

Which of the following best models these data?

A) A linear model, where the wrestler's weight, in pounds, decreases as time increases.
B) A linear model, where the wrestler's weight, in pounds, increases as time increases.
C) An exponential model, where the wrestler's weight, in pounds, decreases as time increases.
D) An exponential model, where the wrestler's weight, in pounds, increases as time increases.

5

The table below displays values of t and $f(t)$. Which of the following correctly characterizes the relationship between t and $f(t)$?

t	$f(t)$
1	20
2	25
3	30
4	35
5	40

A) The relationship is exponential – each time t increases by 1, $f(t)$ increases by 5.
B) The relationship is exponential – each time t increases by 1, $f(t)$ is multiplied by 5.
C) The relationship is linear – each time t increases by 1, $f(t)$ increases by 5.
D) The relationship is linear – each time t increases by 1, $f(t)$ is multiplied by 5.

6

The table below shows values of x and y. Which of the following represents the relationship between x and y?

x	y
1	2
2	4
3	8
4	16
5	32

A) The relationship is exponential – each time x increases by 1, y increases by 2.
B) The relationship is exponential – each time x increases by 1, y is multiplied by 2.
C) The relationship is linear – each time x increases by 1, y increases by 2.
D) The relationship is linear – each time x increases by 1, y is multiplied by 2.

Exponential Functions

lines → $y = mx + b$
$y - y = m(x - x)$

quadratics → $ax^2 + bx + c$
$y = a(x-h) + k$
$y = a(x-x)$

$\boxed{f(x) = ab^x}$

a = initial value
b = multiplier (number we multiply by each time)

a = initial
b = multiply by each time

Modeling Exponential Situations $y = ab^x$

> The average number of fans attending a basketball game is estimated to increase by 15% each year after 2010. In 2010, 100 fans attended each basketball game. Write an equation that models this situation x number of years after 2010.

$a = 100$
$b = 15\%$ increase = 115% → 1.15

$f(x) = 100(1.15)^x$

> The price of a designer purse in 1990 was $155. The purse's value decreases by 5.5% each year. Write an equation that models this situation x years after 1990.

$a = 155$
$b = 5.5\%$ decrease = 94.5% → 0.945

$f(x) = 155(0.945)^x$

> A 45,000-member population of jellyfish halves every 10 years. If x represents the time in 10-year increments, write an equation that models this situation.

$a = 45,000$
$b = 0.5$

$f(x) = 45,000(0.5)^x$

Drill

1

$f(x) = 30(1.6)^x$

A. Initial value = __30__

B. Does this represent a percent **increase** or a percent **decrease**? __increase__

C. What is the percent increase or decrease? __60%__

Questions

1

The function B models the number of bunnies x years after 1990. If the number of bunnies increases by 2.7% each year, what is the value of k?

$$B(x) = 330k^x$$

A) 0.027
B) 0.27
C) 1.027
D) 1.27

2

A certain species of bacteria decreases its population by 17% each hour. There are currently 1,000 bacteria in the population. Which of the following exponential functions models the population $P(t)$ of this bacteria t hours from now?

A) $P(t) = 17(1,000)^t$
B) $P(t) = 1,000(0.17)^t$
C) $P(t) = 1,000(1.17)^t$
D) $P(t) = 1,000(0.83)^t$

3

A certain species of bacteria increases its population by 22% each hour. There are currently 68 bacteria in the population. Which of the following exponential functions models the population $P(t)$ of this bacteria t hours from now?

A) $P(t) = 22(68)^t$
B) $P(t) = 68(0.22)^t$
C) $P(t) = 68(1.22)^t$
D) $P(t) = 68(0.78)^t$

4

A certain species of bacteria doubles its population each hour. There are currently 40 bacteria in the population. Which of the following exponential functions models the population $P(t)$ of this bacteria t hours from now?

A) $P(t) = 40\left(\dfrac{1}{2}\right)^t$
B) $P(t) = 40(2)^t$
C) $P(t) = 2(40)^t$
D) $P(t) = \dfrac{1}{2}(40)^t$

5

$$Z(h) = 400(1.06)^h$$

The function Z gives the approximate number of stripes on a zebra, $Z(h)$, based on the zebra's average daily exposure to sunlight, measured in hours h. Which of the following provides the best interpretation of 1.06 in this context?

A) For each additional hour a zebra spends in the sun each day, on average, the number of stripes the zebra has will increase by 6%.
B) For each additional 1.6 stripes the zebra develops, the zebra's daily sunlight exposure will increase by 1 hour, on average.
C) For each additional hour a zebra spends in the sun each day, on average, the zebra will develop 1.06 more stripes.
D) For each additional stripe the zebra develops, the zebra's daily sunlight exposure, on average, will increase by 6%.

Accounting for Time

Understanding the Powers (Exponents)

t = time in one-year increments

Equation: $y = 7(1.2)^t$

When **no time** has passed (0 years), we just have our initial population of 7	When **one year** has passed, our initial population of 7 is multiplied by 1.2

To see this, we can plug in $t = 0$:

$$y = 7(1.2)^t$$
$$y = 7(1.2)^0$$
$$y = 7$$

To see this, we can plug in $t = 1$:

$$y = 7(1.2)^t$$
$$y = 7(1.2)^1$$
$$y = 7(1.2)$$

***NOTE**: By making the power (exponent) of the equation 1, we indicate that the **first multiplication** of the population by 1.2 has been completed

---

t = time in one-year increments

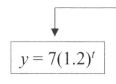

Situation that Models the Equation: There are 7 cats in a population. The population increases by 20% **each year**.

When we plug in $t = 1$, we get $y = 7(1.2)^1$, indicating that after **1 year** we multiply 7 by 1.2 one time.

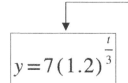

Situation that Models the Equation: There are 7 cats in a population. The population increases by 20% **every 3 years**.

When we plug in $t = 3$, we get $y = 7(1.2)^1$, indicating that after **3 years** we multiply 7 by 1.2 one time.

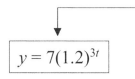

Situation that Models the Equation: There are 7 cats in a population. The population increases by 20% **every $\frac{1}{3}$ of a year**.

When we plug in $t = \frac{1}{3}$, we get $y = 7(1.2)^1$, indicating that after **$\frac{1}{3}$ of a year** we multiply 7 by 1.2 one time.

A local rescue group rehomes dogs. The population of dogs at the start of a mission is 100. Every **month**, the number of dogs in need of a home decreases by 20% from the previous month. Write an equation that models the number of dogs remaining, D after y years.

A) $D = 100(0.80)^{\frac{y}{12}}$

B) $D = 100(0.80)^{12y}$

C) $D = 100\left(\dfrac{0.80}{12}\right)^t$

D) $D = 100(0.80 \times 12)^t$

If the population of dogs decreases by 20% **each month**, it takes **one month** for the population of dogs to complete its **first** multiplication by 0.80. Choices C and D can be eliminated because they do not reflect the correct multiplier of 0.80.

$$\text{In terms of years, a single month} = \frac{1}{12} \text{ year.}$$

Therefore, when we plug $\dfrac{1}{12}$ into the power, we will need the power to equal 1 to indicate that the first multiplication is completed after a month.

$$\text{The only choice that allows this is } \textbf{Choice B}\text{, as } 12 \times \frac{1}{12} = 1.$$

Questions

1

$$R(t) = 30(4)^{\frac{t}{3}}$$

The number of rain droplets R accumulating in a bucket on a rainy day after t minutes can be modeled with the exponential equation shown above. From this model, which of the following is true?

A) The number of rain droplets quadruples every minute.
B) The number of rain droplets quadruples every 3 minutes.
C) The number of rain droplets triples every minute.
D) The number of rain droplets triples every 4 minutes.

2

In 1540, the population of an extraterrestrial species was 799. The population of this species decreases by 40% every quarter of a year. Which of the following exponential functions best models the population $P(t)$ of the extraterrestrial species t years after 1540?

A) $P(t) = 799(0.4)^{\frac{t}{4}}$

B) $P(t) = 799(0.4)^{4t}$

C) $P(t) = 799(0.6)^{\frac{t}{4}}$

D) $P(t) = 799(0.6)^{4t}$

3

$$M = A(1.002)^{\frac{t}{4}}$$

Consider the equation above, which provides a model for the amount of money M, in dollars, in a bank account t years after an initial deposit of A dollars is made. How many months after a deposit is made would the owner of such a bank account see a 0.2% increase in the money in their account if no money is deposited after the initial deposit?

A) 3
B) 4
C) 12
D) 48

4

The equation shown below is used to model the number of weeds W, in hundreds, that will accumulate along the sidewalks of New York City in a given summer after the application of a novel weed killer y years after 1995. Per the equation, the number of weeds is expected to decrease by 25% every d days. What is the value of d?

$$W = 2,500,000(0.75)^{\frac{2y}{5}}$$

A) 146
B) 178
C) 798
D) 912.5

5

An ecologist observes that in the year 2020, there are 890 rats populating the train tracks of a city and that the rat population triples every year. Which of the following equations best models the number of rats, r, d days after 2020?

A) $r = 890(3)^{365d}$

B) $r = 890(3)^{\frac{d}{365}}$

C) $r = 890(3 \times 10)^d$

D) $r = 890\left(\dfrac{3}{10}\right)^d$

Exponential Graphs

There are a few things to consider when determining the equation of a function from a graph:

1) Exponential Growth or Decay

$$f(x) = ab^x$$

Growth

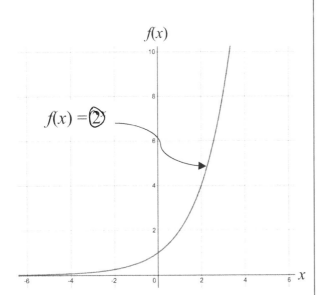

$f(x) = \textcircled{2}^x$

Exponential Growth occurs when the exponent is positive and $b > 1$

Decay

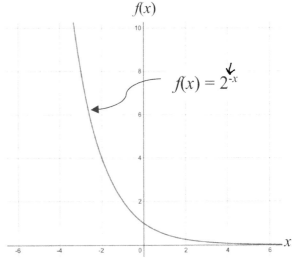

$f(x) = 2^{\downarrow -x}$

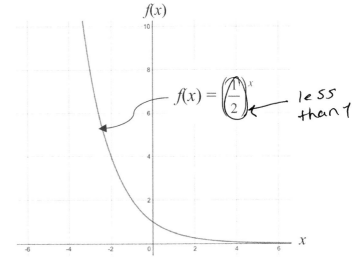

$f(x) = \left(\textcircled{\dfrac{1}{2}}\right)^x$ ← less than 1

Exponential Decay occurs if either…

1. The exponent is negative and $b > 1$

or

2. The exponent is positive but b is a fraction or decimal less than 1

249

2) The y-intercept

$$f(x) = ab^x$$

***NOTE**: Any number raised to the power of 0 will equal 1.

Untranslated Exponential

If a function does **NOT** contain a (an initial value), the y-intercept is 1:

$f(x) = 2^x$ has a y-intercept of 1 because $2^0 = 1$

$f(0) = 2^0 = 1$

If a function does contain a (an initial value), the y-intercept will always equal a:

$f(x) = 3(2)^x$ has a y-intercept of 3

$f(x) = 3(2)^0$

$(3)(1) = 3$

Translated Exponential

A vertical shift in an exponential function will cause the y-intercept to shift up or down.

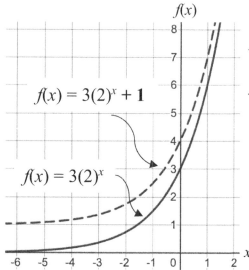

y-intercept of $f(x) = 3(2)^x$ → $3(2)^0 = 3(1) = 3$

y-intercept of $f(x) = 3(2)^x + 1$ → $3(2)^0 + 1 = 3(1) + 1 = 4$

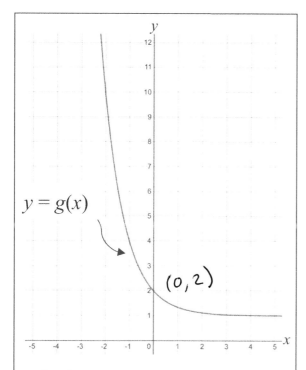

The function g is shown above. Which of the following equations represents g? (-1, 4)

1+2=3
A) $g(x) = 3^{-x} + 2$
B) $g(x) = 2^x - 2$ 1+1=2
C) $g(x) = 2^{-x} + 1$
D) $g(x) = 3^{-x} + 1$ 1+1=2

1) Growth or Decay?

This function represents exponential **decay**. Because b is not a fraction or decimal less than 1 (as per the answer choices), the function must have a negative exponent. **Eliminate B**.

2) The y-intercept

The y-intercept of the graph is 2.

A) y-intercept: $3^{-0} + 2 = 1 + 2 = 3$ **Eliminate A**.
C) y-intercept: $2^{-0} + 1 = 1 + 1 = 2$
D) y-intercept: $3^{-0} + 1 = 1 + 1 = 2$

3) Plug in a point

Pick a known point on the graph and plug it into the two remaining choices: C and D.

Let's use (-1, 4):

C) $g(x) = 2^{-x} + 1$ D) $g(x) = 3^{-x} + 1$
   $4 = 2^{-(-1)} + 1$ $4 = 3^{-(-1)} + 1$
   $4 \neq 3$ $4 = 3 + 1$
                                    $4 = 4$

Therefore, **Choice D** is correct.

Questions

1

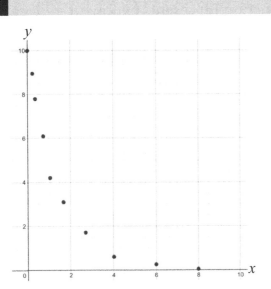

The scatterplot for a data set of a fungal population is shown in the above xy-plane. Which exponential equation best models this data set?

A) $y = 2(10)^{-x}$
B) $y = 2(10)^x$
C) $y = 10(2)^{-x}$
D) $y = 10(2)^x$

2

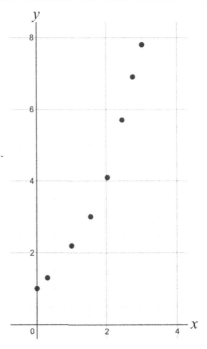

Which exponential equation best models the points shown above?

A) $y = 2^x$
B) $y = 2^{-x}$
C) $y = 3^x$
D) $y = 3^{-x}$

3

In 1840, 35 birch trees existed in a forest. The birch tree population doubles every 85 years. Which of the following graphs best models the population of birch trees?

A)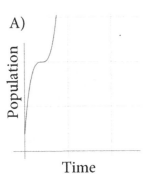
B)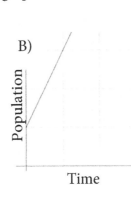
C)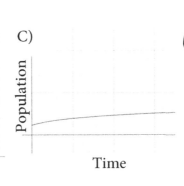
D)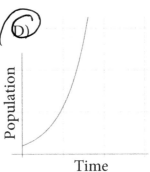

Exponential Tables

There are a few things to consider when determining the equation of a function from a table:

1) Exponential Growth or Decay

$$f(x) = ab^x$$

Table A

x	f(x)
0	150
1	300
2	600
3	1200
4	2400

300/150 = 2

2 = b

This function **grows** as x increases, so $b \geq 1$, and the equation has a positive exponent.

Table B

x	g(x)
-1	12
0	4
1	$\frac{4}{3}$
2	$\frac{4}{9}$
3	$\frac{4}{27}$

This function **decays** as x increases, so either...

1. The exponent is negative and $b > 1$

or

2. The exponent is positive but b is a fraction or decimal less than 1

2) The y-intercept

$$f(x) = ab^x$$

Table A

x	f(x)
0	150
1	300
2	600
3	1200
4	2400

The y-intercept is 150, so $a = 150$.

*As a reminder, the y-intercept occurs when $x = 0$.

Table B

x	g(x)
-1	12
0	4
1	$\frac{4}{3}$
2	$\frac{4}{9}$
3	$\frac{4}{27}$

The y-intercept is 4, so $a = 4$.

3) The multiplier (b)

$$f(x) = ab^x$$

Table A

x	f(x)
0	150
1	300
2	600
3	1200
4	2400

$\dfrac{600}{300} = 2$, so $b = 2$.

Table B

x	g(x)
-1	12
0	4
1	$\dfrac{4}{3}$
2	$\dfrac{4}{9}$
3	$\dfrac{4}{27}$

$\dfrac{4}{12} = \dfrac{1}{3}$, so $b = \dfrac{1}{3}$.

4) Putting It All Together

Table A

x	f(x)
0	150
1	300
2	600
3	1200
4	2400

Proposed Equation:

$f(x) = 150(2)^x$

Table B

x	g(x)
-1	12
0	4
1	$\dfrac{4}{3}$
2	$\dfrac{4}{9}$
3	$\dfrac{4}{27}$

Proposed Equation:

$g(x) = 4\left(\dfrac{1}{3}\right)^x$

1

x	0	1	2
f(x)	3	12	48

The table above shows selected values for the exponential function f. Which of the following correctly defines $f(x)$?

A) $f(x) = 3(4)^x$
B) $f(x) = 3(4)^{-x}$
C) $f(x) = 4(3)^x$
D) $f(x) = 4(3)^{-x}$

2

x	y
0	4
1	6
2	9

The exponential equation represented in the table above can be written as $y = cd^x$. What is the value of d?

6/9 = 2/3

c = 2/3

Answers

For **detailed solutions**, scan the QR code with your phone's camera

or

visit testpreptips.org/exponentials

Questions (Pages 241-242)

1. D
2. D
3. B
4. C
5. C
6. B

Drill (Page 243)

A. 30
B. Increase
C. 60%

Questions (Page 244)

1. C
2. D
3. C
4. B
5. A

Questions (Pages 247-248)

1. B
2. D
3. D
4. D
5. B

Questions (Page 252)

1. C
2. A
3. D

Questions (Pages 255)

1. A
2. $d = \dfrac{3}{2}$

Topic 16: Statistics

Measures of Central Tendency

<u>Mean</u>: the **average** of all numbers in a data set

Data Set: [5, 7, 8, 1, 2, 3, 5, 4, 4, 5, 2, 8, 6]

$$\frac{\text{Sum of Values}}{\text{Number of Values}} = \frac{5+7+8+1+2+3+5+4+4+5+2+8+6}{13} = 4.62$$

<u>Median</u>: the **"middle"** value in a data set

*<u>NOTE</u>: To calculate the median of a data set, we must **first** place the values in **chronological** order

Odd Number of Values

For a data set with an **odd** number of values, the median is the **middle** number.

Data Set: [5, 7, 8, 1, 2, 3, 5, 4, 4, 5, 2, 8, 6] → 13 values

Chronological Version: [1, 2, 2, 3, 4, 4, 5, 5, 5, 6, 7, 8, 8]

Cross out one number on each side until the middle number is reached:

[~~1~~, ~~2~~, ~~2~~, ~~3~~, ~~4~~, ~~4~~, ⑤, ~~5~~, ~~5~~, ~~6~~, ~~7~~, ~~8~~, ~~8~~]

Median = 5

Even Number of Values

For a data set with an **even** number of values, the median is the **average** of the **two middle** numbers.

Data Set: [3, 2, 2, 6, 23, 8, 9, 15, 7, 25] → 10 values

Chronological Version: [2, 2, 3, 6, 7, 8, 9, 15, 23, 25]

Cross out one number on each side until the middle two numbers are reached. Then, take their average.

Average = 7.5

[~~2~~, ~~2~~, ~~3~~, ~~6~~, (7, 8), ~~9~~, ~~15~~, ~~23~~, ~~25~~]

Median = 7.5

257

<u>Mode</u>: the most **common** value in a data set

Data Set: [⑤, 7, 8, 1, 2, 3, ⑤, 4, 4, ⑤, 2, 8, 6]

The most common value is 5 ("5" appears three times).

Mode = 5

A data set can easily **<u>not have a mode</u>**. If each value is different, there will **NOT** be a mode.

Data Set: [7, 15, 8, 9, 3]

There is no most common value, so there is no mode.

Measures of Spread

<u>Range</u>: largest value − smallest value

Data Set: [1, 2, 2, 3, 4, 4, 5, 5, 5, 6, 7, 8, 8]

Smallest Value = 1
Largest Value = 8

Range = (8 − 1) = **7**

<u>Standard Deviation</u>: measures how **spread out** the values are in a data set

Data Set A: [1, 2, 3, 4, 5, 6]   Data Set B: [1, 6, 9, 15, 22, 30]

Data is **less** spread out =   Data is **more** spread out =
SMALLER Standard   **LARGER** Standard Deviation
Deviation

The Standard Deviation of Data Set B is greater than the Standard Deviation of Data Set A because the values of Data Set B are more "spread out" than are those of Data Set A.

*<u>NOTE</u>: The Standard Deviation has **NOTHING** to do with **what** the values are – only how **spread out** they are!

Data Set A: [1, 2, 3, 4, 5, 6]   Data Set C: [101, 102, 103, 104, 105, 106]

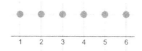   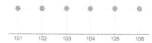

The Standard Deviation of Data Set A is **identical** to the Standard Deviation of Data Set C because both data sets are equally spread out.

# Drills

1

Find the mean, median, mode, and range of the following data set.

2, 6, 10, 11, 15

Mean: __8.8__

Median: __10__

Mode: __None__
(Write "None" if there is no mode)

Range: __13__

2

Find the median of the following data set:

5, 7, 8, 10, 13, 14

9

3

Find the median of the following data set:

6, 1, 13, 2, 5

1 2 5 6 13

5

Questions

1

The prices of two homes in the same neighborhood over time are shown in the table below.

	January 2005	July 2005	January 2007	July 2007	January 2009	July 2009
Price of Home A	$180,050	$206,550	$250,500	$255,900	$295,600	$305,000
Price of Home B	$155,000	$245,750	$345,670	$450,700	$485,000	$585,750

Which of the following statements about the standard deviations of the two homes' prices is true?

A) The standard deviation of Home A's price is greater than Home B's.
B) The standard deviation of Home B's price is greater than Home A's.
C) The standard deviation of Home A's price is equal to Home B's.
D) Not enough information is provided to determine which home's price has a greater standard deviation.

2

Each dot plot shown below represents the number of points a team's best player scored per football game over the course of 20 games.

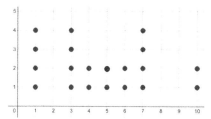

Number of Points Scored – Team A's Best Player

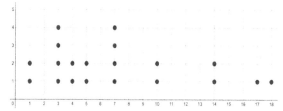

Number of Points Scored – Team B's Best Player

Which of the following statements is true regarding the data shown in the dot plots?

A) There is no difference in the standard deviation of points scored by Team A's best player and Team B's best player.
B) Team A's best player has a greater standard deviation than does Team B's with regards to points scored.
C) Team B's best player has a greater standard deviation than does Team A's with regards to points scored.
D) Additional information is needed to compare the standard deviations of points scored by the players.

3

For the data set provided, x is the mean and y is the median. What is $\dfrac{x}{y}$?

13, 19, 25, 31, 37, 43, 49, 55, 61

A) 0
B) 1
C) 5
D) 6

4

The three dot plots shown below represent the number of points scored in a game of ping pong by three different teams over nine different games.

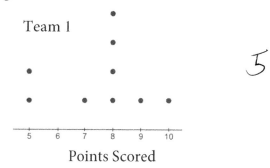

Points Scored

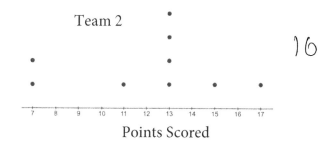

Points Scored

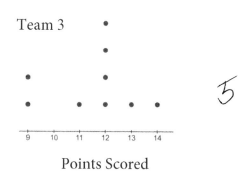

Points Scored

Which of the following statements is true of the range of points scored by these teams?

A) The range of points scored by all three teams is equal.
B) The range of points scored by Teams 1 and 2 is equal but different from that of Team 3.
C) The range of points scored by Teams 1 and 3 is equal but different from that of Team 2.
D) The range of points scored by each team is different.

Modifying Statistics

Least and Greatest Values Changing

When we change either the **least** or **greatest** number in a data set, here's what happens:

> **Mean:** Changes
> **Median:** Unaffected
> **Range:** Changes
> **Standard Deviation:** Changes

Data Set A: [3, 40, 50, 70, 85, 88, 100]

> Data Set A Statistics
> **Mean:** 62.29
> **Median:** 70
> **Range:** 97

Decreasing the Least Value
(Changing 3 → 1)

[①, 40, 50, 70, 85, 88, 100]

> New Statistics
> **Mean:** 62 (decreases)
> **Median:** 70 (same)
> **Range:** 99 (increases)
> **Standard Deviation:** Increases

Explanation

The **mean** decreases because the sum of the numbers decreases.

The **median** remains the same because the middle term is unaffected.

The **range** increases because the lowest number is farther away from the highest.

The **standard deviation** increases because the data is more spread out.

Increasing the Greatest Value
(Changing 100 → 105)

[3, 40, 50, 70, 85, 88, ⑩⑤]

> New Statistics
> **Mean:** 63 (increases)
> **Median:** 70 (same)
> **Range:** 102 (increases)
> **Standard Deviation:** Increases

Explanation

The **mean** increases because the sum of the numbers increases.

The **median** remains the same because the middle term is unaffected.

The **range** increases because the highest number is farther away from the lowest.

The **standard deviation** increases because the data is more spread out.

Inserting an Equal Number of Values Above and Below the Median

Data Set A: [3, 40, 50, ⑦⓪, 85, 88, 100]

(70 is the Median)

- 3 terms **below** median: 3, 40, 50
- 3 terms **above** median: 85, 88, 100

We will now add the following values to the data set: 30, 55, 82, and 86.

NOTICE:
30 and 55 = below median
82 and 86 = above median

We are adding an equal number of terms to each side of the median

New Data Set: [3, 30, 40, 50, 55, ⑦⓪, 82, 85, 86, 88, 100]

(70 is the Median)

- 5 terms **below** median
- 5 terms **above** median

The **median** remains the SAME. If we add the same number of terms below and above the median, the median (middle number) remains **unaffected**.

> A data set with 15 values is modified. Each number less than the median is reduced by 3, and each number greater than the median is increased by 3. What effect would this have on the mean, median, range, and standard deviation of the data set?

We don't **know** any of the actual values, so let's write out our data set in terms of x:

$$[x_1, x_2, x_3, x_4, x_5, x_6, x_7, \overset{\text{Median}}{\widehat{x_8}}, x_9, x_{10}, x_{11}, x_{12}, x_{13}, x_{14}, x_{15}]$$

Let's now modify the data set by subtracting 3 from each number below the median and adding 3 to each number above the median:

$$[\underbrace{x_1, x_2, x_3, x_4, x_5, x_6, x_7}_{-3\ -3\ -3\ -3\ -3\ -3\ -3\ \ \ \ -21}, \overset{\text{Median}}{\widehat{x_8}}, \underbrace{x_9, x_{10}, x_{11}, x_{12}, x_{13}, x_{14}, x_{15}}_{+3\ +3\ +3\ +3\ +3\ +3\ +3\ \ \ \ +21}]$$

The Mean

Because we are subtracting a total of 21 from one side of the median and adding a total of 21 to the other side of the median, the total sum remains unchanged, so the mean remains the same.

The Median

The middle value remains in the middle, so the median remains the same.

The Range

Because the lowest number was decreased by 3 and the greatest number was increased by 3, the range increases by 6.

The Standard Deviation

Because the lowest value is lower and the greatest value is greater, the data is more spread out, so the Standard Deviation increases.

Questions

1

The caloric intake of each of 31 basketball players on a D1 male college basketball team was recorded. The median caloric intake was found to be 3,150 calories. All 31 players had unique caloric intakes. To study how caloric intake affects athletic performance, researchers decided to subtract 500 calories from the diets of players whose caloric intakes were less than the median caloric intake and add 500 calories to the diets of players whose caloric intake was greater than the median caloric intake. Which measures are NOT shared amongst the original caloric intake list and the adjusted, experimental list?

    I. Median
    II. Mean
    III. Sum
    IV. Standard Deviation
    V. Range

A) I, II, and III
B) II, III, and IV
C) II, III, IV, and V
D) IV and V

2

A teacher graded his students' 35 math exams and uploaded the class average, median, range, and standard deviation. After looking through the exams again, he realized that the highest-scoring student actually scored 5 points higher than what he reported. If he were to adjust the statistics he reported for the class, which of the following would NOT be subject to change?

A) The median
B) The mean
C) The range
D) The standard deviation

3

Data Set A consists of 9 unique numbers. The minimum number is 3 and the maximum number is 20. A new data set, Data Set B, consists of the same 9 numbers in Data Set A but with the addition of the numbers 1 and 30. Which statistical measures are NOT shared between the two data sets?

    I. Median
    II. Range
    III. Standard Deviation

A) I
B) II and III
C) I and II
D) I and III

Frequency Charts (Histograms)

The height of each bar indicates the frequency of that value.

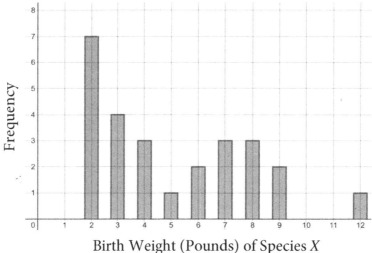

Birth Weight (Pounds) of Species X

> How many members of Species X weighed 8 pounds at birth?

At a weight of 8 pounds (on the *x*-axis), the frequency (on the *y*-axis) is "3," indicating that **3 members** of Species X weighed 8 pounds at birth.

> How many members of Species X were weighed at birth?

To find the total number of members weighed, we need to add up the frequencies of all the bars:

$$7 + 4 + 3 + 1 + 2 + 3 + 3 + 2 + 1 = \textbf{26 members}$$

> What is the mean birth weight amongst Species X members, in pounds?

To calculate the mean birth weight, we will need to add up all the birth weights. The numbers we are going to add are the values on the *x*-axis, but **how many times** we should add each number is indicated by the value on the *y*-axis (the frequency):

$$\frac{(2\text{lbs})(7) + (3\text{lbs})(4) + (4\text{lbs})(3) + (5\text{lbs})(1) + (6\text{lbs})(2) + (7\text{lbs})(3) + (8\text{lbs})(3) + (9\text{lbs})(2) + (12\text{lbs})(1)}{26 \text{ members}}$$

$$\frac{130}{26} = 5 \text{ lbs}$$

Questions

1

The table below displays the scores of 15 Algebra II students on a recent examination. The students' grades were grouped into intervals of 20 points.

Exam Score Interval	Frequency
0 – 20	1
20 – 40	2
40 – 60	4
60 – 80	5
80 – 100	3

Which of the following intervals contains exactly $\frac{1}{5}$ of the values in the data set?

A) 20 – 40
B) 40 – 60
C) 60 – 80
D) 80 – 100

2

The dot plot below shows the number of puppies within a single litter of beagle puppies for 29 different litters.

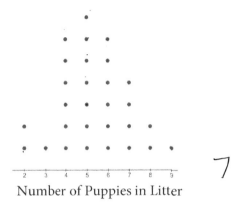

Number of Puppies in Litter

Which of the following statements regarding the mean and range of this data set is accurate?

A) The range is greater than the mean.
B) The mean is greater than the range.
C) The mean is equal to the range.
D) Additional information is necessary to determine the relationship between the mean and range.

The Median Position Formula

The following formula tells us at which position the median falls within a data set:

$$\frac{n+1}{2}$$

n = the number of values in the data set

Let's find the median of the two data sets below by using the Median Position Formula rather than by crossing out numbers on both sides:

Odd Number of Values

Position 3

$[2, 3, \underset{}{⑦}, 10, 12]$ → $n = 5$

$$\frac{5+1}{2} = 3$$

The median falls at Position 3. The number at Position 3 is "7," so the median is 7.

Even Number of Values

Position 3   Position 4

$[2, 3, \widehat{7, 10}, 12, 14]$ → $n = 6$

$$\frac{6+1}{2} = 3.5$$

If we get a number that ends with 0.5, it means that the median is the **average** of the values at the two surrounding positions (here, Positions 3 and 4)

Position 3 = 7
Position 4 = 10

Median = average of 7 and 10 = 8.5

When we have a simple list of data as we did in the previous examples, there is no reason to use the Median Position Formula.

However, when we are working with **larger** data sets (and we cannot possibly write out all the terms and cross them out), the Median Position Formula will be necessary.

The Median Position Formula with Histograms

26 members of Species X were weighed at birth. Their weights are recorded in the histogram below.

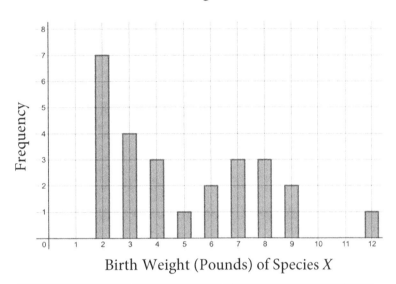

Birth Weight (Pounds) of Species X

What is the median birth weight, in pounds?

$$\frac{26+1}{2} = 13.5$$

The median is the average of the values at Positions 13 and 14

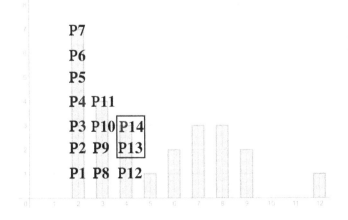

Because both Position 13 and Position 14 have a value of 4 pounds, their average is 4 pounds.

Median = 4 pounds

The Median Position Formula with Frequency Tables

The table below displays the average email response time of 250 workers who work in the same office for the same company.

Average Email Response Time (hours)	Frequency
1	75
2	45
3	52
4	24
5	28
6	14
7	12

What is the median email response time, in hours?

$$\frac{250+1}{2} = 125.5$$

The median is the average of the values at Positions 125 and 126

Average Email Response Time (hours)	Frequency	Running Total of Position Count
1	75	Positions 1-75
2	45	Positions 76-120
3	52	Positions 121-172
4	24	Positions 173-196
5	28	Positions 197-224
6	14	Positions 225-238
7	12	Positions 239-250

Positions 125 and 126 both fall within this group (3 hours).

The average of the two values, then, is 3 hours.

Median = 3 hours

Questions

1

Distribution of Sibling Count

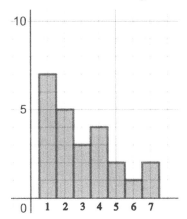

The histogram shown above summarizes the distribution of sibling count for 24 individuals with siblings. The first bar represents the number of students who reported that they have 1 sibling; the second bar represents the number of students who reported that they have 2 siblings, and so on. What is the median of this set of data?

$$\frac{24+1}{2}$$

$$\boxed{12.5}$$

2

Value	Frequency
1	3
2	4
3	2
4	0
5	2

What is the median value in the table above?

A) 1
B) 2
C) 3
D) 4

1 1 1 2 2 2 2 3 3 5 5

Box Plots

A **box plot** uses "boxes" to display the 25th, 50th (median), and 75th percentiles, and "whiskers" to illustrate the range of values.

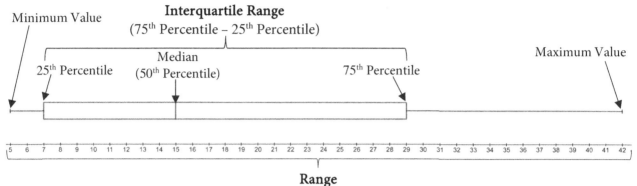

Interpretation

25% of values fall between 5 (minimum) and 7 (25th percentile).
25% of values fall between 7 (25th percentile) and 15 (median).
25% of values fall between 15 (median) and 29 (75th percentile).
25% of values fall between 29 (75th percentile) and 42 (maximum).

Key Data Points

Median = 50th percentile value = 15

Range = 42 − 5 = 37

The **Interquartile Range** (75th percentile − 25th percentile) = 29 − 7 = 22

1

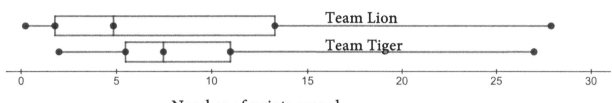

Number of points scored

The box plots displayed above show the distribution of the number of points scored in a year of basketball games for children ages 2 – 5. What is a possible value for the amount by which the median number of points scored in a game for Team Tiger exceeded the median number of points scored in a game for Team Lion? Round your answer to the nearest integer.

Lion M = 5
Tiger M = 7   2

2

For the box plot shown above, identify…

A) The minimum value 5

B) The maximum value 100

C) The median 30

D) The range 95

Table Probability

Probability can be represented as a…

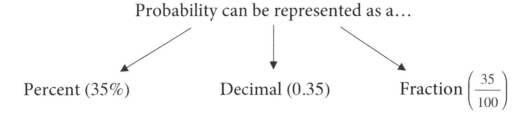

Percent (35%)   Decimal (0.35)   Fraction $\left(\dfrac{35}{100}\right)$

The table below shows the results of a prestigious mathematics exam for three mathlete teams: Mathletes A, B, and C.

	Number of Members Sitting for Exam		
	Placed 95th+ Percentile	Did Not Place 95th+ Percentile	Total
Mathletes A	12	8	20
Mathletes B	13	12	25
Mathletes C	25	15	40
Total	50	35	85

Denominator = Entire Population

> If a mathletes student is selected at random, what is the probability that he or she placed 95th+ percentile?

When we are randomly selecting from the group **as a whole**, we use the entire population defined (here, all the mathletes) as our denominator and use the desired population (here, 95th+ percentile) as our numerator.

Numerator = 50 (50 mathletes placed 95th+ percentile)
Denominator = 85 (85 total mathletes)

Answer: $\dfrac{50}{85}$ or $\dfrac{10}{17}$

Denominator = Subset of Population

	Number of Members Sitting for Exam		
	Placed 95th+ Percentile	Did Not Place 95th+ Percentile	Total
Mathletes A	12	8	20
Mathletes B	13	12	25
Mathletes C	25	15	40
Total	50	35	85

> If a student who did not place 95th+ percentile is randomly selected, what is the probability that the student was a member of the Mathletes A team?

When we are selecting from only a subset of the population (here, students who did not place 95th+ percentile), our denominator will become that subset. The numerator will be the desired value (here, Mathletes A students) of that subset.

<u>Numerator</u> = 8 (8 Mathletes A students did not place 95th+ percentile)
<u>Denominator</u> = 35 (35 students in total did not place 95th+ percentile)

Answer: $\dfrac{8}{35}$

"Given That"

> What is the probability that a student scored 95th+ percentile **given that** the student is a member of Mathletes Team B?

*<u>**NOTE**</u>: "Given That" indicates we are selecting only from the specified subset of the population (here, students who are members of Mathletes Team B).

<u>Numerator</u> = 13 (13 of the students on Mathletes Team B scored 95th+ percentile)
<u>Denominator</u> = 25 (there were 25 total students on Mathletes Team B)

Answer: $\dfrac{13}{25}$

"Or" Probability

	Number of Members Sitting for Exam		
	Placed 95th+ Percentile	Did Not Place 95th+ Percentile	Total
Mathletes A	12	8	20
Mathletes B	13	12	25
Mathletes C	25	15	40
Total	50	35	85

What is the probability that a randomly selected individual **either** was a member of Mathletes Team C and did not place 95th+ percentile **or** that an individual was a member of Mathletes Team B who did place 95th+ percentile?

*__NOTE__: Whenever we have "or" probabilities, we add the two probabilities together.

Because we are randomly selecting individuals from the group **as a whole**, the denominator for each fraction should be 85.

Probability of Mathletes Team C and Did **NOT** Place = $\dfrac{15}{85}$

Probability of Mathletes Team B Who Did Place = $\dfrac{13}{85}$

Answer: $\dfrac{15}{85} + \dfrac{13}{85} = \dfrac{28}{85}$

Questions

1

		Pet	
		Dog	Cat
Age	Young	14	5
	Adult	7	4

The table above shows the results of polling students at a school who responded that they had a cat or dog. Each student had only one pet. Of the students who had a dog, what fraction had one that was an adult?

A) $\frac{7}{30}$

B) $\frac{1}{3}$

C) $\frac{2}{3}$

D) $\frac{7}{11}$

2

The table shown below provides the results of a survey in which 100 entrepreneurs were asked how often they work remotely.

Answer	Number of Responses
Never	35
Rarely	6
Sometimes	14
Usually	19
Always	26

Based on the table, which of the following is closest to the probability that an entrepreneur answered "usually" or "sometimes" given that he or she did not answer "rarely"?

A) 0.15
B) 0.20
C) 0.33
D) 0.35

$\frac{19+14}{19+26+14+35}$

3

A group of 2,633 adults in Central Park was surveyed. Participants were asked which flavor of ice cream they preferred from a total of 4 choices: chocolate, vanilla, strawberry, and coffee. After providing a response, participants were sorted based on their age group and gender.

	Chocolate	Vanilla	Strawberry	Coffee	Total
Female, 18-35	356	201	46	142	745
Female, 36-64	227	230	166	134	757
Male, 18-35	167	255	93	58	573
Male, 36-64	104	289	67	98	558
Total	854	975	372	432	2,633

Based on the data shown above, which of the following is closest to the probability that a randomly selected adult from the 2,633 adults surveyed is a female and prefers strawberry ice cream?

A) 0.017
B) 0.063
C) 0.081
D) 0.141

Questions 4 and 5 refer to the following information.

Students in Bulldog High School were surveyed about their favorite sport. The table below indicates the responses to this survey by grade-level.

Grade	Favorite Sport				
	Football	Baseball	Soccer	Other	Total
9	24	39	22	35	120
10	50	16	20	45	131
11	32	29	16	32	109
12	41	27	19	38	125
Total	147	111	77	150	485

4

A student who indicated football as a favorite sport is selected at random. What is the probability that the student is in Grade 9? Round your answer to the nearest hundredth.

$$\frac{24}{485} = .049$$

.05

5

A student from Bulldog High School is selected at random. What is the probability that baseball is their favorite sport? Round your answer to the nearest hundredth.

$$\frac{111}{485}$$

= .22

= .23

Surveys

Accurate Surveys

For a survey to be statistically accurate, it must meet a few criteria:

1. Random selection

    - <u>Principle</u>: Within the population a surveyor is intending to survey, the selection of participants must be **random**
    - <u>Example</u>: If Joe, a restaurant manager, wants to know if customers were satisfied with the quality of service, he could survey every 3rd person leaving the restaurant, ensuring that his selection of candidates is random.

2. No Bias

    - <u>Principle</u>: Bias occurs when the candidates selected for surveying are not representative of the entire population that is being surveyed
    - <u>Example</u>: If Jamie, a sports researcher, wants to know what sporting event Americans prefer attending, she should **not** survey people inside of a soccer stadium. This will produce biased results, as the majority surveyed will likely respond "soccer" when this may not be representative of Americans as a whole.

Survey Response Generalization

<u>Generalization</u> – applying the results of a survey to the **entire** population from which candidates were randomly selected

> An online fashion store wants to know what its customers think of its clothing quality. From a list of all customers' emails (obtained at checkout), the store randomly selects customers from the list and emails a customer satisfaction survey. All customers who received the email provide a complete reply. What is the largest population the results of this survey can be applied to?
>
> A) The fashion store customers who participated in the study
> B) All customers of the fashion store
> C) All individuals who have viewed the fashion store website
> D) All individuals who have purchased clothing online

We can apply the results of a survey to the entire population (here, customers of the online fashion store) from which candidates were randomly selected. Therefore, we can generalize the results of this survey to all customers of the online fashion store. **Choice B.**

Questions

1

A PTA mom designed jewelry that she planned to sell to students at the annual bookfair. To determine if her items would actually sell, she randomly pulled 30 students in the school to the side to see if they liked her jewelry. 9 out of every 10 students said that they liked it and would consider purchasing it. What is the largest group to which the responses could be generalized?

A) The 30 students questioned
B) All students in the school
C) All students in the county
D) All PTA moms

2

A beverage researcher trying to determine people's favorite drinks went to a local coffee shop and received a response from 180 of the 195 individuals to which he proposed his research question. Why would his study likely not produce accurate or reliable conclusions?

A) Sample size was too small
B) Setting in which the survey was administered would produce biased results
C) Lack of response amongst almost 8% of all who were proposed the survey question
D) Research question was flawed

3

A local elementary school is considering upgrading its playground, but it first wants to see how parents of the school feel about the proposal. Which of the following methods would result in a random sample of all parents of elementary school attendees for that particular elementary school?

A) Acquire a list of all parents of the elementary school attendees. Survey the first 50 who appear on the list alphabetically.
B) Put the email addresses of parents who have chosen to keep their emails on file with the school into a random generator and survey those individuals.
C) Randomly survey the first 50 parents who come to pick their children up from the elementary school.
D) Put all names of parents of the elementary school attendees into a random generator and survey those individuals.

4

At a football game, 80 fans of the losing team were selected at random and asked if they thought the referee made fair calls throughout the game. Of the 80 fans questioned, 70 said that they did not consider the calls to be fair. Which of the following is the largest population to which the results obtained can be applied?

A) All sports' fans
B) All fans of the winning team
C) All fans of the losing team
D) All fans of the losing team at the game

281

Margin of Error

Not every randomly selected group of individuals will 100% accurately reflect what is true of the entire population they were selected from.

We must account for this using the **Margin of Error**.

> New York Residents were selected at random and asked if they were satisfied with the NYS Anti-Pollution Program. As determined from the survey, the program had a 65% satisfaction rating, with a 2.5% margin of error.

Interpretation: Of the individuals who were randomly selected for the survey, 65% were satisfied with the program. This does **NOT**, however, mean that if we surveyed **every** New-Yorker that **exactly** 65% would express satisfaction.

Margin of Error (MOE): The Margin of Error (2.5%) exists to account for random sampling error. Not every random sample is going to be perfectly accurate. Perhaps, the people who were randomly selected are very invested in the environment. The Margin of Error allows for us to account for this chance.

$$\text{Reported Rating} - \text{MOE} = 62.5\%$$
$$(65\%) \quad (2.5\%)$$

$$\text{Reported Rating} + \text{MOE} = 67.5\%$$
$$(65\%) \quad (2.5\%)$$

The 2.5% Margin of Error tells us it is likely that out of **ALL** New-Yorkers, between 62.5% and 67.5% are satisfied with the program.

How can we decrease the Margin of Error?

The Margin of Error decreases when the sample size of those surveyed **increases** because there will be less uncertainty.

Is the Margin of Error ever 0?

The only way the Margin of Error is 0 is if **every** member of the intended survey population is surveyed and provides a response. That way, there is absolutely **no** uncertainty.

> At the end of the semester, Mr. Robbins, who teaches a 750-student introductory course, randomly selects 100 students in the course and administers an academic satisfaction survey. The survey asks for students to rate the course from 1-10. The mean response was 8.2, with a Margin of Error of 0.6. Which of the following best interprets Mr. Robbins' study results?
>
> A) All surveyed students likely responded with a score between 7.6 and 8.8
> B) The mean of the surveyed students' responses is likely between 7.6 and 8.8
> C) All students would likely respond with a score between 7.6 and 8.8
> D) The mean of all the students' responses would likely be between 7.6 and 8.8

Choice A: **incorrect**. The reported result was the **mean** response (not individual responses). This choice does not even mention the mean.

Choice B: **incorrect**. The Margin of Error provides a likely range for the entire population from which candidates were selected - not the surveyed individuals.

Choice C: **incorrect**. The reported result was the **mean** response (not individual responses). This choice does not even mention the mean.

Choice D: **correct**. The Margin of Error tells us what is likely true of the entire population from which candidates were selected. Because the mean response was 8.2, adding and subtracting the Margin of Error gives us the likely range of 7.6 – 8.8 as the mean rating.

> An aeronautical researcher wants to know what percent of the world's 25,000 commercial aircraft use a 3-seat model rather than a 2-seat model. After observing 1,000 planes, she concludes that 83% of commercial planes use a 3-seat model with a 3% margin of error. What is the range of values between which the **actual** number of aircraft that use a 3-seat model likely falls?

83% of commercial aircraft the researcher directly observed used a 3-seat model. To generalize this to all 25,000 commercial aircraft, we will incorporate the Margin of Error. The Margin of Error indicates to us that the **actual** percent of aircraft that use a 3-seat model likely falls between 80% (83% – 3%) and 86% (83% + 3%).

Multiplying each percentage by the 25,000 commercial aircraft, we find that the range is (0.80)(25,000) = 20,000 to (0.86)(25,000) = 21,500.

20,000 to 21,500 commercial aircraft

Questions

1

Patrons entering a local ice cream shop were surveyed to assess the level of interest in a new flavor of ice cream. 50 patrons responded to the survey. 82% responded favorably to the new ice cream proposal. With the incorporation of the margin of error, the surveyor correctly predicts that between 73% and 91% of all patrons would respond favorably to the new flavor. What is the margin of error?

A) 9%
B) 18%
C) 82%
D) 91%

2

A sushi restaurant manager, after realizing that her restaurant was not profiting on sashimi, decided to weigh the sashimi portions of 20 random sashimi plates leaving the kitchen in a given night. Of those sampled, the mean sashimi piece weighed 0.70 ounces, with a margin of error of 0.05 ounces. Which of the following is the best interpretation of the manager's findings?

A) All sashimi pieces in the sample weigh between 0.65 and 0.75 ounces.
B) The majority of sashimi pieces that leave the kitchen weigh between 0.65 and 0.75 ounces.
C) The mean mass of all sashimi leaving the kitchen is likely between 0.65 and 0.75 ounces.
D) The sashimi in the sample likely has a mean mass anywhere between 0.65 and 0.75 ounces.

3

	Sample Average Birth Weight (pounds)	Margin of Error
Brian's Sample	7.15	.19
Shane's Sample	7.42	.17

Brian and Shane are both statisticians measuring the average birth weight of babies in America. The table above shows the average birth weight, in pounds, of each statistician's sample along with the associated margin of error. B and S are the sample sizes of Brian's sample and Shane's sample, respectively. Which of the following must be true regarding the sizes of B and S?

A) B > S
B) B < S
C) B = S
D) Cannot be determined

Answers

For **detailed solutions**, scan the QR code with your phone's camera

or

visit testpreptips.org/statistics

Drills (Page 260)

1. <u>Mean</u>: 8.8
   <u>Median</u>: 10
   <u>Mode</u>: None
   <u>Range</u>: 13
2. 9
3. 5

Questions (Pages 260-261)

1. B
2. C
3. B
4. C

Questions (Page 265)

1. D
2. A
3. B

Questions (Page 267)

1. D
2. A

Questions (Page 271)

1. 2.5 siblings
2. B

Drills (Page 273)

1. 2 or 3
2. <u>Minimum</u>: 5
   <u>Maximum</u>: 100
   <u>Median</u>: 30
   <u>Range</u>: 95

Questions (Pages 277-278)

1. B
2. D
3. C
4. 0.16
5. 0.23

Questions (Page 281)

1. B
2. B
3. D
4. D

Questions (Page 284)

1. A
2. C
3. B

Topic 17: Geometry
Part I: Definitions, Area, and Perimeter
Terms and Symbols

Symbol	Meaning	Visual
$\parallel$	**Parallel** – parallel lines "rise" / "fall" together Mathematically, parallel lines have the same slope and different y-intercepts.	(two parallel lines)
$\perp$	**Perpendicular** – perpendicular lines "cross" each other and create four right (90°) angles. Mathematically, perpendicular lines have slopes that are negative reciprocals.	(two perpendicular lines)
$\sim$	**Similar** - triangles that are similar have sides that are "scaled" versions of one other. The angles across from each pair of corresponding ("matching") sides are identical. Mathematically, the sides are proportional, and all angles opposite corresponding sides are equal.	$\triangle ABC$ with sides 2, 3, 4; $\triangle XYZ$ with sides 4, 6, 8. All sides of $\triangle XYZ$ are double those of $\triangle ABC$. Regarding angles, $\angle A = \angle X, \angle B = \angle Y, \angle C = \angle Z$
$\cong$	**Congruent** – sides or angles are equal	(two congruent triangles)

287

Term	Meaning
Bisect	To cut an angle into two **equal** halves
Vertex	The "corner" of a shape (i.e. the point where two sides of a square meet)
Acute Angle	An angle less than 90° (i.e. 65°)
Obtuse Angle	An angle greater than 90° (i.e. 140°)
Right Angle	A 90° angle

Symbols on Shapes

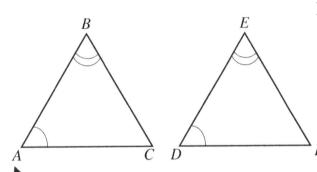

If the angles in a figure are labeled with the same number of "curves," it indicates that they are equal:

$\angle A = \angle D$

$\angle B = \angle E$

***NOTE**: This angle can be referred to as either $\angle A$, $\angle BAC$, or $\angle CAB$. If the angle is referred to by its three-letter name, the desired angle will always be the **middle** letter.

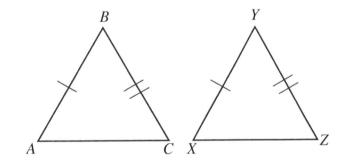

If the sides in a figure are labeled with the same number of "dashes," it indicates that they are equal:

$\overline{AB} = \overline{XY}$

$\overline{BC} = \overline{YZ}$

Area and Perimeter of Shapes

The Height

*<u>NOTE</u>: The height of a shape is always **perpendicular** to its base.

Examples: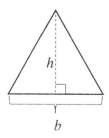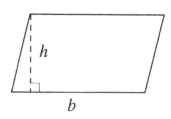

Triangles

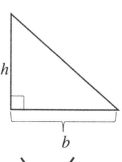 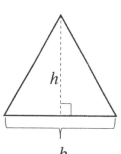 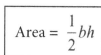

$$\text{Area} = \frac{1}{2}bh$$

 Drills

1
Calculate the area of the triangle shown below.

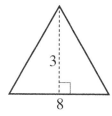

Area: _____

2
Calculate the area of the triangle shown below.

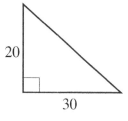

Area: _____

289

3

Calculate the area **and** perimeter of the triangle shown below.

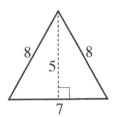

Area: _____

Perimeter: _____

Squares

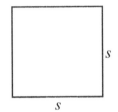

Area = s^2
Perimeter = $4s$

Properties

All sides are equal

All angles are 90°

 Drills

1

Calculate the area **and** perimeter of the square shown below.

Area: _____

Perimeter: _____

2

The area of a square is 49. What is the perimeter of the square?

Rectangles

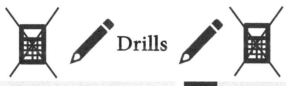

Area = lw
Perimeter = $2l + 2w$

Properties

Opposite sides are equal

All angles are 90°

Drills

1

Calculate the area **and** perimeter of the rectangle shown below.

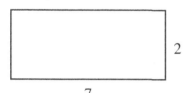

Area: _____

Perimeter: _____

2

Calculate the area **and** perimeter of the rectangle shown below.

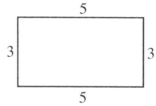

Area: _____

Perimeter: _____

Parallelograms

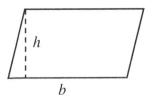 

Properties

Opposite sides are equal and parallel

 Drills

1

Calculate the area of the parallelogram shown below.

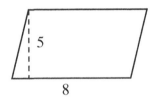

Area: _____

2

Calculate the area of the parallelogram shown below.

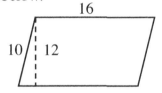

Area: _____

Trapezoids

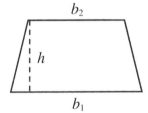 

Properties

Bases are parallel

 Drills

1

Calculate the area of the trapezoid shown below.

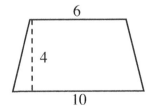

Area: _____

2

Calculate the area of the trapezoid shown below.

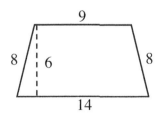

Area: _____

Answers

For **detailed solutions**, scan the QR code with your phone's camera

or

visit testpreptips.org/geometry1

Drills (Pages 289-290 [Top])

1. <u>Area</u>: 12
2. <u>Area</u>: 300
3. <u>Area</u>: 17.5
   <u>Perimeter</u>: 23

Drills (Page 291)

1. <u>Area</u>: 14
   <u>Perimeter</u>: 18
2. <u>Area</u>: 15
   <u>Perimeter</u>: 16

Drills (Page 292 [Bottom])

1. <u>Area</u>: 32
2. <u>Area</u>: 69

Drills (Page 290 [Bottom])

1. <u>Area</u>: 9
   <u>Perimeter</u>: 12
2. <u>Perimeter</u>: 28

Drills (Page 292 [Top])

1. <u>Area</u>: 40
2. <u>Area</u>: 192

Part II: Lines and Angles

Rule 1: All angles in a **Line Split** add to 180°

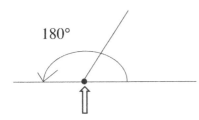
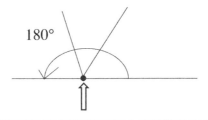

"**Line Split**" = a straight line cut up by one or more other lines emerging from the same point

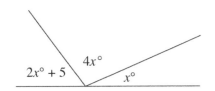

What is the measure of the largest angle in the figure shown to the left?

The angles are a **Line Split**, so we know they add to 180°:

$$(2x + 5) + 4x + x = 180$$
$$7x = 175°$$
$$x = 25°$$

Largest angle = $4x = 4(25°) = 100°$

Rule 2: All right angles are 90°

What is the measure of the smallest angle in the figure shown to the left?

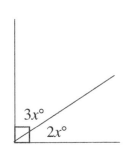

Both angles form a right angle, which is 90°:

$$3x + 2x = 90°$$
$$5x = 90°$$
$$x = 18°$$

Smallest angle = $2x = 2(18°) = 36°$

Rule 3: The three angles in a triangle sum to 180°

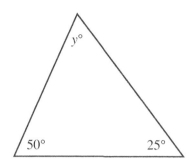

What is the measure of angle y?

All three angles must sum to 180°:

$$50° + 25° + y° = 180°$$
$$y = 105°$$

Questions

1

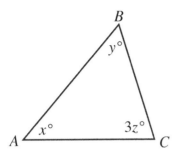

In the triangle above, $y = 88°$. If $z = x$, what is the value of $\angle BCA$?

A) 23°
B) 69°
C) 88°
D) 92°

2

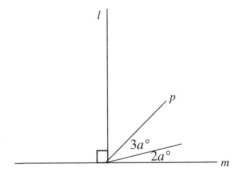

In the figure shown above, line p bisects the angle formed by the intersection of lines l and m. What is the value of the larger of the two unknown angles?

A) 9
B) 18
C) 27
D) 54

3

In triangle QRS, $\overline{QT}$ is a straight line that contains $\overline{QS}$. $\overline{VS}$ bisects $\angle RST$. What is the measure of $\angle RSV$?

Note: Figure below is not drawn to scale.

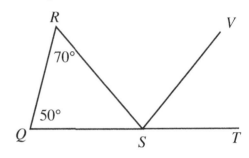

A) 30°
B) 40°
C) 60°
D) 70°

4

What is the value of x?

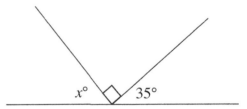

5

What is the value of *x*?

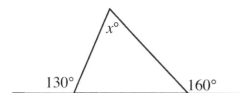

6

What is the value of *a*?

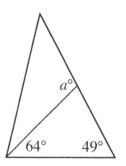

Opposite Angles

Rule 4: All angles that are "opposite" one another are equal

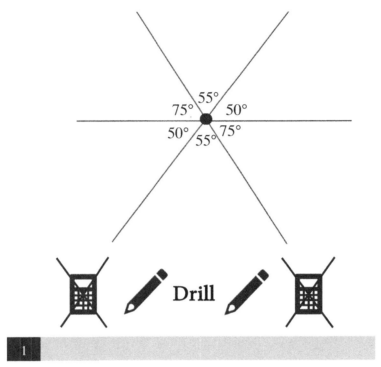

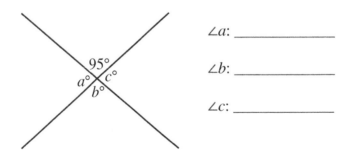

1

What is the measure of ∠a, ∠b, and ∠c?

∠a: _____

∠b: _____

∠c: _____

Parallel Lines

Rule 5: All **alternate interior angles** have the same measure

Alternate interior angles refer to angles that are either **within** the "Z" or **within** the backwards "Z"

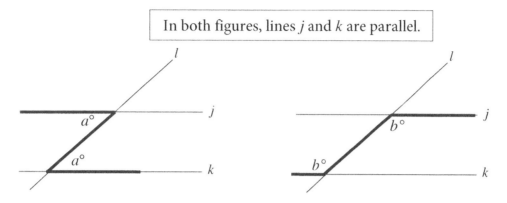

In both figures, lines j and k are parallel.

Rule 6: All **corresponding angles** have the same measure

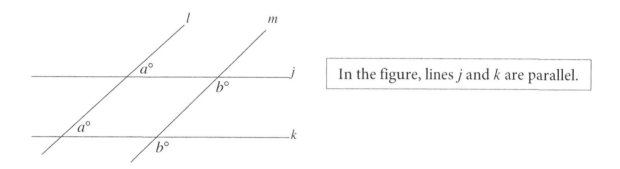

In the figure, lines j and k are parallel.

*__NOTE__: We oftentimes have **corresponding angles** when one triangle is **inside** of another triangle and the triangles have a pair of parallel sides

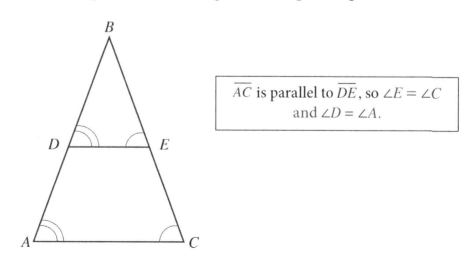

$\overline{AC}$ is parallel to $\overline{DE}$, so $\angle E = \angle C$ and $\angle D = \angle A$.

Drills

1

Identify the relationship between the angle pairs listed below from the following options: **alternate interior**, **corresponding**, **line split**, or **opposite**.

∠a and ∠d: _____

∠d and ∠e: _____

∠f and ∠h: _____

∠c and ∠g: _____

In the figure, lines X and Y are parallel.

∠c and ∠f: _____

2

Identify the measure of ∠a, ∠b, ∠c, ∠d, ∠e, ∠f, and ∠g.

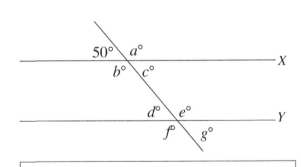

∠a: _____

∠b: _____

∠c: _____

∠d: _____

∠e: _____

∠f: _____

In the figure, lines X and Y are parallel.

∠g: _____

Questions

1

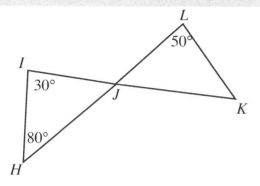

Note: Figure not drawn to scale.

In the figure above, *J* is the point of intersection of $\overline{HL}$ and $\overline{IK}$. What is the value of ∠*LKJ*?

A) 20°
B) 60°
C) 70°
D) 80°

2

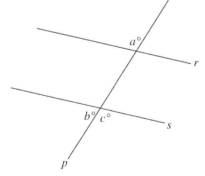

Which of the following statements, if true, would indicate that lines *r* and *s* are parallel lines?

I. $a = c$
II. $a = b$
III. $a = 180 - b$
IV. $b + c = 180$

A) I only
B) I and II only
C) I and III only
D) III and IV only

3

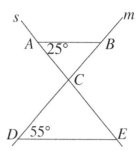

Note: Figure not drawn to scale.

The figure shown above contains 2 triangles: *ABC* and *CDE*. $\overline{AB}$ is parallel to $\overline{DE}$. What is the measure of ∠*ACB*?

A) 25°
B) 55°
C) 80°
D) 100°

4

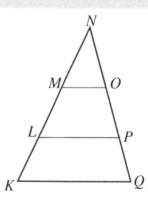

$\overline{KQ}$, $\overline{LP}$, and $\overline{MO}$ are parallel. If ∠*NPL* = 27°, and ∠*NKQ* = 82°, then what is the measure of ∠*KNQ*? Ignore the degree sign when answering.

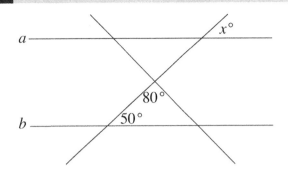

Lines *a* and *b* are parallel. What is the value of *x*?

General Shapes

Regular and Irregular

A **polygon** is an enclosed figure with straight sides.

*<u>NOTE</u>: In a **regular polygon**, the sum of the angles is split **evenly** between the angles.

Regular Polygon

All sides and angles are equal

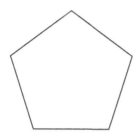

Shown above is a **regular pentagon** (5 sides)

Irregular Polygon

Neither all the angles nor all the sides are equal

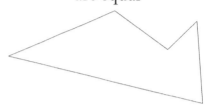

Shown above is an **irregular** pentagon.

Sum of the Interior Angles

The sum of the interior angles of any polygon is represented by

$$180°(n-2)$$

where n is the number of sides

You should memorize that a…

3-sided shape has 180°
4-sided shape has 360°

 Drills

1

What is the total number of degrees in a...

A. Rectangle: _____

B. Triangle: _____

C. Square: _____

D. Parallelogram: _____

E. Pentagon (5 sides): _____

F. Hexagon (6 sides): _____

2

Shown below is a regular hexagon. How many degrees is the labeled angle?

3

What is the value of the largest angle in the figure shown below?

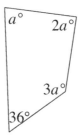

A) 36
B) 54
C) 108
D) 162

Answers

For **detailed solutions**, scan the QR code with your phone's camera

or

visit **testpreptips.org/geometry2**

Questions (Pages 296-297)

1. B
2. C
3. C
4. 55
5. 110
6. 113

Drill (Page 298)

1.

∠a: 85°
∠b: 95°
∠c: 85°

Drills (Page 300)

1.

∠a and ∠d: <u>opposite</u>
∠d and ∠e: <u>alternate interior</u>
∠f and ∠h: <u>line split</u>
∠c and ∠g: <u>corresponding</u>
∠c and ∠f: <u>alternate interior</u>

2.

∠a: 130°
∠b: 130°
∠c: 50°
∠d: 50°
∠e: 130°
∠f: 130°
∠g: 50°

Questions (Pages 301-302)

1. B
2. C
3. D
4. 71
5. 50

Drills (Page 304)

1.

A. Rectangle: 360°
B. Triangle: 180°
C. Square: 360°
D. Parallelogram: 360°
E. Pentagon (5 sides): 540°
F. Hexagon (6 sides): 720°

2. 120
3. D

Part III: Triangles
Angles and Sides

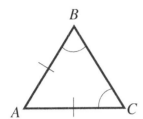

The angles opposite equal sides are equal
(because $AB = AC$, $\angle B = \angle C$)

Types of Triangles

Equilateral

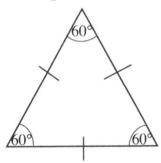

All sides are equal.
All angles are equal.
Each angle is 60°.

Isosceles

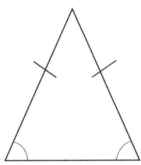

Two of the three sides are equal.
The angles opposite the equal sides have the same measure.

Scalene

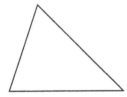

NO sides (and therefore **NO** angles) are equal.

Right

90°

One angle is a right angle.
The other two non-right angles are acute.

Drill

1

Indicate if each triangle is equilateral, isosceles, or scalene.

A.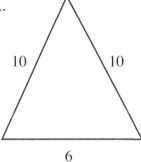

equilateral / isosceles / scalene

B.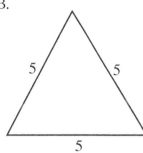

equilateral / isosceles / scalene

C.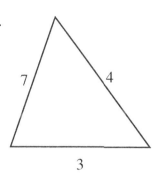

equilateral / isosceles / scalene

D.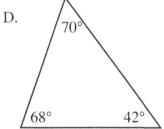

equilateral / isosceles / scalene

E.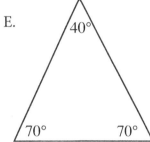

equilateral / isosceles / scalene

F.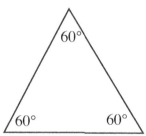

equilateral / isosceles / scalene

The Pythagorean Theorem

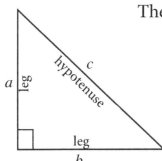

The Pythagorean Theorem helps us find a missing **third** side of a **right** triangle when we already know two sides.

$$a^2 + b^2 = c^2$$

a = one of the legs
b = one of the legs
c = the hypotenuse

What is the value of x?

7 = one of the legs
24 = one of the legs
x = the hypotenuse

$(7)^2 + (24)^2 = (x)^2$
$49 + 576 = x^2$
$625 = x^2$
$x = 25$

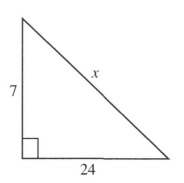

What is the value of x?

x = one of the legs
40 = one of the legs
41 = the hypotenuse

$(x)^2 + (40)^2 = (41)^2$
$x^2 + 1600 = 1681$
$x^2 = 81$
$x = 9$

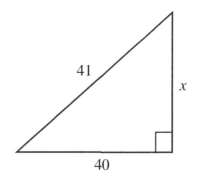

Pythagorean Triples

Rather than use the Pythagorean Theorem each time we want to calculate a side, we can memorize two common Pythagorean Triples:

3 – 4 – 5 and 5 – 12 – 13

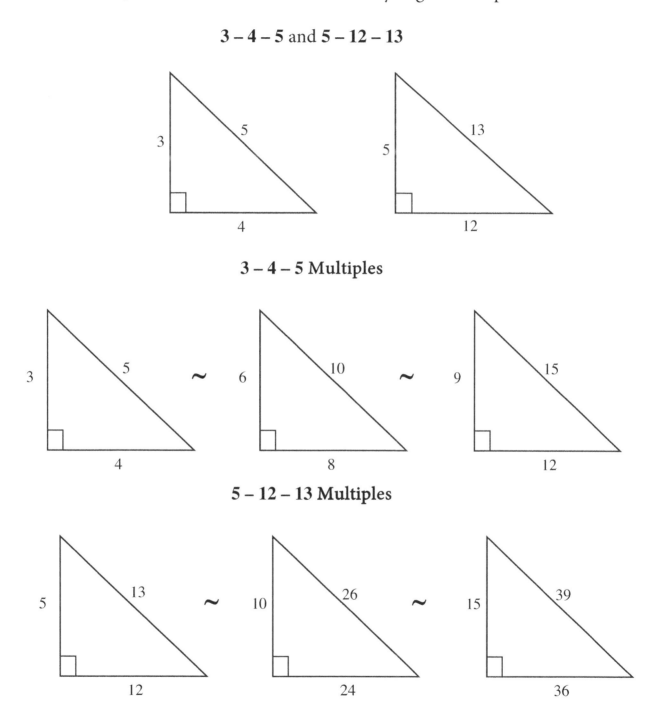

*Whenever you see a right triangle with **two** of the **three** sides in one of the Pythagorean Triples shown above, you automatically know the third side*

Questions

1
Find the value of x.

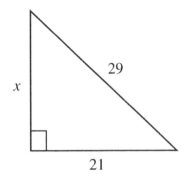

2
Find the value of x.

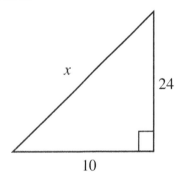

3
Find the value of x.

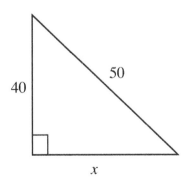

4
Find the value of x.

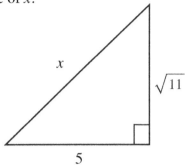

5

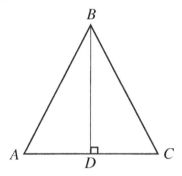

In triangle ABC, $\overline{AB}=\overline{BC}$. If $AB = 10$ and $AC = 12$, what is the length of $\overline{BD}$?

Special Right Triangles

Shown below are the two Special Right Triangles you must be familiar with:

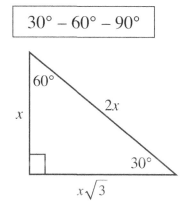
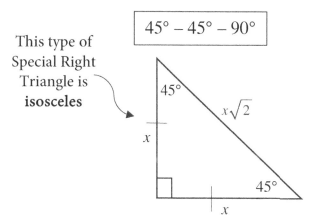

This type of Special Right Triangle is **isosceles**

***NOTE**: The two Special Right Triangles shown above are provided on the "Reference" pages before Sections 3 and 4. Therefore, you do not need to memorize them and should instead focus on how to work with them.

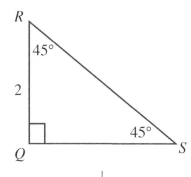

Find the lengths of $\overline{QS}$ and $\overline{RS}$.

The side opposite 45° corresponds with x.

Therefore, $x = 2$

The other side opposite 45° also corresponds with x.

$QS = x = 2$

The side opposite 90° corresponds with $x\sqrt{2}$.

$RS = x\sqrt{2} = 2\sqrt{2}$.

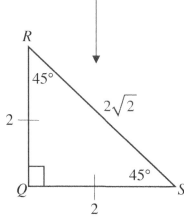

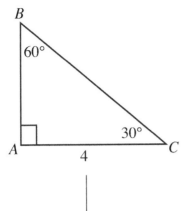

Find the lengths of $\overline{AB}$ and $\overline{BC}$.

The side opposite 60° corresponds with $x\sqrt{3}$.

Therefore, $x\sqrt{3} = 4$, so $x = \dfrac{4}{\sqrt{3}}$.

The side opposite 30° corresponds with x.
$$AB = x = \dfrac{4}{\sqrt{3}}.$$

The side opposite 90° corresponds with $2x$.
$$BC = 2x = \dfrac{8}{\sqrt{3}}.$$

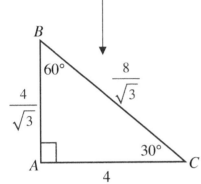

Questions

1

Find the value of AC and BC.

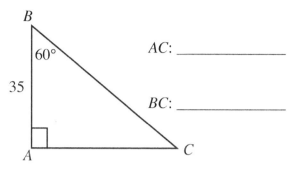

AC: _____

BC: _____

2

Find the value of AE and AI.

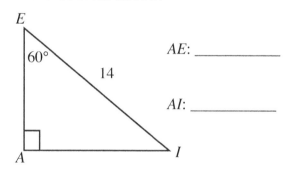

AE: _____

AI: _____

3

Find the value of GH and GI.

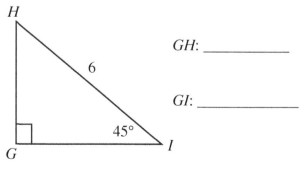

GH: _____

GI: _____

4

Find the value of JL and KL.

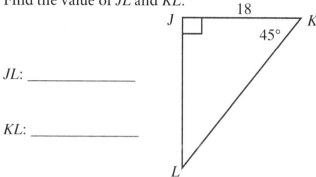

JL: _____

KL: _____

5

Find the value of TS and TU.

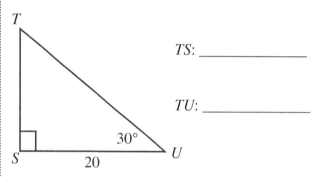

TS: _____

TU: _____

6

Square $ABCD$ has diagonal $\overline{BD}$. If $BD = 10\sqrt{2}$, then what is the length of $\overline{CD}$?

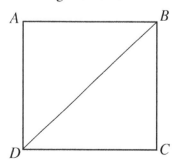

Similar Triangles

Similar Triangles have...

1. Corresponding ("matching") sides that are proportional

and

2. Corresponding ("matching") angles that are equal in measure

*__NOTE__: Corresponding sides are opposite corresponding angles

---

$\triangle ABC \sim \triangle XYZ$

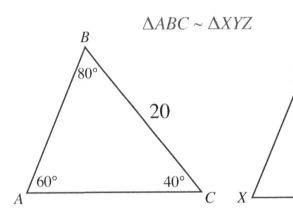

| Find the length of $\overline{AC}$. | What is the measure of $\angle Z$?
What is the measure of $\angle Y$? |

$\overline{BC}$ corresponds with $\overline{YZ}$.
$\overline{AC}$ corresponds with $\overline{XZ}$.

The sides are proportional, so we can set up a proportion:

$$\frac{BC}{YZ} = \frac{AC}{XZ}$$

$$\frac{20}{4} = \frac{AC}{6}$$

$$AC = 30$$

The angles in the same position (**corresponding angles**) are equal.

Therefore, $\angle Z$ is 40° and $\angle Y$ is 80°.

Drills

1

$\triangle QRS \sim \triangle TUV$

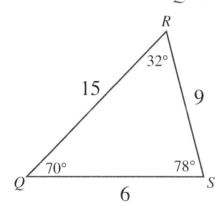
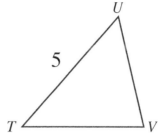

A. ∠T = _____ °

B. ∠U = _____ °

C. ∠V = _____ °

D. TV = _____

E. UV = _____

2

$\triangle QRS \sim \triangle TUV$

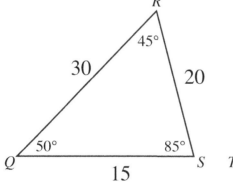
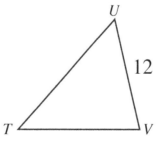

A. ∠T = _____ °

B. ∠U = _____ °

C. ∠V = _____ °

D. TV = _____

E. TU = _____

Two Pairs of Congruent Angles = Similar Triangles

*RULE: If triangles have **two pairs of congruent angles**, they are **similar**.

All three examples shown below illustrate similar triangles.

A.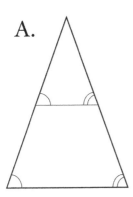
B.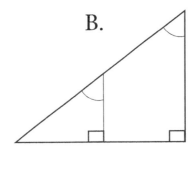
C.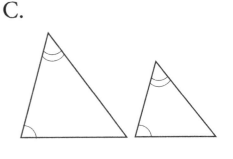

🔆 Strategy: Identifying Similar Triangles 🔆

If a smaller triangle sits <u>inside</u> of another larger triangle (as is the case for Examples A and B shown above), it's very likely that the triangles are similar.

> In $\triangle ABC$, $\overline{AB}$ is parallel to $\overline{DE}$, $AB = 10$, $CD = 5$, and $DE = 7.5$. What is the length of $\overline{AC}$?

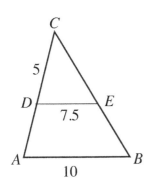

A smaller triangle within a larger triangle likely indicates Similar Triangles

$\angle CDE = \angle CAB$ (parallel lines)
$\angle CED = \angle CBA$ (parallel lines)

Because the triangles have two pairs of congruent angles, they are indeed similar.

Because the triangles are similar, we know that their sides are proportional:

$$\frac{DE}{AB} = \frac{CD}{AC} \rightarrow \frac{7.5}{10} = \frac{5}{AC} \rightarrow AC = \frac{20}{3}$$

Questions

1

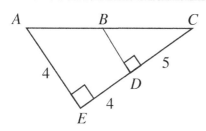

ACE and BCD are both triangles. What is the length of $\overline{BD}$?

A) 5

B) $\dfrac{20}{9}$

C) $\dfrac{36}{5}$

D) 9

2

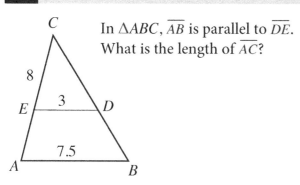

In $\triangle ABC$, $\overline{AB}$ is parallel to $\overline{DE}$. What is the length of $\overline{AC}$?

3

Triangle QRS is similar to triangle TUV. Q corresponds to T, and R corresponds to U. If $QR = 2TU$ and $\angle T = 24°$, then which of the following must be true?

I. $\angle Q = 48°$

II. $RS = 2UV$

A) I

B) II

C) I and II

D) None of the above

4

In $\triangle HIJ$, $\angle H$ is $40°$ and $\angle I$ is $94°$. $\triangle HIJ$ is similar to $\triangle KLM$, where $\dfrac{HI}{KL} = \dfrac{IJ}{LM} = \dfrac{HJ}{KM}$. Angle M is equal to $x°$. What is the value of x?

5

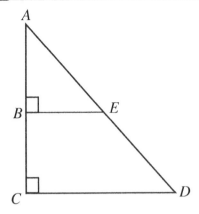

In the figure above, B is the midpoint of $\overline{AC}$. If $BE = 10$, what is the length of $\overline{CD}$?

6

$\triangle QRS$ and $\triangle XYZ$ are similar right triangles. $\overline{RS}$ corresponds with $\overline{YZ}$. $\overline{RS}$ is the hypotenuse of $\triangle QRS$, and $\overline{YZ}$ is the hypotenuse of $\triangle XYZ$. If $QR = \frac{1}{4}XY$, the perimeter of $\triangle XYZ$ is how many times the perimeter of $\triangle QRS$?

7

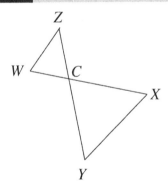

In the figure, $\overline{WZ}$ is parallel to $\overline{YX}$. Lines $\overline{WX}$ and $\overline{ZY}$ intersect at C. If $WC = 5$, $ZC = 4$, and $CX = 25$, what is the length of $\overline{CY}$?

The Triangle Inequality

> *__RULE__: The sum of any two sides of a triangle must be **greater than** the third side.

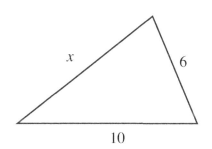

Because 6 and 10 sum to 16, x must be **less than** 16: x could be 5, 6, 8, 11, or even 15.99.

The value of x **CANNOT** be too low, though: if, for example, $x = 3$, we would violate the Triangle Inequality because $3 + 6$ is **not** greater than 10.

 Drill

1

Triangle *ABC* has two known sides: 18 and 17. Which of the following options are possible values for the third side? (Circle all that apply)

    A) 30
    B) 34
    C) 35
    D) 40
    E) 45

Answers

For **detailed solutions**, scan the QR code with your phone's camera

or

visit testpreptips.org/geometry3

Drills (Page 307)

A. isosceles
B. equilateral
C. scalene
D. scalene
E. isosceles
F. equilateral

Questions (Page 313)

1. AC: $35\sqrt{3}$
   BC: 70
2. AE: 7
   AI: $7\sqrt{3}$
3. GH: $\dfrac{6}{\sqrt{2}}$
   GI: $\dfrac{6}{\sqrt{2}}$
4. JL: 18
   KL: $18\sqrt{2}$
5. TS: $\dfrac{20}{\sqrt{3}}$
   TU: $\dfrac{40}{\sqrt{3}}$
6. $CD = 10$

Questions (Page 310)

1. $x = 20$
2. $x = 26$
3. $x = 30$
4. $x = 6$
5. $BD = 8$

Drills (Page 315)

1.

A. 70°
B. 32°
C. 78°
D. 2
E. 3

2.

A. 50°
B. 45°
C. 85°
D. 9
E. 18

Questions (Pages 317-318)

1. B
2. $AC = 20$
3. B
4. 46
5. $CD = 20$
6. 4
7. $CY = 20$

Drill (Page 319)

1. A and B

Part IV: Circles

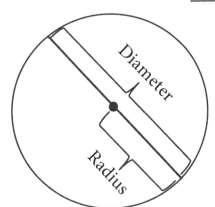

Diameter – a line that passes through the center of the circle with endpoints on the rim of the circle

Radius – a line that goes from the center of the circle to the rim of the circle

Half the length of the diameter

Area and Circumference

Key Formulas

Area = πr^2

Circumference = $2\pi r$

The <u>area</u> of a circle is the amount of space the circle occupies (the gray region)

The <u>circumference</u> of a circle is the length of its "rim" (the black outline)

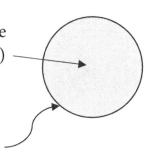

A circle has a radius of 3 inches. Find the **area** and **circumference** of the circle.

<u>Area</u>

Area = πr^2
Area = $\pi(3)^2$
Area = 9π inches^2

<u>Circumference</u>

Circumference = $2\pi r$
Circumference = $2\pi(3)$
Circumference = 6π inches

The area of a circle is 49π square centimeters. What is the **circumference** of the circle?

The area and circumference formulas are related in that we can find the radius from the area formula and then use that radius in the circumference formula.

<u>Area</u>

Area = πr^2
$49\pi = \pi r^2$
$49 = r^2$
$r = 7$

<u>Circumference</u>

Circumference = $2\pi r$
$C = 2\pi r$
$C = 2\pi(7)$
$C = 14\pi$

Questions

1
What is the area of a circle whose radius has a length of 7?

2
The circumference of a circle is 8π. What is the area of this circle?

3
What is the circumference of a circle whose diameter has a length of 18?

4
The area of a circle is 50π. The circumference of this circle is equal to $a\sqrt{b}\,\pi$. What is the value of a^2b?

Equation of a Circle

$$(x - h)^2 + (y - k)^2 = r^2$$

(h, k) = center of circle
r = radius

The center of Circle O is located at $(-5, 2)$, and Circle O has a radius of 2. What equation represents Circle O?

$$(x+5)^2 + (y-2)^2 = (2)^2$$
$$(x+5)^2 + (y-2)^2 = 4$$

A circle has the equation $(x - 3)^2 + (y + 4)^2 = 25$. What are the center and radius of this circle?

<u>Center</u>: $(3, -4)$
<u>Radius</u>: $r^2 = 25 \rightarrow r = \sqrt{25} \rightarrow r = 5$

Drills

1

<u>Instructions</u>: State the center and radius of each circle.

A. $(x - 7)^2 + (y + 5)^2 = 16$ Center: (__7__, __-5__)   Radius: __4__

B. $(x + 4)^2 + (y - 8)^2 = 49$ Center: (__-4__, __8__)   Radius: __7__

C. $(x - 9)^2 + y^2 = 25$ Center: (__9__, __0__)   Radius: __5__

D. $x^2 + y^2 = 4$ Center: (__0__, __0__)   Radius: __2__

E. $x^2 + y^2 = 7$ Center: (__0__, __0__)   Radius: __$\sqrt{7}$__

2

Instructions: Write the equation of each circle given the information provided.

A. Center: (2, 5)   Radius: 6   Equation: $(x-2)^2 + (y-5)^2 = 36$

B. Center: (-7, -3)   Radius: 3   Equation: $(x+7)^2 + (y+3)^2 = 9$

C. Center: (4, 0)   Radius: 1   Equation: $(x-4)^2 + y^2 = 1$

D. Center: (0, 0)   Radius: 5   Equation: $x^2 + y^2 = 25$

E. Center: (7, -4)   Radius: $\sqrt{3}$ Equation: $(x-7)^2 + (x+4)^2 = 3$

Endpoints and Midpoints

Case 1
Given: Two Endpoints
Desired: Center

When graphed in the *xy*-plane, the diameter of a circle has endpoints at (-2, 4) and (10, -4). What is the center of this circle?

*The center is the **midpoint** of the diameter*

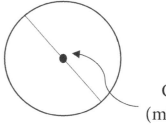

Center (midpoint)

Therefore, we can use the **Midpoint Formula** to determine the center of the circle:

Midpoint Formula

$\left(\dfrac{x_1+x_2}{2}, \dfrac{y_1+y_2}{2}\right)$

$x_1 = -2$
$y_1 = 4$
$x_2 = 10$
$y_2 = -4$

$\left(\dfrac{-2+10}{2}, \dfrac{4+(-4)}{2}\right) = \dfrac{8}{2}, \dfrac{0}{2} = (4,0)$

Drill

1

Instructions: Find the center of the circle that has a diameter with the following endpoints for each circle.

A. Endpoint 1: (2, 5)   Endpoint 2: (6, 11)   Center: (__4__ , __8__)

4, 8

B. Endpoint 1: (-3, 1)   Endpoint 2: (7, -3)   Center: (__2__ , __-1__)

C. Endpoint 1: (11, -4)   Endpoint 2: (6, 6)   Center: (__$\frac{17}{2}$__ , __1__)

$$\frac{x_1 + x_2}{2}, \frac{y_1 + y_2}{2}$$

__8__

Case 2

Given: One Endpoint and Center
Desired: Other Endpoint

$\overline{AB}$ is the diameter of a circle. The center of the circle, C, has coordinates (2, 9), and Point A has coordinates (10, 3). What are the coordinates of Point B?

If $\overline{AB}$ is the diameter of the circle, then C is the **midpoint** of $\overline{AB}$.

First, let's think about the shift from A (an endpoint) → C (the center)

x-coordinates: A → C (10 → 2)   **Subtract 8 (-8)**

y-coordinates: A → C (3 → 9)   **Add 6 (+6)**

If we apply this same shift to C (the center), we will get B (the other endpoint)

x-coordinates: C → B   Subtract 8 from C → 2 – 8 = **-6**
y-coordinates: C → B   Add 6 to C: 9 + 6 = **15**

Coordinates of B: (-6, 15)

Here is a graphical representation to contextualize what we've discussed:

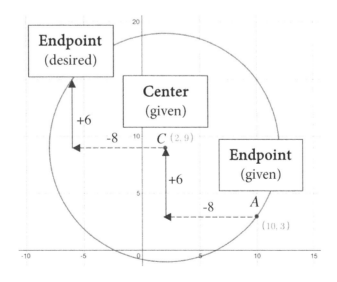

1

<u>Instructions</u>: Find the missing diameter endpoint given the following center and other diameter endpoint for each circle.

A. <u>Center</u>: (2, 5)   <u>Endpoint 1</u>: (0, 1)   Missing Endpoint: (____, ____)

B. <u>Center</u>: (-3, 6)   <u>Endpoint 1</u>: (-10, -2)   Missing Endpoint: (____, ____)

C. <u>Center</u>: (5, -5)   <u>Endpoint 1</u>: (-2, -1)   Missing Endpoint: (____, ____)

D. <u>Center</u>: (10, 8)   <u>Endpoint 1</u>: (9, 12)   Missing Endpoint: (____, ____)

Case 3
Desired: Radius

The easiest way to do find the radius is to use the **Pythagorean Theorem** (**NOT** the Distance Formula).

Given: One Endpoint and Center	Given: Two Endpoints
Endpoint: (-2, 4) Center: (4, 0)	Endpoint A: (-2, 4) Endpoint B: (10, -4)

x-coordinate:

Endpoint → Center: (-2 → 4) = +6

y-coordinate:

Endpoint → Center: (4 → 0) = -4

These distances represent the legs of a right triangle. We can use the **Pythagorean Theorem** to find the hypotenuse (which is the **radius**):

$$a^2 + b^2 = c^2$$
$$6^2 + (-4)^2 = r^2$$
$$52 = r^2$$
$$r = \sqrt{52} \rightarrow r = 2\sqrt{13}$$

x-coordinate:

A → B: (-2 → 10) = +12

y-coordinate:

A → B: (4 → -4) = -8

These distances represent the legs of a right triangle. We can use the **Pythagorean Theorem** to find the hypotenuse (which is the **diameter**):

$$a^2 + b^2 = c^2$$
$$12^2 + (-8)^2 = d^2$$
$$208 = d^2$$
$$d = \sqrt{208} \rightarrow 4\sqrt{13}$$

Divide by 2 to get radius: $r = 2\sqrt{13}$

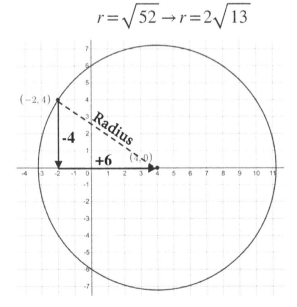
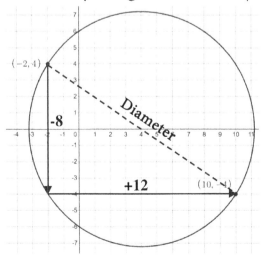

1

Instructions: Find the length of the radius given the center and endpoint for each circle.

A. Center: (1, 2)   Endpoint 1: (4, -2)   Radius: _____

B. Center: (-3, -5)   Endpoint 1: (3, 1)   Radius: _____

2

Circle O has a diameter with endpoints (-3, 2) and (5, -4). What is the length of the radius of Circle O?

Completing the Square

"Completing the Square" problems will present the Equation of a Circle in a weird form. Here's an example:

> What are the **center** and **radius** of a circle with the equation $x^2 + y^2 + 6x - 10y - 3 = 0$?

To find the center and radius, we must first convert the equation provided into the form we're used to by completing the following steps:

Step 1: Rearrange the provided equation to group all x's and y's and leave a blank space after both the x- and y-variables. Then, move the constant to the other side of the equation and leave two blank spaces.

$$x^2 + 6x \_\_\_ + y^2 - 10y + \_\_\_ = 3 + \_\_\_ + \_\_\_$$

Step 2: To turn our equation into a pair of **squared binomials** [ex: $(x + 5)^2$], we first need two **complete trinomials** [ex: $x^2 + 10x + 25$]. Currently, we have the a and b terms for both the x- and y-variables, but both variables are missing the c term.

$$\underline{\text{Standard Form for } x \text{ variable}}: ax^2 + bx + c$$
$$\underline{\text{Standard Form for } y \text{ variable}}: ay^2 + by + c$$

*__RULE__: To find the c term, divide the b term by 2 and square the result:

$$\boxed{x}: \frac{6}{2} = 3 \rightarrow (3)^2 = 9 \;\rightarrow\; x^2 + 6x + \underline{\mathbf{9}}$$

$$\boxed{y}: \frac{-10}{2} = -5 \rightarrow (-5)^2 = 25 \;\rightarrow\; y^2 - 10y + \underline{\mathbf{25}}$$

$$(x^2 + 6x + \underline{\mathbf{9}}) + (y^2 - 10y + \underline{\mathbf{25}}) = 3 + \underline{\mathbf{9}} + \underline{\mathbf{25}}$$

Because we added 9 and 25 to the left-hand side of the equation to get two **complete trinomials**, we must add 9 and 25 to the righthand side. Whenever we add a number to **one side** of the equation, we must do the same to the **other side** of the equation.

Step 3: Now that we have our **complete trinomials**, we can **convert** them into **squared binomials**.

$(x^2 + 6x + \underline{\mathbf{9}}) \rightarrow (x + 3)^2 \qquad (y^2 - 10y + \underline{\mathbf{25}}) \rightarrow (y - 5)^2 \qquad r^2 = 3 + 9 + 25 = 37$

> __Equation__: $(x + 3)^2 + (y - 5)^2 = 37$ $\longrightarrow$ __Center__: $(-3, 5)$ __Radius__: $\sqrt{37}$

Questions

1

What is the radius of a circle that has the equation $x^2 - 6x + y^2 + 8y - 25 = 0$?

A) 3
B) $5\sqrt{2}$
C) $\sqrt{39}$
D) $3\sqrt{3}$

2

A. What is the center of the circle with equation $x^2 + y^2 + 2x - 10y = -3$?

A) (2, -10)
B) (-2, 10)
C) (-1, 5)
D) (1, -5)

B. What is the radius of the circle with equation $x^2 + y^2 + 2x - 10y = -3$?

A) $\sqrt{23}$
B) 3
C) 9
D) 23

Tangent Lines

If a line is drawn **tangent** to a circle, the line is **perpendicular** to the **radius**.

Therefore, the tangent line and the radius form a **90° angle**.

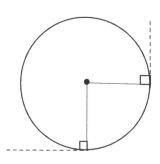

Both dashed lines are drawn tangent to the circle.

> In the figure shown below, Point P is the center of the circle, and $\overline{QR}$ is tangent to the circle at Point Q. If $PQ = 10$ and $QR = 20$, what is the length of $\overline{PR}$?

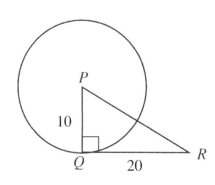

$\overline{PQ}$ is the **radius**, so $\angle PQR$ is a 90° angle.

Therefore, we are working with a right triangle and can use the **Pythagorean Theorem** to find $\overline{PR}$:

$$10^2 + 20^2 = (PR)^2$$
$$500 = (PR)^2$$
$$PR = \sqrt{500} \to 10\sqrt{5}$$

Drill

1

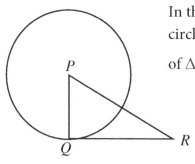

In the figure, P is the center of the circle and $\overline{QR}$ is tangent to the circle at Point Q. If the circumference of the circle is 16π and the area of $\triangle PQR$ is 20, the length of $\overline{PR}$ is $\sqrt{x}$. What is the value of x?

Note: Figure not drawn to scale.

Circle Ratios

Arc Length

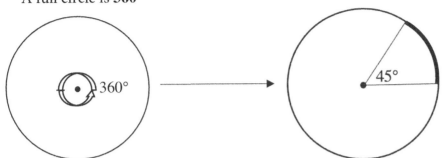

A full circle is **360°**

The **circumference** of a circle **is** the length of a 360° arc of the circle.

Because 45° is $\frac{1}{8}$ of 360°, the length of the arc associated with this angle will simply be $\frac{1}{8}$ of the circumference.

The **arc** (portion of a circle's rim) of a circle is **directly proportional** to the number of degrees of its **central angle**.

Find the arc length of the bolded arc shown below.

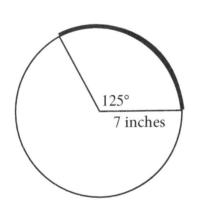

$$\frac{\text{arc length}}{\text{circumference}} = \frac{\text{arc degrees}}{360°}$$

$$\frac{x}{2\pi(7)} = \frac{125°}{360°}$$

$$\frac{x}{14\pi} = \frac{125°}{360°}$$

$$x = \frac{175}{36}\pi$$

Sector Area

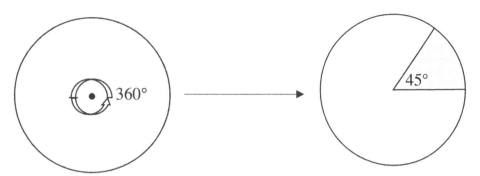

The **area** of a circle is the full amount of "space" the 360° occupies

Because 45° is $\frac{1}{8}$ of 360°, the area of the sector associated with this angle will simply be $\frac{1}{8}$ the area of the whole circle.

The **area of the sector** (portion of a circle's area) is **directly proportional** to the number of degrees of its **central angle**

Find the area of the shaded sector shown below.

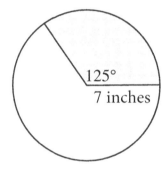

$$\frac{\text{sector area}}{\text{total area}} = \frac{\text{sector degrees}}{360°}$$

$$\frac{x}{\pi(7)^2} = \frac{125°}{360°}$$

$$\frac{x}{49\pi} = \frac{125°}{360°}$$

$$x = \frac{1225}{72}\pi$$

Questions

1

The circumference of Circle O is 32π. What is the length of arc MN?

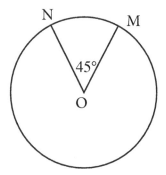

2

The area of the shaded sector is 15π. What is the area of Circle O?

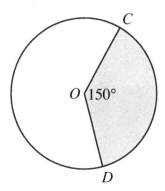

3

In the circle shown below, central angle $\angle AOB$ measures $45°$, and arc AB equals π. What is the circumference of the circle?

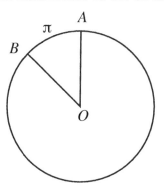

4

The radius of Circle O is 6. What is the area of the shaded sector?

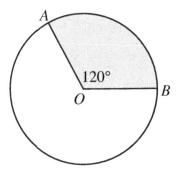

5

The length of $\overline{AO}$ is 4, and O is the center of the circle. The area of the shaded sector is 2π. What is the measure of $\angle AOB$?

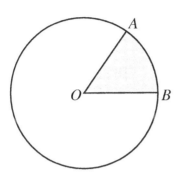

6

If the length of arc AB is $\dfrac{2}{5}$ the circumference of Circle O, what is the measure of $\angle AOB$?

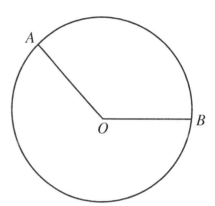

Answers

For **detailed solutions**, scan the QR code with your phone's camera

or

visit testpreptips.org/geometry4

Questions (Page 323)

1. 49π
2. 16π
3. 18π
4. 200

Drill (Page 326)

A. <u>Center</u>: (4, 8)
B. <u>Center</u>: (2, -1)
C. <u>Center</u>: (8.5, 1)

Drill (Page 328)

A. <u>Endpoint</u>: (4, 9)
B. <u>Endpoint</u>: (4, 14)
C. <u>Endpoint</u>: (12, -9)
D. <u>Endpoint</u>: (11, 4)

Drills (Page 330)

1.

A. <u>Radius</u>: 5
B. <u>Radius</u>: $6\sqrt{2}$

2. 5

Drills (Pages 324-325)

1.

A. <u>Center</u>: (7, -5)
   <u>Radius</u>: 4
B. <u>Center</u>: (-4, 8)
   <u>Radius</u>: 7
C. <u>Center</u>: (9, 0)
   <u>Radius</u>: 5
D. <u>Center</u>: (0, 0)
   <u>Radius</u>: 2
E. <u>Center</u>: (0, 0)
   <u>Radius</u>: $\sqrt{7}$

2.

A. <u>Equation</u>: $(x - 2)^2 + (y - 5)^2 = 36$
B. <u>Equation</u>: $(x + 7)^2 + (y + 3)^2 = 9$
C. <u>Equation</u>: $(x - 4)^2 + y^2 = 1$
D. <u>Equation</u>: $x^2 + y^2 = 25$
E. <u>Equation</u>: $(x - 7)^2 + (y + 4)^2 = 3$

Questions (Page 332)

1. B
2. <u>Part A</u>: C
   <u>Part B</u>: A

Questions (Page 336-337)

1. 4π
2. 36π
3. 8π
4. 12π
5. $45°$
6. $144°$

Drill (Pages 333)

1. 89

Topic 18: Right Triangle Trigonometry
SOHCAHTOA

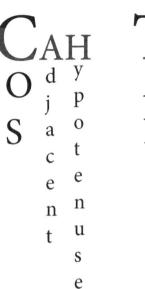

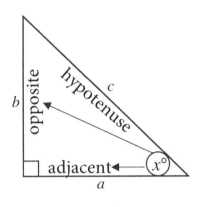

Side a is **adjacent** to (next to) angle x.
Side b is **opposite** angle x.
Side c is the **hypotenuse**.

*NOTE: SOHCAHTOA can only be applied to **right triangles**.

What is the value of x in the figure?

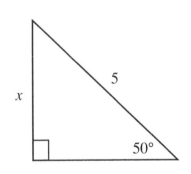

Sides: x and 5
Angle: 50°

The unknown side (x) = **opposite** 50°
The known side (5) = **hypotenuse**

We need to use a function that relates the **opposite** side to the **hypotenuse**: the <u>sin</u> function.

$$\sin(\text{angle}) = \frac{\text{opposite}}{\text{hypotenuse}}$$

$$\sin(50°) = \frac{x}{5} \rightarrow x = 5\sin(50°)$$

A right triangle has two acute angles: x and y. If $\cos(x) = \dfrac{3}{5}$, what is $\tan(y)$?

*RECALL: An acute angle is an angle less than 90°.

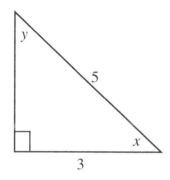

$$\cos(x) = \dfrac{\text{adjacent}}{\text{hypotenuse}} = \dfrac{3}{5}$$

This means the side **adjacent** to x is 3, and the **hypotenuse** is 5 (as labeled in the figure).

To find the **tangent** of y, we will need the side **opposite** y (which we already know is 3) and the side adjacent to y (currently unknown).

To find the side adjacent to y, we can use the Pythagorean Theorem:

$$3^2 + (\text{side})^2 = 5^2$$
$$(\text{side})^2 = 16$$
$$\text{adjacent side} = 4$$

Alternatively, we can recognize that this is a 3 – 4 – 5 Right Triangle and conclude that the unknown side is 4.

$$\tan(y) = \dfrac{\text{opposite}}{\text{adjacent}} = \dfrac{3}{4}$$

Instructions: First, complete Parts A and B by stating the relation of each side to the angle (adjacent, opposite, or hypotenuse). Then, for Part C, circle which function relates the angle to the two sides. Finally, for Part D, state the value of x. Leave your answer in terms of sin / cos / tan of the angle.

1

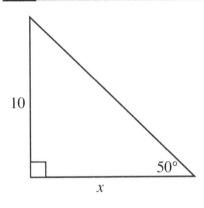

A. Relation of "x" to Angle:
_____

B. Relation of "10" to Angle:
_____

C. Function (circle one):
sin / cos / tan

D. $x =$ _____

2

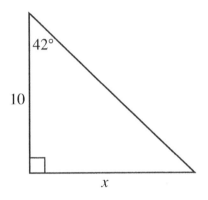

A. Relation of "x" to Angle:
_____

B. Relation of "10" to Angle:
_____

C. Function (circle one):
sin / cos / tan

D. $x =$ _____

3	4
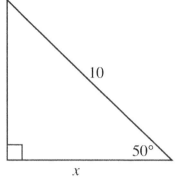	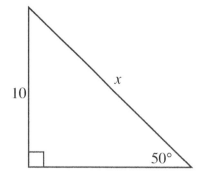
A. Relation of "x" to Angle: _____	A. Relation of "x" to Angle: _____
B. Relation of "10" to Angle: _____	B. Relation of "10" to Angle: _____
C. Function (circle one): sin / cos / tan	C. Function (circle one): sin / cos / tan
D. $x =$ _____	D. $x =$ _____

Questions

1

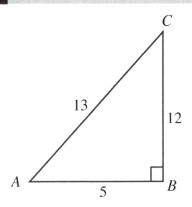

In triangle *ABC* shown above, what is the value of tan*A*?

$\frac{12}{5}$

2 700+

In triangle *ABC* shown below, $\sin A = \frac{3}{5}$, and $\overline{BC}$ is 6 feet. What is the length, in feet, of $\overline{AC}$?

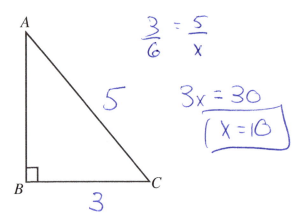

$\frac{3}{6} = \frac{5}{x}$

$3x = 30$

$\boxed{x = 10}$

3

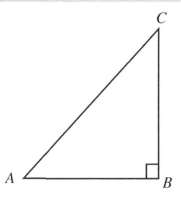

In triangle *ABC* shown above, which of the following is equal to $\frac{AB}{BC}$?

A) cos*A* $\frac{AB}{AC}$
B) cos*C* $\frac{CB}{CA}$ $\frac{AB}{CB}$
C) tan*A*
D) tan*C* $\frac{CB}{AB}$

4

Triangle *TUV* has right angle *U*. If $\sin T = \frac{3}{5}$, what is the value of cos*T*?

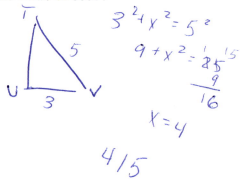

$3^2 + x^2 = 5^2$

$9 + x^2 = 25$

$x^2 = 16$

$x = 4$

$4/5$

5

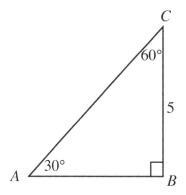

In triangle *ABC* shown above, what is tan*A*?

A) $\dfrac{1}{2}$

B) $\dfrac{1}{\sqrt{3}}$

C) $\sqrt{3}$

D) 2

6

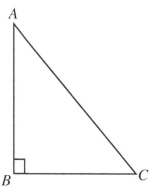

Which of the following must be equal to the length of side $\overline{AC}$ in right triangle *ABC* shown above?

A) $BC\cos(A)$

B) $\dfrac{BC}{\cos(A)}$

C) $BC\sin(A)$

D) $\dfrac{BC}{\sin(A)}$

 The Unit Circle

The **Unit Circle** is a circle centered at the origin $(0, 0)$ with a radius of 1.

The Unit Circle

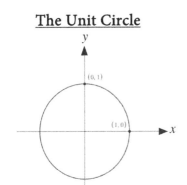

***NOTE**: You may not be told directly that you have a Unit Circle, but if you see the coordinates $(1, 0)$ or $(0, 1)$ labeled on the circle, it means that you are working with a Unit Circle because the radius is 1.

In the Unit Circle...

x represents $\cos\theta$

y represents $\sin\theta$

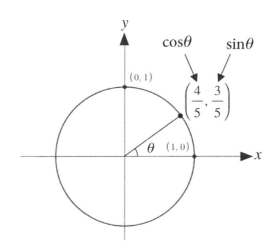

346

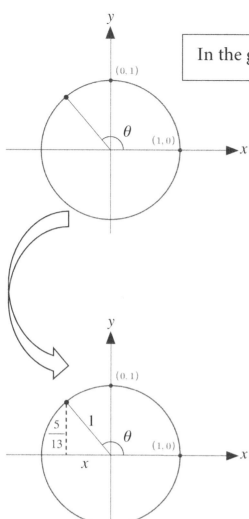

In the given figure, $\sin\theta = \frac{5}{13}$. What is the value of $\cos\theta$?

When we are given the value of either sin or cos and asked for the other value, we must create a right triangle by connecting the provided point to the *x*-axis.

The legs of the resultant triangle become the *x* (cos) and *y* (sin) coordinates.

Because we are given sin, we will label the vertical leg (*y*) as $\frac{5}{13}$.

Now, we can use the **Pythagorean Theorem** to find the horizontal leg (*x*). The hypotenuse (the radius of the Unit Circle) = 1.

$$\left(\frac{5}{13}\right)^2 + x^2 = 1^2$$

$$\frac{25}{169} + x^2 = 1 \rightarrow x = \frac{12}{13}$$

*<u>NOTE</u>: We must, however, account for the fact that the *x*-coordinate is **NEGATIVE** in the figure.

Therefore, $x = -\frac{12}{13}$, so $\cos\theta = -\frac{12}{13}$

347

Questions

1

In the *xy*-plane, the unit circle with center at the origin O contains point A with coordinates $(1, 0)$ and point B with coordinates $\left(\dfrac{12}{13}, \dfrac{5}{13}\right)$. What is the value of the sin and cos of $\angle AOB$?

Sin: _____

Cos: _____

2

In the given figure, point P has coordinates $\left(a, -\dfrac{\sqrt{3}}{2}\right)$. What is the value of a?

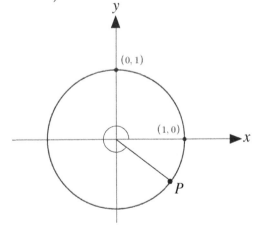

3

In the figure shown, θ is an angle. If $\cos\theta = \dfrac{4}{5}$, what is $\sin\theta$?

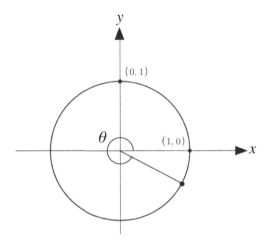

Sine and Cosine Properties

Property 1:

$\cos(x) = \sin(90 - x)$
$\sin(x) = \cos(90 - x)$

Property 2:

Let *x* and *y* represent the **two acute angles** of a right triangle.

If $\sin(x) = \cos(y)$, then $x + y = 90°$
(If sin of one angle = cos of other angle, the sum of the two angles is 90°)

If $x + y = 90°$, then $\sin(x) = \cos(y)$.
(If the two angles sum to 90°, then sin of one angle = cos of other angle)

In right triangle ABC, $\cos(90 - x) = \dfrac{3}{5}$. A. What is $\sin(x)$? B. What is $\cos(x)$?

A. Finding $\sin(x)$:

Recall **Property 1**: $\cos(90 - x) = \sin(x)$

If $\cos(90 - x) = \dfrac{3}{5}$, then $\sin(x) = \dfrac{3}{5}$

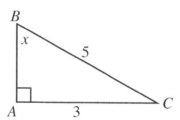

B. Finding $\cos(x)$:

We know that $\sin(x) = \dfrac{3}{5}$, which means that the side opposite x is 3 and the hypotenuse is 5.

Therefore, this is a 3 – 4 – 5 Right Triangle → $\cos(x) = \dfrac{4}{5}$.

x and *y* are acute angles and $\cos(x) = \sin(y)$. If $x = 3b + 10$ and $y = 2b - 5$, what is the value of the larger of the two angles?

Recall **Property 2**: If $\cos(x) = \sin(y)$, then $x + y = 90°$.

$x + y = 90°$
$(3b + 10) + (2b - 5) = 90°$
$5b + 5 = 90°$
$5b = 85°$
$b = 17°$

The larger angle is $3b + 10$, which equals $3(17°) + 10° = 51° + 10° = \mathbf{61°}$.

Drills

1

x is the degree measure of one of the acute angles in triangle ABC. $\sin(90 - x) = \frac{3}{5}$. What is the value of $\cos(x)$?

2

x and y are the degree measures of two acute angles, and $\sin(x°) = \cos(y°)$. If $x = 3k - 10$ and $y = 4k + 30$, what is the value of k?

Answers

For **detailed solutions**, scan the QR code with your phone's camera

or

visit testpreptips.org/trigonometry

Drills (Pages 342-343)

1.
A. Adjacent
B. Opposite
C. tan
D. $x = \dfrac{10}{\tan 50}$

2.
A. Opposite
B. Adjacent
C. tan
D. $x = 10\tan 42$

3.
A. Adjacent
B. Hypotenuse
C. cos
D. $x = 10\cos 50$

4.
A. Hypotenuse
B. Opposite
C. sin
D. $x = \dfrac{10}{\sin 50}$

Questions (Pages 344-345)

1. $\dfrac{12}{5}$
2. $AC = 10$
3. D
4. $\dfrac{4}{5}$
5. B
6. D

Questions (Page 348)

1.

Sin: $\dfrac{5}{13}$

Cos: $\dfrac{12}{13}$

2. $a = \dfrac{1}{2}$

3. $\sin\theta = -\dfrac{3}{5}$

Drills (Page 350)

1. $\cos(x) = \dfrac{3}{5}$
2. $k = 10$

Topic 19: Imaginary and Complex Numbers

Imaginary Numbers

A number is **imaginary** if a negative number appears under the square root sign. We CANNOT take the square root of a negative number.

$\sqrt{-2}$, $\sqrt{-18}$, and $\sqrt{-300}$ are all examples of imaginary numbers.

i is a particular imaginary number: it is equal to the square root of -1.

$$\boxed{i = \sqrt{-1}}$$

Powers of Imaginary Numbers

$i^1 = i$	$i^2 = -1$	$i^3 = -i$	$i^4 = 1$

*__NOTE__: You must memorize the powers of i from i^1 to i^4

There are only **four** unique values a power of i can take on:
i, -1, -i, and 1

After i^4, the cycle repeats again (i^5 has the same value as i, i^6 has the same value as i^2, etc.)

cycle repeats every 4

$= i$	$= -1$	$= -i$	$= 1$
i^1	i^2	i^3	i^4
i^5	i^6	i^7	i^8
i^9	i^{10}	i^{11}	i^{12}...

We can use the fact that the value of *i* "repeats" every 4 powers to find the value of *i* raised to larger powers, like i^{23} or i^{100}

To do this, we will divide the power by 4 and pay careful attention to the remainder (or the lack of a remainder)

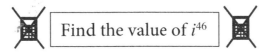
Find the value of i^{46}

Step 1: Divide the power by 4

$$\begin{array}{r} 11R2 \\ 4\overline{)46} \\ \underline{-4} \\ 6 \\ \underline{-4} \\ 2 \end{array}$$

Step 2: *i* raised to the power originally provided (here, 46) equals *i* raised to the remainder (here, 2)

$$i^{46} = i^2 = -1$$

Find the value of i^{32}

Step 1: Divide the power by 4

$$4\overline{)32} = 8$$

Step 2: If there is **NO** remainder, *i* raised to that power equals 1, so $i^{32} = 1$.

Operations with Imaginary Numbers

Addition & Subtraction

When adding / subtracting terms with *i* raised to different powers, we need to first **simplify** each term.

Calculate the value of $i^{14} + i^{12}$

$i^{14} \rightarrow \dfrac{14}{4} = 3R2 \rightarrow i^2 = -1 \qquad i^{12} \rightarrow \dfrac{12}{4} = 3$ (no remainder) $\rightarrow i^{12} = 1$

$-1 + 1 = 0$

Calculate the value of $5i^{25} - i^{27} + i^{26}$

$i^{25} \rightarrow \dfrac{25}{4} = 6R1 \rightarrow i^1 = i \qquad i^{27} \rightarrow \dfrac{27}{4} = 6R3 \rightarrow i^3 = -i \qquad i^{26} \rightarrow \dfrac{26}{4} = 6R2 \rightarrow i^2 = -1$

$5(i) - (-i) - 1 = 6i - 1$

Multiplication & Division

When multiplying / dividing terms with *i* raised to different powers, we can add / subtract the exponents because the bases are identical (base = *i*):

Calculate the value of $(6i^5)(i^8)$

$(6i^5)(i^8) = 6i^{13}$

$i^{13} \rightarrow \dfrac{13}{4} = 3R1 \rightarrow i^1 = i$

$6(i) = 6i$

Calculate the value of $\dfrac{10i^{20}}{5i^6}$

$\dfrac{10i^{20}}{5i^6} = 2i^{14}$

$i^{14} \rightarrow \dfrac{14}{4} = 3R2 \rightarrow i^2 = -1$

$2(-1) = -2$

Drills

Instructions: Determine the value of i in each of the following examples.

1
i^{11}

2
i^8

3
i^{17}

4
i^{10}

5
$5i^{16} + 8i^2$

6
$(4i^{40})(i^{19})$

7
$\dfrac{3i^{15}}{6i^9}$

8
$i^{18} - 10i^6 + 6i^{23}$

9
$(7i^{25})(8i^{10})$

10
$\dfrac{20i^{20}}{4i^{12}}$

Complex Numbers

$$a + bi$$

a = real component
b = imaginary component

A **complex number** can be thought of as a hybrid form of a real and imaginary number.

$3 + 4i$, $19 - i$, and $-8 + i$ are all examples of complex numbers.

Addition & Subtraction
Method: Combine Like Terms

What is $(3 - 5i) + (-6 + 4i)$?	What is $(3 - 5i) - (-6 + 4i)$?
$3 + (-6) = -3$	$3 - (-6) = 9$
$-5i + 4i = -i$	$-5i - 4i = -9i$
$= -3 - i$	$= 9 - 9i$

Multiplication
Method: Distribution

Simplify $i(2+3i)$

$= 2i + 3i^2 = 2i + 3(-1) = 2i - 3$

Method: "FOIL"

We can multiply complex numbers by using the same "FOIL" method we use for any binomial [like $(x + 3)(x - 5)$].

Simplify $(5 + 6i)(4 - 7i)$

$(5 + 6i)(4 - 7i)$
$= 20 - 35i + 24i - 42i^2$
$= 20 - 11i - 42(-1)$
$= 62 - 11i$

Division

When we are dividing imaginary numbers, we must **remove** all i's from the denominator.

*<u>RECALL</u>: i^2 = a real number (-1). We can use this fact as a tool to remove imaginary components from the denominator.

$$\boxed{\text{Simplify } \frac{15}{7i}}$$

To remove i from the denominator, we can multiply the denominator by i to give us i^2 (which is a real number: -1)

$$\frac{15}{7i} \rightarrow \frac{15}{7i}\left(\frac{i}{i}\right) \rightarrow \frac{15i}{7i^2} \rightarrow \frac{15i}{7(-1)} \rightarrow -\frac{15i}{7}$$

The Conjugate

A **conjugate** is created by taking the sign between the two terms of a binomial and **negating** it.

<u>Ex</u>: the conjugate of $x + 3$ is $x - 3$
<u>Ex</u>: the conjugate of $8 + 4i$ is $8 - 4i$
<u>Ex</u>: the conjugate of $-10 - 9i$ is $-10 + 9i$

The conjugate is important because it allows us to **eliminate the middle term of two multiplied binomials**:

$$(x + 3)(x - 3) = x^2 + \cancel{3x} - \cancel{3x} - 9 = x^2 - 9$$

The Conjugate with Complex Numbers

The only way to remove i from the denominator shown below (which contains a complex number) is by multiplying by the **conjugate** of the denominator:

$$\frac{4+i}{2-3i} \rightarrow \frac{4+i}{2-3i}\left(\frac{2+3i}{2+3i}\right) \rightarrow \frac{8+12i+2i+3i^2}{4+\boxed{6i-6i}-9i^2} \rightarrow \frac{14i+8+3(-1)}{4-9(-1)} \rightarrow \frac{14i+5}{13}$$

Instructions: Perform the requested operation on the complex numbers provided.

1

$(4 + 5i) + (7 + 6i)$

2

$(3 - 2i) - (5 + 3i)$

3

$(2 + i)(5 + 2i)$

4

$i(4 - i)$

5

$(2 + 6i)(3 - 4i)$

Instructions: Remove i from the denominator to simplify each expression.

1

$$\frac{4 + 3i}{2i}$$

2

$$\frac{4 - i}{9 + 3i}$$

3

$$\frac{3 - i}{5 + 4i}$$

Answers

For **detailed solutions**, scan the QR code with your phone's camera

or

visit testpreptips.org/imaginarynumbers

Drills (Page 355)

1. $-i$
2. 1
3. i
4. -1
5. -3
6. $-4i$
7. $-\frac{1}{2}$
8. $9 - 6i$
9. $-56i$
10. 5

Drills (Page 358 [Top])

Instructions: Perform the requested operation on the complex numbers provided.

1. $11 + 11i$
2. $-2 - 5i$
3. $8 + 9i$
4. $4i + 1$
5. $30 + 10i$

Drills (Page 358 [Bottom])

Instructions: Remove i from the denominator to simplify each expression.

1. $-\dfrac{4i - 3}{2}$
2. $\dfrac{33 - 21i}{90}$
3. $\dfrac{11 - 17i}{41}$

Topic 20: Absolute Value

The output of an absolute value function will **always** be positive, regardless of the sign of its input.

$$|9| = 9$$
$$|-9| = 9$$

Solving Absolute Value Equations

We will obtain **two** equations when solving for a variable within an absolute value.

$$|x+4| = 9$$

$x + 4 = 9$ $x + 4 = -9$
$x = 5$ $x = -13$

<u>Logic</u>: If $|x+4| = 9$, $x + 4$ can either equal 9 (since $|9| = 9$) or -9 (since $|-9| = 9$)

To find the two values of *x* that satisfy the absolute value equation, we must solve two different equations.

The **absolute value** must always be **isolated** before we can obtain the two equations we'll need to solve for *x*. We may need to add, subtract, multiply, or divide on both sides to isolate the absolute value.

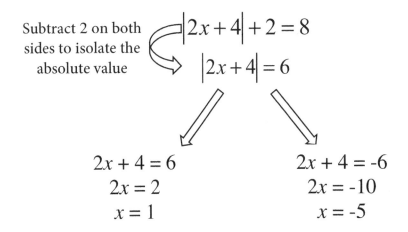

Subtract 2 on both sides to isolate the absolute value

$|2x+4| + 2 = 8$
$|2x+4| = 6$

$2x + 4 = 6$ $2x + 4 = -6$
$2x = 2$ $2x = -10$
$x = 1$ $x = -5$

*NOTE: An absolute value function **always** produces a positive output.

For this reason, we **CANNOT** solve for *x* if the absolute value is EQUAL to a negative number.

$$|x+4|=-5$$

The above equation is **INVALID**: there is no number we can insert for *x* to obtain -5. There are **NO** solutions to this equation.

$$|x+5|+6=4$$

The above equation is a less obvious version of an **INVALID** equation. Watch what happens when we isolate the absolute value by subtracting 6 from both sides:

We get $|x+5|=-2$

Again, there are no values of *x* that will satisfy this equation.

Questions

1

$$\left|6 - \frac{3}{2}x\right| = 3$$

Which of the following values of x satisfies the equation shown above?

I. 2
II. -2
III. 6
IV. -6

A) II and IV
B) I and III
C) I and IV
D) II and III

2

$$|4x - 1| + 3 = 0$$

Which of the following values of x satisfies the equation shown above?

I. 1
II. -1
III. $-\frac{1}{2}$

A) I and II
B) I and III
C) II and III
D) None of the above

3

Which of the following equations has a solution?

A) $|x + 2| + 2 = 0$
B) $|2x - 2| + 2 = 0$
C) $|4x - 2| + 2 = 0$
D) $|4x - 2| - 2 = 0$

4

$$|3x + 2| = 8$$

If q and p are the solutions to the equation shown above, what is the value of $|qp|$?

5

$$|4x+2|=14$$

If j and k are both solutions to the above equation and $j > k$, what is the value of $j - k$?

6

If $|2a-2|=10$ and $|2b+4|=16$, what is a possible value of $|ab|$?

7

$$|x-8|=5$$

There are two solutions to the above equation, one of which is $x = 13$. What is the value of the other solution?

8

$$2|x-3|+5=25$$

What positive x value satisfies the above equation?

9

How many solutions are there to the equation $|x-5|=-2$?

Answers

For **detailed solutions**, scan the QR code with your phone's camera

or

visit testpreptips.org/absolutevalue

Questions (Pages 362-363)

1. B
2. D
3. D
4. $\dfrac{20}{3}$
5. 7
6. 24, 36, 40, or 60
7. 3
8. $9 - 6i$
9. 13
10. 0

Made in United States
North Haven, CT
04 October 2022